Woman as Healer

Woman as Healer

Jeanne Achterberg

Shambhala
Boston & Shaftesbury
1990

Shambhala Publications, Inc.
Horticultural Hall
300 Massachusetts Avenue
Boston, Massachusetts 02115

Shambhala Publications, Inc.
The Old School House
The Courtyard, Bell Street
Shaftesbury, Dorset SP7 8BP

9 8 7 6 5 4 3 2 1

First Edition

Printed in the United States of America on acid-free paper

Distributed in the United States by Random House
and in Canada by Random House of Canada Ltd.
Distributed in the United Kingdom by Element Books Ltd.

Library of Congress Cataloging-in-Publication Data

Achterberg, Jeanne.
    Woman as healer / Jeanne Achterberg. — 1st ed.
        p.   cm.
    Includes bibliographical references.
    ISBN 0-87773-444-5 (alk. paper)
    1. Women in medicine.   2. Women healers.   I. Title.
    R692.A24   1990
    610'.82—dc20   89-43314
                                                          CIP

To Frank: gentle and compassionate healer

Contents

List of Illustrations   ix
Acknowledgments   xi
Introduction   1

Part One
Medicine Woman: The Ancient Cosmic Connection   7

1. The Primeval Turning Points   9
2. Sumer: The Birth and Death of a Culture   14
3. Denmark: Woman as Shaman   20
4. The Healing Legacy from Greece   29
5. Women of Rome   34
6. Brilliant Early Christian Flowering   38
7. Medieval Christian Cosmology   41

Part Two
Woman and the Genesis of Scientific Thought   61

8. The Tapestry   63
9. Women Healers as Heretics: Philosophic Foundation   65
10. Fate of the Wise Women   76
11. Absent at the Birth of Modern Medicine   99

Part Three
Women and the Professionalization of the Healing Arts   113

12. Gender and the Health Professions   115
13. Midwifery: The Mysterious Office   118
14. Every Woman Her Own Doctor: The Popular Health Movement   133
15. The Warriors: Doctors, Nurses, and Ministers   144

Part Four
Twentieth-Century Women and the State of
   the Healing Arts and Sciences   169
16. Woman as Health-Care Provider: Realities of the Marketplace   171
17. Life in the Balance   187

Notes   207
Bibliography   223
Index   233

Illustrations

Following p. 98

Venus of Willendorf
Snake Goddess
Radiant Inanna, Queen of Heaven and Earth
Athena
Hygeia
Saint Felicity of Carthage
Saint Lucy
Birth Scene from the Uttenheimer Altar
Medieval Childbirth Scene
Lady Mary Wortley Montagu
Dr. Elizabeth Blackwell
Dr. Harriot K. Hunt
Dr. Marie Zakrzewska
Cornell Surgical Clinic
Dr. Mary Putnam Jacobi
Florence Nightingale
Hannah Maria Young
The Visiting Nurse

Acknowledgments

RESEARCHING AND WRITING the story of woman as healer was a very personal journey, facilitating a dramatic mid-life, mid-career transformation. It became necessary for me to understand and express more fully the past, present, and potential of women healers, as well as take the time to look with clarity at my own experiences as a woman, a healer, and a scientist. Information was difficult to come by, and I was both empowered and disturbed by what I found. The emotional impact of the project, as well as its girth and complexity, required the goodwill, inspiration, and able scholarship of many individuals.

My husband, Frank, showed concern and infinite patience, and provided me with the opportunity to leave full-time academic work in order to complete this task. He facilitated my living and writing for extended periods in the majestic solitude of Big Sur, where I experienced the healing that comes from being connected to the earth—one of the underlying themes of the book. As our bonded relationship matured and deepened over these years of our life-change, I was profoundly and repeatedly reminded that the healing of people, our relationships, institutions, and indeed, our world, depends entirely on loving partnership between men and women, and on honoring the traditional values associated with both sexes.

The work itself was enriched by women healers—students, mentors, colleagues—with whom I have had contact over the years. Many women connected with me for the first time after learning of the book-in-progress. I am touched by their strength, their stories, and their wisdom. I continue to be in awe of the instant recognition we have for one another, regardless of professional affiliation. I owe a very special thanks to Mary Stowell, Gail Swift, and Susan Luck, who reviewed earlier drafts and continue to bring new materials on this topic to my attention. They, Rachel Naomi Remen, Angie Arrien, Marion Woodman, Joan Borysenko, Stephanie Simonton, Barbie Dossey, Dee Krieger, and legions of nurse healers inspired me by their examples.

Furthermore, I owe debts of scholarship to many contemporary writers, as well as several scholars of centuries past who sought to make women's experience known. I have noted their work throughout the text. In particular, the passionate and careful work of Jules Michelet, Matilda Gage, Katherine Hurd-Mead, and Lynn Thorndike, mostly forgotten or out-of-print, deserves special recognition. Hopefully, women's experience will not always be buried in dusty archives or obscure tomes.

The notion of adding balance to healing by the inclusion of the traditional feminine principles and practices was supported by several men who see this as integral to the field of medicine. I would especially like to thank Andrew Weil for reviewing the botanical aspects of the manuscript, and Michael Samuels and Larry Dossey for their constant encouragement and their eminent and balanced commentaries in the field of medicine.

Finally, I am grateful for the visionary editing of Emily Hilburn Sell. We have now worked together on two books, and both have been nurtured, clarified, and greatly enhanced by her excellent advice.

Woman as Healer

Introduction

WOMEN HAVE ALWAYS been healers. Cultural myths from around the world describe a time when only women knew the secrets of life and death, and therefore they alone could practice the magical art of healing. In crises and calamity, or so some of the stories go, women's revered position as keepers of the sacred wisdom was deliberately and forcibly wrested away from them. At other places, in other eras, women's legal right to practice the healing vocations was gradually eroded by changing mores and religious dogma.

Today, over 80 percent of the workers in the health system in the United States are women. Without women, hospitals, laboratories, and social agencies could not operate. Nevertheless, women in general have limited professional independence and authority, and are, in some instances, legally constrained in practicing the skills associated with their training. For most of the history of the Western world, women who worked as healers in their own right have been exceptional people who defied custom in order to share their creative and intellectual gifts. More often, women healers have simply joined a large and exploited corps of handmaidens.

The dissonance between women's talents and women's fate bears closer attention, as it reflects the evolution of institutions that lack the feminine voice. The absence of balance in these institutions has perpetrated a crisis that now extends alarmingly through all levels of health—from the health of cells, tissues, mind, and relationships, to the health of the environment upon which life itself is dependent.

THIS BOOK EXAMINES the role of the feminine in the Western healing traditions. With all respect to the compassionate and gentle men who identify with so many aspects of women healers—and to the complex continuum of gender itself—I have written about woman as woman. Having a woman's body, being faced with myriad social and biological proscriptions as well as the magnificent abilities associated with that body, creates a uniqueness that need not be generalized or diluted in any way.

As healers, we crave empowerment from the past. Yet, for women, the past has not been well told—and for good reason. Women were often forbidden to speak or write in Latin, the language of the scholar and of the professions. The information presented here had to be carefully teased out of a few surviving works written by women healers, from relics and artifacts, from myth and song, and from what was written about women. The experience of women healers, like the experience of women in general, is a shadow throughout the record of the world that must be sought at the interface of many disciplines: history, anthropology, botany, archaeology, and the behavioral sciences.

The text focuses on women's role in the heritage of Western civilization, and on the events and ideas that directly affect women healers in the United States. Eastern systems of healing, and even tribal customs of North America, often more adequately reflect the positive characteristics of the feminine aspects of healing, but they have had little impact on women working within the cultural confines of American institutions. I have also concentrated on women in those professions most commonly associated with the restoration and preservation of physical health as a means of further confining the topic to a workable format.

The available information on woman as healer in the Western tradition spans several thousand years, stretching far back into prehistory when conditions were likely to support women as independent and honored healers. During and following those very early years, the role of women healers has been inexorably married to shifts in the ecology, the economy, and the politics of the area in which they lived. Examining the events of the past brings two timely points into bold relief: *the intimate connection between women healers and the cosmology,* and a *thread of consciousness* that links the feminine aspects of healing.

WOMEN HEALERS AND THE COSMOLOGY

The cosmology of a culture is the belief system that describes the nature of the universe, including creation myths. The cosmic story ascribes a meaning to life, defining what lies in the invisible spaces that are beyond the range of human perception. It also determines, and is determined by, the relationship humans have with one another, and their regard for the nonliving and living things of the earth.

The story is told and embellished by priests, shamans, scientists, politicians, philosophers, poets, and any granted the power to see and work with unseen worlds. It is born from observation, intuition, divine revelation, and from ideas deliberately contrived to meet a certain end. What is good and what is evil—the faces of gods and of demons—arise from cosmology.

A culture's cosmology determines who assumes positions of leadership and honor. Almost always those individuals must have the face of god(s). Since the vocation of healer, particularly, is associated with the sacred, and the healing beliefs of any culture directly reflect the nature of the gods, only in those times when the reigning deity has had a feminine, bisexual, or androgynous nature have women been able to exercise the healing arts with freedom and power.

The cosmology upon which the foundations of the Western world rest evolved thousands of years ago. The Great Mother or Great Goddess was unseated from her reign in favor of a single male god who resided outside and above the earth. The essence of the new cosmology came from the religious stories of the Near East, from the mythologies of ancient Europe, and from the sciences that grew from Christian theologies.

The Western cosmology supports a hierarchy that popularly holds that man is superior to woman, but that woman is more connected to the earth. For this and other complex reasons, women, and what is typically regarded as the feminine perspective, bear the brunt of ecological stresses. The fate of woman and the fate of the earth are inseparable, perpetually linked by the metaphors of woman as nature and nature as female.

"Woman as healer" is antithetical to the cosmological structure that binds the Western world. Throughout civilization, scientific, civic, and ecclesiastical bodies have closely watched the activities of women healers. Vigilance has been followed by legal restraint, persecution, and finally, by the enactment of laws and customs that prohibit women from practicing publicly. This cycle can be traced from the European heritage into the American tradition of allopathic medicine. Women and the values associated with the feminine were deliberately expunged from the institutions of society. In order for true progress—true healing in a global sense—to take place, Western cosmology must change. Women can no longer be seen as the problem, but as part of the solution to the crises facing the health of humankind.

THE THREAD OF CONSCIOUSNESS OF WOMAN AS HEALER

A thread of consciousness weaves through the centuries, connecting one era of women healers to the next. It relates to the feminine myth—the behaviors, abilities, and belief systems traditionally associated with women. Whether the myth originates in culture or biology is debatable and somewhat irrelevant—it simply is. In terms of healing, the feminine myth relates to such attributes as intuition, nurturance, and compassion. When expressed in professional practice, it supports the virtues of nature as healing resources, and the curative aspects of caring.

Women demonstrate the feminine myth in their choice of healing techniques and medicaments. They tend to be empiricists, observing at the bedside what soothes and heals and what does not. Their choice of profession is based on these observations; they gravitate to fields emphasizing prevention and the gentler botanics (rather than aggressive procedures), and to those serving the needs of other women and their children. The feminine myth supports the use of ritual at life's passages to acknowledge human bonds and the infinite connection of life.

Now and again, the feminine healing myth—the consciousness of woman as healer—moves brilliantly ungirded into the world, touching and changing and healing the space of humanity in ever-widening circles. Then, trapped by twisted logic and primal fears, by power's perverse seduction of human beings, it retreats. This book outlines this ebb and flow through the years of Western civilization, ending with the present—a time of critical juncture of events.

During the past few years, the expression of the feminine myth in healing has become more resolute and has taken on new dimensions. Women of a special caliber—the vast majority well-trained professionals—are appearing in great numbers.

They can be found working in hospital emergency rooms, and well-baby clinics, and hospices. They staff shelters for battered women and victims of rape. They minister to congregations and teach students. They are everywhere—in the creative arts, in the social sciences, in allied health professions. They heal with their hands and their words and their deep conviction that they have a knowledge or talent that will help others in some way.

Their work is likely to reflect a broad sense of healing that aspires to wholeness or harmony within the self, the family, and the global community. They see body, mind, and spirit as the inseparable nature of humankind; they believe that any healing ministrations have an impact on each element of this triune nature. They regard sickness as a potential catalyst for both emotional and spiritual growth, among other things. These healers have chosen to accompany, help, lead, teach, and care for others who seek wholeness.

These women view healing not as something one does to another, but as a process that takes place through the healer/healee relationship. Healing relates not so much to techniques as to philosophic and spiritual foundations. The bond that is established between the healer of this genre and the healee is life-giving and life-enriching for both. The relationship, itself, is held in reverence, with the awareness that it is made of trust, love, and hope. They aver that they are, indeed, working in sacred space.

The emergence of women whose consciousness blends with the ancient

---

themes of healing is the single most promising event in health care, for the lack of a feminine point of view is the most abject omission in American institutions and at the heart of the problems in American medicine. The manifestation of feminine values in medicine is critical for the health of the planet.

The women healers who share the thread of consciousness have taken a major leap forward from the past: they know that the feminine myth must influence, but not replace, advanced technology and sound, scientific strategies for helping and healing at all levels—physical, mental, and spiritual. The invisible spaces are seen as sacred, but so is good medicine, good counseling, good science, or whatever is being used to facilitate wellness. To return exclusively to the feminine myth in healing is to return to the Dark Ages. It is to be expected, then, that women healers are being joined in their mission by compassionate, nurturing, intuitive men who desire balance in their lives and in their professions.

The story of woman as healer will be told in four major sections: (1) The ancient and enduring relationship between Western cosmologies and woman healers; (2) the birth of science and the world events that justified the persecution of women healers; (3) the development of women's healing professions, including midwifery and nursing; and (4) observations from the modern era, and postulations for the future of women who practice the arts and sciences of health.

The information is presented chronologically, with the assumption that a consideration of both past and present are necessary to establish new institutions that nurture the essentials of humanity. Armed with facts and wisdom, women can begin to heal themselves and their professions from centuries of despair and successfully advocate change. Elizabeth Blackwell, the first woman to be awarded a medical degree in this country, stated in 1889 that "methods and conclusions formed by one-half of the race only, must necessarily require revision as the other half of humanity rises into conscious responsibility."[1] The purpose of the research and writing of this book was to assist in gathering an information base for all who choose actively to exercise "conscious responsibility" for a functional, balanced, and humane system of healing.

Part One

Medicine Woman:
The Ancient Cosmic
Connection

I The Primeval Turning Points

THE EARTH HAS BEEN bountiful in its healing prescriptions. In every part of the world, antiseptics, analgesics, diuretics, and emetics can be found. Weeds grow that can staunch the flow of blood and lower fevers. Nature provides tools for surgery and manipulation of the human body: pincers, lancets, needles, sutures, and splints.

Within the vast depths of the human mind are skills for observation, for making conclusions about how to care for each other to sustain life and enhance well-being. Creative juices flow into curative rites. During prehistorical times, the healing arts combined all of these—pharmacy, manipulation, and ritual. And it was woman, as it is today in tribal cultures, whose task it was to tend the sick, manage labors, and ease loved ones through their last repose. She sought the medicaments of the earth and the healing magic stored in the human mind. The medicine man appeared only when a louder voice or stronger hand was needed.

At the very dawn of humankind, the human female was regarded as a prodigious source of wisdom and power. She could bring life and save life, and therefore was the healer of sick bodies and wandering souls. She could also maim and take life away, and thus served as the gateway to dreams and vision and the world beyond the senses. Woman, particularly woman who gave birth and nurtured her babies with her own body, was mysterious and powerful.

A large number of diverse, widely placed cultures (such as the Amazon and Ona of South America, and the civilizations of ancient Crete and eastern Europe) have myths or artifacts from a very early time when women were the sole keepers of the magical arts. This suggests only that women served in the esteemed roles of healer and priestess and not necessarily as dominant tribal heads. No convincing finds have come to light that would support the existence of a matriarchy at any time or place. The history of the goddess and her living representatives, though, is long and sprinkled liberally over the planet.

Thousands of corpulent female figurines that date far back into the Stone

Age have been unearthed on the European and Asian continents. Carved of stone, ivory, or bone, they are the earliest detectable expression of woman as the embodiment of the beginning and continuance of life, and the symbol of immortality.[1] The "Venus" figures were placed on household altars and shrines, and were clearly part of the ceremonial life of early humans. The female, not the male, served in the most sacred capacity. For millennia, even until the Greek mythological era, woman was surrounded by common motifs, including animals of many types, snakes, and a labyrinth into the earth. These represent woman's connection to life, regeneration, wisdom, and the mysteries of her inner being.

Then, rather abruptly, at different times around the planet, the penis, not the vagina, became the sacred object of worship. Woman's magic was conscripted. Some of the feminine religious objects from the Stone Age show definite signs of having been attacked and deliberately damaged. Why? Changes in the ecology and economy, as well as invasions, played a major role. Furthermore, women and the products of their labors were placed in a secondary position of importance as humans began to feed themselves in ways that honored the male contribution. During the Stone Age, the bulk of foodstuffs was gathered and even grown by women using primitive methods of gardening. Man, who hunted with crude tools, was not able to provide food with any consistency. Given that the male's role in reproduction was also uncertain, men were probably viewed as basically superfluous to the health and continuance of the species. Men's adoption of herding and animal husbandry increased their worth significantly. When a glimmer of the truth of their reproductive function came to the conscious fore, men may have begun to regard themselves as the creative, generative force of the universe.

Fundamental to this idea was the establishment of men's lodges or secret cults, which had a deliberate and conscious goal of achieving power though subjugating and terrorizing women.[2] Membership in the cults was by election or decree, and by no means open to all men. From the closed fraternities, new and highly contrived cosmologies or creation stories emerged. The cosmologies were organized into actively propagandistic, patriarchal religions, which sought converts far beyond the local tribes. These religions developed myths on the origin of humanity and promoted a creator in man's own image.

Man's superiority was ordained in all matters of life. The lodges or cults became increasingly common, and included the ancient Hebrew tribes from whom our modern creation myths are derived. Some tribes, such as the Ona of Tierra del Fuego, have legends of a massacre conducted by the members of the lodge that destroyed the age of woman's magic. In Stone Age cave temples in southern France and elsewhere in Europe, the decimated remains of the female figurines suggest a similar violent overthrow. In other instances, a more benign cultural transformation took place.

These are the legends of the primeval turning point. However, the events are both ancient history and modern drama, acted and reenacted throughout the record of humankind. Invariably, the deities of the old ways become demons in the new; what was good becomes evil. Woman, as chief representative of the old ways, suffers the consequences as the ancient mother goddess figure is blamed for man's fall from grace. Even the pangs of birth, rather than part of the divine act of producing a miracle, became woman's just deserts. Life, procreation, sensual love between man and woman, all revert to a lowly, unholy status when the cosmic story excludes the divinity of the female. Women are viewed as ominous threats to the established order, and within a cosmological framework such as this, women cannot perform the sacred arts of healing.

As the homage to the goddess of the earth ceased, men looked to the heavens for succor. The male gods were of air and wind and thunder, all elements of the sky. Even the megalithic structures in Britain—sacred sites such as Stonehenge that were adopted by a succession of cultures for thousands of years—show evidence of these changes. The areas were redesigned over and over again in accordance with the existing gods. Pits and burrows in the earth gave way to stone arrangements that captured the light of the sun and the path of the stars. Gods no longer resided in the belly of the earth and in women but in the heavens and in the hearts of men.

Respected scholar of mythic traditions J. E. Harrison believes that the power of the male gods—Zeus, Apollo, or Yahweh—reflects that they are of a force greater than one that is earthbound. They stand

> first and foremost as a protest against the worship of Earth and the daimones
> of the fertility of the earth. A worship of the powers of fertility which
> includes all plant and animal life is broad enough to be sound and healthy,
> but as man's attention centers more and more on his own humanity, such a
> worship is an obvious source of danger and disease.[3]

Joseph Campbell identifies four types or stages of cosmology or creation stories that are generic for most cultures: belief in (1) a world born of a goddess without a consort, (2) a world born of a goddess fecundated by a consort, (3) a world fashioned from the body of a goddess by a male warrior god, and (4) the world created unaided by a male god.[4]

As cultures moved to the final stage of monotheism, every institution of the society became patriarchal in form. Sexual subordination was institutionalized in the earliest codes of law. These laws established legal dominion over women's reproductive function. This is a necessary step in a patrilineage, otherwise men could never be certain of which children were from their bloodlines.

Women's relatively smaller body mass, their biological bond to constant childbearing and nursing, as well as their enormous value as barter made them prime targets for domination and control. It was another 3,500 years before large numbers of women began to question their subordinate position in society. There may not have been an "overthrow" of women as such, but rather a process that developed over several thousand years.

Having been deprived of their own past and excluded from interpreting history, their voice was muted by the dominant male myth. "Where there is no precedent, one cannot imagine alternatives to existing conditions."[5]

In this section, six cultures will be described that demonstrate the relationship between women healers and cosmology. The first two, located in ancient Sumer and the vicinity of Denmark, are of special significance because of recent archaeological finds. There is no reason to believe that the events that took place there are in any way unique to the Western world, but, owing to geographic conditions, the earth has provided evidence substantiating the circumstances of women healers with more clarity here than in other prehistoric cultural locations.

We will also discuss ancient Greek culture, Roman culture around the time of the birth of Christ, the early Christian culture, and Christian Europe during the Middle Ages. The cosmologies from these eras are the foundation for the healing arts of Western civilization. They predetermined woman's role as healer even into modern times.

Within these cultural contexts, the pivotal processes that had such an impact on healers and dictated the future of Western civilization will be discussed. The themes that will be explored through the material are these:

1. In all cultures, women were associated with nature, a factor that initially deified them, and then served as the basis for their condemnation.
2. Healing is considered a divine function everywhere, in every time. Only those created in the image of the chief deity(ies) are legally or socially sanctioned to serve as healers.
3. There are many reasons for the image of God to shift from that of a nurturing, healing mother to that of a monotheistic male god: invasions, famine, disease, natural cataclysm, and deliberate counterfeit of new cosmologies in order to seize power.
4. The need for power and domination crept in as civilization progressed from being a hunter-gatherer society to a stable agrarian and, finally, a technological society. Women were subjugated in deference to power needs.

The final common pathway of these pivotal events was that women were forbidden entrance to the institution of healing as it evolved. The view of the world became fixed, distinguished by "setting apart of all pairs of opposites—male and female, life and death, true and false, good and evil—as though they were absolutes in themselves and not merely aspects of the larger entity of life."[6] On the other hand, when the Great Mother preponderates, "even the dualism of life and death dissolves in the rapture of her solace; the worlds of nature and the spirit are not separated . . . and there prevails an implicit confidence in the spontaneity of nature, both in its negative, killing, sacrifical aspect . . . and its productive and reproductive aspect."[7]

2 Sumer: The Birth and Death of a Culture

THE MOST PROMINENT city-state in Mesopotamia was Sumer, which reached a remarkable degree of development over six thousand years ago. Two major changes that altered the course of human history happened relatively early here: animals and plants began to be systematically grown for food about 7500 B.C., and around 3500 B.C. the fundamental arts of all high civilization came into being: writing, math, architecture, heavenly observation, temple worship, and government.[1]

Ancient Sumer, located in the approximate vicinity of modern Iraq, was hidden by layer upon layer of mud until it was discovered in excavations less than one hundred years ago. The voice of the Sumerians was never silent, however. Their culture sent fingers of myth into the succession of people who populated the land (the Babylonians, Assyrians, and Chaldeans), influencing the institutions and methods of healing that are the heritage of the Western world. The Sumerians, and not the ancient Greeks and Romans, are the parents of Western healing systems.

Until about 2000 B.C., women participated fully in sacred activities, owned property and business, and, if they were unmarried, could serve as priestess-physicians. In examining the turning point of this relatively advanced civilization, we witness the transformation of the Sumerian feminine myth, the loss of women's connection to the divinity, and hence loss of recognition of their natural gifts in the realm of healing.

CREATED IN DIVINE IMAGE

The pantheon of ancient Sumer was diverse; gods and goddesses of every conceivable nature breathed their spirit into daily life. As the deities touched and were integrated into the lives of the succeeding inhabitants of the land, their names and activities changed. Over time, the deities evolved into one male god whose divinity could be mirrored only by his sons. But in the peak of Sumer's civilization, both goddesses and women healers were recognized and, in some instances, were exceptionally revered.

The story of the rise and fall of women's divinity is best told through a brief overview of the myth of Inanna, or Ishtar, as she was later known to the Assyrians. Of all the gods and goddesses, Inanna has been the most honored with the written word. Known as the Queen of Heaven and Earth, the Lady of the Evening, and the Morning Star, Inanna was considered to be cosmic force propelling order and civilization among these advanced people. Her temple, the House of Heaven, was enormous—thirty by eighty meters. She embodied the trinity of love, healing, and birth, which speaks to their natural association. Her empathy for the suffering multitudes was legend.

In Mesopotamia the biological aspects of procreation were understood, and it was known that beings could not be conceived without the male and female. Reflecting this knowledge, their creation myths involved both sexes, and the female gave birth to the world. So, Inanna was in the lineage of the co-creators of the universe. It was only in much later cosmic interpretations that the universe was created single-handedly by a male god—an idea that is sustained through the curious logic of philosophers from Aristotle to Aquinas to modern-day theologians.

In Sumer the most sacred of all acts—sexual union—was celebrated as the green shoots pushed through the spring soil, giving promise of the harvest to come. The union of male and female was enacted to encourage the birth and growth of all that sustained life. It was, indeed, an act representing love, healing, and birth—the trifold province of Inanna.

Inanna, by her several names and through her mortal representatives, participated fully in these sacred marriage rites. Her votaries chose their own male consorts and explicitly, actively, and skillfully engaged in making love with them. Hymns and poetry from that time are an erotic tribute to these rites.[2]

Inanna calls to her "honey man" who, she says, "sweetens me always." And the king went to her holy loins with lifted head, opening his arms wide to the Priestess of Heaven.

> He shaped my loins with his fair hands,
> The shepherd Dumuzi filled my lap with cream and milk,
> He stroked my pubic hair,
> He watered my womb.
> He laid his hands on my holy vulva,
> He smoothed my black boat with cream,
> He quickened my narrow boat with milk,
> He caressed me on the bed.
> Now I will caress my high priest on the bed,

I will caress the faithful shepherd Dumuzi,
I will caress his loins, the shepherdship of the land,
I will decree a sweet fate for him.[3]

It is difficult to imagine the degree of empowerment such a cultural myth with its erotic imagery would have on contemporary women. A woman was a reigning and supreme deity who pleasured herself, rejoiced with birth, and whose body danced with the cycles of the moon. Mortal women would be called healers because they too knew of these mysteries and with wisdom could watch the ebb and flow of life.

Inanna, in one of the oldest stories, went down into the netherworld. There, as she passed through the gates, she was divested of her divine powers. According to the laws of the nether region, she could not return to the land of living. Or, if she was somehow retrieved, she must appoint a substitute to hold her place below. It was a curse to all humankind. Enki, the god of wisdom, interpreted this as meaning that if Inanna should not return, the progress of civilization would be reversed to its most primitive stages.[4] The myth was prophetic. Civilization did retreat when the feminine spirit was forced underground.

Gula, who embodied some of the persona of Inanna for the Assyrians, was viewed as a primary healer, and the goddess of death and resurrection. Temples were built in her honor, and litanies were sung to praise her cures. If she failed, a thousand lesser gods were required to intercede. Gula knew the herbal remedies and the poisons—often one and the same. She advocated the use of dreams for divination and diagnosis. She and Ishtar, together with the sun god Ea, would be viewed as a healing team with whom women might serve an apprenticeship.

Ishtar was likewise held in high esteem as a heavenly monarch. It was to her that the kings' secular power was attributed. Her temples have been found at virtually every level of excavation. Ishtar, too, was a compassionate, healing deity. A song to her follows:

Where you cast your glance, the dead awaken, the sick arise;
The bewildered, beholding your face, find the right way.
I appear to you, miserable and distraught,
Tortured by pain, your servant,
Be merciful and hear my prayer.[5]

As the land of Sumer became a perpetual battlefield (beginning in about the third millennium B.C.), it was to Ishtar that supplications were made. She became the goddess of war and destiny, and slowly, insidiously, there crept in more praises for her sexuality, and fewer for her healing nature.

The Epic of Gilgamesh, written in about 2000 B.C., describes what seems to be an inevitable consequence of adored and divine femininity. Here King Gilgamesh calls Ishtar a predatory and promiscuous woman, and rebukes her advances. In retaliation, Ishtar threatens to unleash the bull of heaven to destroy the city. The goddess of all things light and dark became the untamed goddess of the terrible.

The Istaritu were holy women of the temples who represented Ishtar in the act of consummating the sacred marriage. In the early times they embodied the essence of the deity and showered blessing upon the men who sought their presence. As Ishtar was seen as more sexual and promiscuous, the holy women were transformed into harlots associated with decadence and orgies, devoid of any holy significance. All of this was in concert with the dying of the Sumerian civilization.

The civilization that was Sumer ended about 1000 B.C. It died as do most societies, with disorder, injustice, inequality, and an unrecoverable imbalance in the ecology.

THE HEALING LEGACY

The Sumerian legacy to the healing arts was profound and enduring. Theories of body function and disease were carried via trade routes to the Phoenicians, Egyptians, and Greeks. The Sumerians thought that disease was caused by some sin, worm, or insect—ideas that permeate the Judeo-Christian teachings, as well as acknowledge the widespread parasitic diseases and malaria endemic to the region.

Prescriptions for stopping pain, written on clay biscuit-shaped pads, were found in the grave site of Queen Shubad of Ur (3500 B.C.). In the same grave were found what could be surgical tools made of flint and bronze, as well as charms and amulets. A clay pot that was likely used for distillation of plant essences into medicines was found in another grave site, which dated back to 5500 B.C.

Over eight hundred prescriptions have been recovered from this ancient part of the world, and have been translated by Assyrian scholars. What is referred to as the oldest medical text in existence was found on two tablets from the Sumerian period.

For two to three thousand years—at least until the Semitic invasions in about 2600 B.C.—women were allowed to practice healing with little or no restriction. Female occupations included doctor, scribe, barber, and cook. That women were allowed to be scribes is of great importance and most unusual, because it shows that women had the power to transcribe the culture through their own senses.[6]

By around 1000 B.C., as the society careened into decadence, women were excluded from formal education. By 700 B.C., neither scribe nor doctor were listed as women's occupations. The variety of classes of work available to women included several types of entertainer, transvestite, midwife, nurse, sorceress, wet nurse, and two kinds of prostitute. Woman's participation in the healing arts had been swiftly downgraded to one of service only. And, while women were still acting as midwives, this profession had probably lost stature as procreation and birth were seen less as a miracle and more as a shameful, degrading activity.

In any case, during the years when women's work in healing was relatively unrestricted, there were two categories of practitioners: the Ashipu and the Asu. The Ashipu knew the invisible (or magical) realm, and treated those aspects of disease. The Asu knew the botanical prescriptions and the other paraphernalia that were believed to influence the physical course of health.

In most tribal cultures there is a hierarchy of healers, with those who function in a capacity similar to the Sumerian Ashipu serving in the most venerated role. Those whose activities resemble the Asu practice the simpler, more mechanical type of medicine, and are of lesser stature.

In the land of Sumer, prescriptions for healing the invisible and the visible aspects of disease were regarded as of equal importance. Both may appear together on the same clay biscuit. The prescription for eye inflammation, for instance, included the following advice: insert a hot antimony needle in the cornea, or heat castor oil and pour it into the eye. The proper incantation is

O clear eye, O doubly clear eye, O eye of clear sight!
O darkened eye, O doubly darkened eye, O eye of darkened sight!
Like a cup of sour wine thrown away,
Gula quicken the recovery, thy gift.[7]

Modern interpretations of the Sumerian categories of healer tend to reverse the hierarchal structure. "Magic" is therefore equated with bad medicine, and the first-aid sort of practice with "good" medicine, or at least "better" medicine. The Ashipu, from this point of view, are seen as illiterate, dirty, ignorant, and superstitious.[8]

Several hundred healing plants were listed in the Sumerian pharmacopoeia. Many of these have been found to contain active ingredients that soothe, facilitate healing, and disinfect. The Sumerians had knowledge of the uses of opium and featured the poppy on their works of art.

THE DISAPPEARANCE OF WOMEN HEALERS

The status of women was, and usually is, a barometer of the degree of civilization in a culture. In Sumer, their status reached its maximum at the apex of the civilization, and declined in tandem with the culture. Women's role as healers was also an intimate reflection of the prevailing cosmology in Sumer—an association found in all places, at all times.

Women were also annihilated from their rightful place in healing by the scribes in Sumer. Samuel Noah Kramer, an Assyrian scholar, believes that the priests and scribes of Sumer were selectively and deliberately recording myths in such a way as to further their political ends. For example, by 3000 B.C., the Mother Goddess is replaced in the records of the Near East by a male god—usually of wind, air, or thunder. The goddesses have become wives and daughters. Namu, Mother Goddess, formerly hailed as the creator of the universe and mother of gods, is omitted altogether from the lists.[9]

Modern scribes are no less at fault for their selective omission of women in their recordings of medical history. What is written in this section on Sumer is well-documented in the Sumerian literature. Yet the emphasis on women is significantly different in two of the most popular texts on medical history, both written by male physicians. Lyons and Petrucelli, in their *Medicine: An Illustrated History,* invoke the Sumerian "cosmic ancestry" of today's physician, and refer to the sun god Ea.[10] They ignore the feminine healing pantheon, even though the goddesses are generally regarded as the patrons of healing. They make no mention of women's medicine in Sumer, and dedicate only a thin chapter to women in the 600-page text. Nevertheless, their bibliography lists authors such as Kate Campbell Hurd-Mead, M.D., and others who have carefully documented the work of thousands of women healers.[11]

Guido Majno, in *The Healing Hand: Man and Wound in the Ancient World,* makes only passing mention of the influential female deities of ancient Sumer, although he discusses the medicine of that time in lively detail.[12] He does cite a reference to the priestesses, however, in conjunction with a discussion of an Akkadian treatise on prognosis. "If his testicles are inflamed, if his penis is covered with sores, he has gone in to the high priestess of his god." Majno wisecracks, though, that the reader should ignore the comment on the "high priestess," because she was but one step beyond "the call of duty" (prostitution).[13]

The written record, then, is vague and full of projection and selective perception. Regardless of this, the connection between women healers and the religious beliefs of Sumer transcends the discrepancies in telling the story.

The next culture to be discussed, that of ancient Denmark, had no contemporary scribes to leave a written record. Instead, these are artifacts and the well-preserved remains of human bodies from which the correlation between woman as healer and the deities can be deduced.

3 Denmark: Woman as Shaman

THE PEAT BOGS and marshes of modern Denmark, which include the Jutland peninsula extending north from Germany and many surrounding islands, have begun to reveal their ancient hoard. Just as the layers of mud protected the lore of ancient Sumer, the tannic acid of the peat and the highly acidic ground waters in these areas captured life and held its story.

By now, approximately two thousand graves and seven hundred bodies in a remarkable state of preservation have been found, together with artifacts and sacrificial objects. People buried in mounds that jut over the rolling countryside were wealthy or esteemed individuals who apparently died from natural causes. Those found in the bogs were likely to have been sacrificed in goddess-worshipping rites or murdered for practicing witchcraft, adultery, or unknown crimes.[1]

Several of the bodies have been studied by teams of archeologists, historians, physicians, radiologists, parisitologists, anthropologists, botanists, specialists in nutrition and forensic medicine, and others who have added useful information about what life must have been like in those times. Hair, eyes, brains, skin, clothing, the last meal still partially digested in the gut, even the expression on faces leave a haunting memory of conditions of life. From these human remains, and in the artifacts and legends that accompany their era, we witness relatively recent evidence that points to the worship of a powerful female deity.

ANCIENT DANISH WOMAN AND HER HEALING LORE

Only the distinguished representatives of womanhood who were accorded the mound burials left a record of their appearance and life during the Bronze Age. The peasantry, then as always, left little or nothing to posterity. The women of means, even during this early time, were elaborately coiffed and bejeweled and were buried with prized possessions.

A description of a young woman found in a mound near Skrydstrup reads:

> Her hair had been piled up high to rest above her forehead on a hair pad
> . . . and covered with a square-meshed hair-net . . . held in place by cords

bound several times around the head. . . . [It was] ash blonde with a reddish glint. . . . An elaborately woven bonnet made by the "sprung" technique lay rolled up under her left cheek . . . rings of gold wire twisted in spirals were coiled round the ears. . . . [She had] outstandingly beautiful teeth, coated with strong enamel entirely free from caries or any other dental infection . . . in build she was tall and slender, being slightly more than five feet seven inches in height.[2]

This elegant woman, judged to be about eighteen years old, had a "well-shaped face, long and narrow and of Nordic type," and wore an embroidered tunic with a long belted skirt, to which a horn comb in fretted work was attached. From this and similar grave finds from the era, we know that Bronze Age women had time and skills to make beautiful things, and that for some, anyway, life was not consumed by toil.

Women during this time practiced healing with a number of herbal remedies. Yarrow, chamomile, chervil, fern, and other plants with known medicinal value were often buried with them. Henbane was found in a woman's grave located in a fortress at Fyrkat. In Denmark, and virtually all agrarian societies where women are involved in gathering or growing plants, they have knowledge of the plants' habits, as well as their nutritive and healing properties.

The country has over six hundred springs, which have been used for healing purposes since antiquity. The water coming from the belly of mother earth is believed to be inhabited by feminine spirits, and has always been associated with fertility. Offerings were placed in and around them to ensure safe childbirth, to supplicate for health, or to offer thanks.[3]

We can assume that women of ancient Denmark attended births and deaths, and served as caregivers in the general way that women do. However, no evidence has emerged showing that women served as shamans or priestesses, until around 500 B.C. The medicine bags, amulets, and other objects used in healing rituals that have been recovered from thirty of the two thousand graves dated before 500 B.C. have all been found in the graves of men identified as chieftains or priests. One of the coffins contained what seem to be surgical instruments; another contained "medicine" articles associated with rituals in cultures all over the world: amber beads, a conch shell, a small cube of wood, a number of dried roots, bark, the tail of a grass snake, a falcon's claw, and the jaw of a squirrel.[4]

MIND MEDICINE

Botanics containing high levels of alkaloids, such as henbane, which play a major role in woman's medicine through time, were known to the ancient

Danes. These plants have psychoactive and narcotic properties. In careful measure, they are useful for pain and suffering. In larger doses, they are poisons, causing delirium and even death.

The effects of the mushroom *Amanita muscaria* were also understood by the Danes, as well as by many tribes throughout the Northern Hemisphere. They are used in healing ritual and by those wishing to establish contact with the supernatural. Certain Danish soldiers may have eaten the mushrooms prior to battle.[5] The frenzy and exhilaration exhibited by these fearless troops earned them the name "berserkers," or "beserks of Odin," who also had the reputation of being able to shapeshift into animals.[6]

DISEASES AND CAUSES OF DEATH

Trauma was a major cause of death, particularly of the people found in the bogs. Childbearing has always been hazardous to women's health and life, but these women were large, strong, and relatively well nourished, and therefore probably survived childbearing better than women of other times. One young woman was found buried with the remains of a newborn infant. It is unlikely that she died in childbirth, however. Her hair had been closely cropped in the manner of an adulteress, and she had probably been thrown in the bog after her secret was discovered.[7]

The bog bodies do show evidence of having had several types of parasites, problems associated with irregular nutrition, such as rickets, and minor deformities, which were probably asymptomatic. Lower back pain must have plagued many as it does today. Several of the spines examined show evidence of vertebral spurs, Schmorl's nodes, and other indications of biomechanical problems. Several types of arthritis have also been identified, as well as limb and skull deformities which may have been caused by birth trauma. Pathology of some nature—hematoma or other brain injury, headache, mental illness, or even demon possession—resulted in numerous instances of trephination, or cutting and drilling a hole in the skull.[8]

COSMOLOGY AND THE TURNING POINT FOR WOMEN

Around 1200 B.C., the Danes abruptly began to cremate their dead instead of using the mound burials. The change indicates a dramatic shift to a belief that souls were more likely freed from the body by burning than by burial. The celestial flight was aided by including wings of birds with the ashes.[9]

A new god had come to the North. She was called Nerthus, of the lineage of Inanna and Ishtar. Her entry is depicted in bronze statuary, carved on rocks, and imprinted on razors. She is shown on a barge, one hand outstretched in greeting, another grasping a coiled serpent. On holy days, the mortal representative of Nerthus would assume this posture as she rode through the village on a wagon pulled by a team of oxen. One of the first figures in Norse myth, she was considered the mother of the earth.

Nerthus herself is only a superimposition of a stronger personality on a long-existing deity. The Earth Mother was worshipped as far back as the Paleolithic era, and her form appears on pottery found throughout northern Europe dating to that time. By the end of the Stone Age in ancient Denmark, she was carried in amulet form and carved into pendants of schist, a fine crystalline rock.[10]

Nerthus's close resemblance to the Sumerian goddesses was not accidental. The Danes were seafaring traders who came in contact with the cultures of the Near East, where the dead were cremated and the memory of Inanna and her successors lingered on. The Indo-European tribes were restless migrators, and could also have brought the old myths to the North. Like Inanna and Ishtar of ancient Sumer, Nerthus was a healer who granted her skills to mortals formed in her image, i.e., women. Too, she chose her consort and celebrated the sacred marriage in a ritual intended to initiate the beginnings of all life. The consummation of the marriage between Nerthus in her mortal form and the man of her choice assured that the bounty of the earth would be reaped as the seasons passed.

In early spring, several tribes from the Scandinavian countries and northern Germany met together to feast and drink and celebrate the sacred union. Weapons were laid aside in this time of hope and peace. The chosen mate ate a sacramental meal of many types of seeds in order to ensure that there would be foodstuffs available during the short, dim days of winter. Then the eternal rite of procreation was performed. Afterward, the mate was sacrifically offered to the Earth Mother, and the bog became his eternal resting place.

After the ceremony, the chariot or wagon, the vestments, and the representative of the goddess herself were cleansed in a secluded lake, a service performed by slaves who were drowned immediately afterward.

The earliest written record of these Danish customs comes from Tacitus, a Roman who, around A.D. 100, published the lengthy description of his travels in several volumes entitled *Germania*.[11] Evidence from the bog bodies supports his report of the powerful female deity Nerthus and her rituals. An example is the Danish Tollund Man, who died around 294 B.C., with a gentle and content expression on his face. His stomach contents show that his last meal was a gruel made from sixty-five types of seeds of the plants commonly used for food. Around his neck he wore the torque associated with the goddess in works of art, which may have been used as a garrote. This handsome man was no laborer lost in the fen; his hands and feet were remarkably free from calluses, and his nails well manicured.[12]

Lindow Man (300 B.C.), found recently in northern Germany, also testifies to ritual sacrifice. The contents of his last meal included mistletoe pollen and charred bread. Mistletoe has been used ceremonially by Druids and others, and is widely believed to have magical properties. In ancient Beltane festivals, a special bread was broken up and distributed. The one who got the burnt portion was called the "devoted" and was sacrificed to the gods. Whether these northern Europeans were practicing similar rites is not known, but the evidence suggests that they were.[13]

Bloodletting was an important aspect of the rite dedicating a man to the goddess. Lindow Man and others had had their arteries severed and their blood drained into the earth. A man found near Schleswig, Germany, not only had his throat slit, but his genitals removed, thus diffusing his procreative power. Emasculation also assured that his seed remained with the goddess alone. This man, like Tollund Man, was no commoner. His fine golden hair was carefully tied in an intricate Swabian knot, and his hands and feet were neatly manicured.

WOMAN AS SHAMAN

Influence of female deities increased steadily from the beginning of the cremation period, and by 500 B.C. they dominated religious expression. Grave finds indicate that at the same time, the role of medicine man was assumed by medicine woman.

In a coffin containing a woman's charred remains were also found her belt box, knife, and bronze fibula. Another box made of bronze and decorated with stars contained two horse's teeth, weasel bones, a cat's claw joint, a bird's windpipe, snake vertebrae, twigs of mountain ash, charred aspen, quartz crystals, clay, pyrite, and a bronze wire bent into a hook. These are the accoutrements of a medicine woman or shaman.[14]

In areas scattered across the world, the shamans typically serve as revered healers and sages dedicated to the well-being of the community. As "technicians of the sacred," they are able to commune with the realm of the supernatural and heal problems of the most difficult or spiritual nature.[15] The objects found in the woman's coffin have spiritual significance, are believed to be imbued with the potential for divination, healing, or protection, and are used in healing rituals. The animal parts, such as the weasel bones or the horse's teeth, usually represent an animal fetish or totem or spirit ally that aids in the shaman's work.

The fact that women were shamans during this period indicates they had entered into the most authoritative and honored ranks of healers. The shaman in ancient or tribal cultures is at the top of the healing hierarchy, and his or her skills are considered more advanced than those of either the herbalist or the bonesetter.

The shift in cosmology that is associated with women's elevation in the hierarchy has been documented through an inventory of the sacrificial objects found in the sacred springs, groves, and bogs. In the first period of the Bronze Age (which began in Denmark about 1500 B.C.) all the gifts were offered to male deities. But in the second and third periods, 60 percent of the offerings were to female deities. In the fourth and fifth periods, female deities received 75 percent of the gifts. By the end of the Bronze Age (around 500 B.C.) 90 percent of the offerings were made to female deities. Jewelry, ornamental vessels, cooking pots, parts of looms, and other domestic tools were given in honor of the female god; weapons, ships, and razors were typical offerings to the male.[16]

The Betrayal by Mother Earth: Enter the Gods of War

The beginning of Nerthus's reign was a time of peace and prosperity associated with a stable, developing civilization in which the creative arts were evolving. Even the sudden change in cosmology upon her arrival seemingly caused no cultural upheaval.

Around 500 B.C. cataclysmic geological events occurred. The temperature dropped, and the Scandinavian glaciers began their descent. By 300 B.C. the groundwater began to rise, eliminating significant portions of fertile soil. The hostile seas encroached on the lands, destroying harbors and pushing villages inland to higher ground, finally to be abandoned altogether for several centuries. Only the tenacious weeds and rye survived the short summers and the long, dark winters, and the bones of the children were bent from malnutrition. Many of the Danes left, seeking kinder terrains in Switzerland and France.

Those who stayed behind offered Nerthus, the Earth Mother, many votives so that she would calm the seas and bring back the warm sun. The bogs have yielded the simple metal adornments of peasants, as well the jewels of kings and queens. Amber—the most precious trading commodity of ancient Denmark—and articles of bronze and gold were given in abundance in intercessory ritual. The silver Gundestrup cauldron, one of several vessels in contention as the Holy Grail, was offered during this time of tribulation— dismantled, with pieces neatly stacked.

Nerthus was not appeased, and meanwhile the troubled culture was also faced with invasions of marauding tribes. As the Iron Age drew to a close, offerings to the male god(s) of war increased significantly. Single caches of

---

great size, containing hundreds of weapons and war booty, have been uncovered, as well as Roman coins, silver helmets, coats of mail, spearheads, a sixty-five-foot war canoe filled with swords and shields, and even a dismembered horse. These deposits are evidence of troubled times and of the influence of the gods of war upon men's minds. Odin and Thor, gods of thunder and destruction, usurped Nerthus's reign, and her fertility function was assumed by the male deity Njord.

SHAMANIC PRACTICES IN THE CHRISTIAN ERA

The harsh barriers of land and sea, plus the independent nature of the men and women of the North, prevented these areas from ever becoming a part of the Roman Empire. Their relative isolation also prevented them from becoming officially Christianized until A.D. 980. Visits to the healing springs, the old gods, and the sacred stones were allowed until the first few years of the second millennium, when they were finally banned by Knud the Great. Indeed, there is evidence that the punitive god of the Israelites blended into a hybrid with the personality of the Norse gods: sacred objects bore both the cross and the hammer.

The colorful Norse pantheon was not readily dismissed, and even in the twelfth century there was still interest in the "heathen" legends. Sensing that the old stories were fading, a gifted Icelandic scholar, Snorri Sturluson, determined to preserve them for poets and intellectuals, and as a guide to imagery of the past. His work, the *Prose Edda,* written about A.D. 1220, tells us that Nerthus was revived in the form of the goddess Freyja, and "that she was the most renowned of the goddesses, and that she alone of the gods yet lived."[17]

Freyja was the leader of the Vanir, a group of agricultural and matriarchal goddesses who were represented in mortal form by women who practiced a type of shamanism called *seidhr,* or *seiðr.* The women journeyed from village to village in their wagons, accompanied by a large group that provided music. Elaborately dressed, the women sat regally on high cushions stuffed with chicken feathers. During special songs and chants, their souls left their bodies to travel through space, assuming the form of an animal. While in a state of trance, the women were said to cure the sick and divine the future with significant reliability. The Vanir were occasionally described as rivals of the cult of Odin, and as practitioners of witchcraft or harmful magic.[18]

The ceremonies made a considerable impact on the sagas from the northern regions, and have been recently documented by grave finds. A woman of high rank, believed to be a priestess of the Vanir, was buried in a delicately carved ceremonial wagon found in a ship at Oseberg. The find—dated about

A.D. 800—included tapestries and fine wooden objects. How long after that the shamanic practices continued in secret among the women of Denmark is not known.[19]

WOMEN'S PLACE

What was happening to women during the changeover of the gods? As one might expect, given the episodic reemergence of the Earth Mother, they fared surprisingly well. Tacitus claims they were even able to own property, practice in the professions, and obtain divorce—very unusual for any era.

Both Tacitus and Julius Caesar observed that these people did not marry in haste, but only after a suitable exchange of dowry (usually weapons of war), and relatively late in life. The virility, youthful physique, and strength of both the men and women were attributed to their living chaste well into their twenties. The men were content with one woman, which Tacitus found unique among the "barbarians."

Tacitus also observed that these northern tribes "believe that there resides in women an element of holiness and prophecy, and so they do not scorn to ask their advice or lightly disregard their replies."[20] Strabo, in *Geography*, written about the time of Christ, noted that among the women who accompanied the men into battle were prophetesses and priestesses. They were gray with age, wore white clothes, cloaks of fine linen, had metal belts, and were barefoot. As they entered camp with swords in hand, they approached the prisoners, crowned them, and led them to a bronze vessel. One of the women would mount a step and, leaning over the cauldron, cut the prisoner's throat, bleeding him into the vessel's rim. Others cut open his body and inspected the entrails to divine the army's next strategy.[21]

This type of divination is not uncommon in native cultures, and those who perform it generally diagnose disease also. Whether these women were functioning within the mainstream of their culture, or on the fringe, is debatable.

As recently as the eighteenth century, physician and historian William Alexander complained about the Danes' reverence for their enchantresses. In *The History of Women: From the Earliest Antiquity to the Present Time Giving Some Account of Almost Every Interesting Particular Concerning that Sex, Among All Nations, Ancient and Modern*, he notes that poetry and divination were particularly sacred in these northern areas, and that the people were "dupes of superstition," venerating every female who dealt in charms and divination. The problem with the women, that they should be so given to spells, was probably their vegetable diet, among other things. He mentions Thorbioga, a Danish woman who was especially honored, and kept company with the nobility and wore robes and headdresses that made her a legend in her own time:[22]

> She was dressed in a gown of green cloth, buttoned from top to bottom, had a string of glass beads about her neck, and her head covered with the skin of a black lamb, lined with the skin of a white cat; her shoes were made of calf's skin, with the hair on it, tied with thongs, and fastened with brass buttons; on her hands she had a pair of gloves, of a white cat's skin, with the fur inward; about her waist, she wore an Hunlandic girdle, at which hung a bag containing her magical instruments; and she supported her feeble limbs by leaning on a staff, adorned with many knobs of brass.[23]

Alexander goes on to say that when Thorbioga entered a hall, the whole company would rise in salute. She was known far and wide for her soothsaying ability, wielding power through her visions of the future.

Although the voice of the goddess eventually receded, she lived far longer in the hearts of these northern women than in their sisters' in other lands. Traces may still live on. According to one leading scholar of ancient Denmark, "Midsummer Night's bonfires still blaze from the heights and along the coast all over the country on the night when all the powers of witchcraft were let loose, but when also the healing powers of wild herbs were at their greatest and the water in the sacred springs strongest in miraculous power."[24]

THE PIVOTAL TIMES

These two instances from prehistory were chosen to describe a time when women were omnipotent in myth, cherished for their connection to nature, regarded as healers, and believed to hold power in the invisible realm.

What happened in both cultures was complex: a goddess-worshipping, peaceful, thriving, people were hit by disaster on all flanks. The seasons were changing, the earth itself was showing signs of great upheaval, there was famine and sickness, and there were hungry marauders on the horizon. The Great Mother as healer and creator was worshipped more and more intensely. When conditions didn't change, she was given warlike characteristics in hopes that she would intercede in battle. Ultimately, she was replaced by other gods—whichever male, angry, and warlike gods were worshipped by those who had the best fortune in battle—and finally by a single male god. In the process, the magical arts practiced by women—including the art of healing—were banned.

4   *The Healing Legacy from Greece*

THE GREEK TRADITIONS formed what was considered the epitome of healing practices in Western civilization until about four hundred years ago. Even though the roots of modern healing practices go back as far as Sumer, Greek physicians are popularly considered the fathers of Western medicine. A brief review of the role women inherited from an earlier Grecian era, seen through the legend and cosmology of the times, is therefore in order. The era we are discussing—ancient Greece—is generally regarded to have begun about 2000 B.C., and ended with the fall of Corinth in 146 B.C.

The Greek women had a healing predecessor in Helen of Troy, who may have lived about 2000 B.C. She was a student of Polydamna, physician and queen of Egypt. According to the fourth book of Homer's *Odyssey*, when Telemachus and his companions visited Helen in Sparta, they were distraught over the fate of Telemachus' missing father, Odysseus. To soothe their misery, Helen "cast a drug into the wine whereof they drank, a drug to lull all pain and anger, and bring forgetfulness of every sorrow."[1] This drug was the legendary nepenthe, which Plutarch suggests was verbena, adiantum, and wine; Dioscordes and Galen believe it was from a root called oinopia; still others think it could have been datura, poppy (opium), or evening primrose.

Helen and other Homeric heroes had a creditable pharmacopoeia, particularly for relieving pain and altering moods. Mention is made of hellebore, burned sulphur, mandrake, and poppy juice (inhaled from a steaming sponge).

Women healers probably enjoyed the height of their glory at this time. Some scholars believe them largely responsible for the initial development of surgical techniques and therapeutics, which made Greek medicine the most advanced in the ancient world.[2]

The Greek cosmology abounded with healing goddesses. However, by 1000 B.C. the feminine deities were significantly less powerful than the masculine gods who were ascribed an angry, vengeful, and often cruel nature. A list of the healing pantheon includes Demeter, caretaker of women and children; Persephone, who could cure sore teeth and eyes; Genetyllis, prayed to for problems of infertility; Hecate, specialist in diseases of children; Athena, who cured blindness; Medea and Circe, whose special knowledge was poisons and their antidotes; Leto, the surgeon; and Eileithyia, who was midwife of the gods. Hera was the chief healing deity at Argos, and Isis, although a foreign goddess, was considered by the Greeks of Corinth to be among the greatest of healers.[3]

The legend of Asclepius and the women in his family continues to penetrate Western medical tradition. These "sainted mortals" probably lived around 900 B.C., and it is to them that the Hippocratic Oath, the ethical code of honor taken by every physician today, is recited. The oath begins, "I swear by Apollo the physician, by Asclepius, by Hygeia and Panacea and by all the Gods and Goddesses making them my witnesses, that I will fulfill according to my ability and judgment this oath and this covenant." Asclepius' daughters, Hygeia and Panacea, have long represented prevention and cure, and his wife Epione was the patron saint for those in pain.

Over three hundred magnificently built and beautifully sited temples or sanitariums dedicated to this family have been located. The primary healing arena was the *abaton,* a large room where patients drifted into twilight, or "incubation" sleep. During this altered state of consciousness, the retinue of gods and goddesses (or their earthly representatives) would appear and minister cures.

Each woman in the Asclepian family had her own caduceus—the snake-entwined staff that to this day symbolizes medicine. The Greek women healers are often pictured as keepers of the snakes, as were women elsewhere—in Crete, Canaan, Egypt, and even as far north as Germany and Scandinavia. Numerous statues have been found of Hygeia, a beautiful and modest-looking figure who holds a dish from which she feeds the serpent coiled by her side. In these we see the continuity of the snake motif representing feminine healing energy.

A type of yellow snake (probably now extinct) was regarded as so sacred that when some escaped from a Greek sailing vessel into a cave nearby on the Italian shore, an Asclepian temple was built immediately on the spot. The snakes were trained to lick the eyelids and sores of patients during healing ceremonies. Snake venom may have been used to induce healing imagery during the incubation sleep. The venom of many poisonous snakes (cobras, kraits, and probably rattlesnakes) has hallucinogenic properties. Victims who have survived snakebites and are thus immunized report feelings of euphoria and revelatory visions.[4] The healers, too, may have allowed themselves to be bitten in order to perceive the supernatural realms of altered consciousness, where virtually all ancient peoples believe healing information is available.

Prior to the seventh century B.C., the women of this healing family were often depicted on pottery, statuary, and frescoes as ministering their healing art alone. After that time they were rarely shown except in the presence of their father. Their role was modified to that of handmaiden; they are shown carrying baskets of herbs, introducing Asclepius to a patient, or working under his guidance. Concomitantly, regard for women healers was on a swift decline. The downgrading of Hygeia is a reflection of Western medicine to this day. The principles that she represents—prevention, sanitation, nutrition, and the general prescriptions for healthy living—are not taken as primary medical tools. Instead, the Western healing tradition has identified with active intervention methods, such as surgery and medication, promoted by the Greek fathers of medicine.

At Delphi, picturesquely located on a hillside above the blue waters of the bay of Corinth, stands another shrine in testimony to the Grecian belief in woman's healing abilities. During the earliest times, the spot was identified with Gaia, the earth goddess. It has always been held as a site of oracular or divinatory power. The oracles were given by a woman, called the Pythia, who perched on a stool around which a snake called the Python was wrapped. The mumblings of the Pythia were not intelligible to all mortals, and required interpretation, first by priestesses, and later by priests. The devoted would travel in processions from great distances to receive treatment or prophesies. The primary methods of treatment were similar to that of the Asclepian temples: the nature of diagnosis, possible treatments, and even sudden cures would occur in the imagery state of near sleep or incubation sleep. Herbal remedies, baths, exercise, water from sacred springs, purges, bleedings, and perhaps even surgery, as well as games and entertainment, took place in the buildings on the site.

The shrine was reassigned to Apollo, who, legend says, found it necessary to kill the Python. Around the shrine are numerous sculptures and reliefs of women—the "Amazons"—fighting men, which may depict the initial seizure of the shrine.[5] Here, as in legends of very primitive cultures such as that of Tierra del Fuego, women's magic was violently conscripted.

By the time of Aristotle (born around 384 B.C.) and Hippocrates (born in 460 B.C.)—the fathers of medicine—Greek women were little more than slaves. Their involvement in healing arts was minimal compared to the legendary days of Helen and the priestesses of Delphi. Despite this, they did make a contribution, albeit forgotten, to the basis of Western medical science. Pythias, for example, worked alongside her husband, Aristotle. He referred to her as his "assistant." They spent their honeymoon on Sappho's island, studying plant and animal life, and together wrote an encyclopedia of their observations. Pythias was particularly involved in studies of tissues and reproduction and detailed her findings from studies of chicken and human embryos.

The healing skills of a Greek queen, Artemsia (about 350 B.C.) were praised by Pliny, Strabo, and Theophrastus. She was credited with discovering wormwood as a cure for a wide range of disorders. Several species of the flower named for her were prescribed for women's health problems, including delayed menses and prevention of abortion. (Artemis, the goddess, has been given similar attributes.)

Pliny, writing in about A.D. 50, mentions several women who wrote medical books. He claimed that one of them, Elephantis, was so beautiful that she was obliged to lecture behind a curtain so as not to distract the attention of her students. A woman of Pliny's time named Lais wrote on abortions and was famed for her cures of malaria using menstrual blood![6]

One of the better-known woman physicians of all time was named Agnodice, a great favorite among the women she treated. She wore men's clothing, probably trying to disguise her sex. By then (the third or fourth centuries B.C.), women were in disrepute as healers, and her disguise may have allowed her to practice with less scrutiny. Agnodice was forced to stand trial when her ruse was discovered. The women of Athens rushed to the tribunal with vociferous declarations of loyalty. According to legend, they threatened to condemn their husbands and withhold certain favors if she were not released immediately. The strategy was effective. Agnodice was released and allowed to continue to practice, and to dress in whatever way she chose.

The stories about her are no doubt apocryphal, but a few such stories about women healers are most welcome, given the scarcity of information. It is said that after her release, she lifted her skirts to proudly display her womanhood. Whatever the truth, there is agreement that she was well trained in the tradition of the master teacher Herophilus. From him she learned how to perform cesarean sections, embryotomy, and other medical procedures.

Many, many other women are mentioned during these years in Greece.[7] Even Seneca (4 B.C.–A.D. 65) wrote of the skillful fingers of his woman doctor; St. Paul and Pliny acknowledged the prowess of the midwives. None of the women's names, though, have attained any lasting status.

It is widely assumed that the large volumes attributed to Aristotle, Hippocrates, Galen, and others were not written singlehandedly but were a compilation of the works of many writers. Women like Pythias may well have written lengthy portions of the prolific writings of the fathers of medicine, but documentation of this is scant.

Evidence also suggests that a few women were making original contributions, but they were obscured by centuries of plagiarism and confusion over authorship. For example, a woman named Cleopatra wrote a book on

Woman as Healer

gynecology that was used as a reference for fifteen or sixteen hundred years. She was a healer who was often confused by historians with other Cleopatras, including the queen (who did know something of poisons), several healers who lived in Galen's time, and even a writer on magic of later centuries. In the sixth century A.D. her work was falsely attributed to a male writer named Moschion. It wasn't until the sixteenth century that her identity as author was restored.

A Greek woman named Metrodora wrote a treatise on diseases of the uterus, stomach, and kidneys. The manuscript—still preserved in Florence, Italy—was written around the first century A.D., and is believed to be the oldest medical text written by a woman. But soon after it was written, the text was attributed to a man named Metrodorus. The prevailing belief system simply did not allow that women could write anything of medical value. Metrodora's work met what was, in those days, a common fate: it was reattributed to a male.

Scattered evidence such as I have cited suggests that women healers played a role in the genesis of Western medicine, despite male domination of the nascent healing sciences and legal proscriptions against women practitioners.

5   Women of Rome

THE MYTHS AND STORIES of the feminine healing contribution from Rome surface during the two hundred years before the birth of Christ. Healing practices during this time were more fully and creatively developed in the supernatural area than in the physical realm. Ancient Roman historians had little regard for medicine or its practitioners. Cato (234–149 B.C.) classified all medical people with mountebanks and robbers; women healers, particularly, were dismissed as poisoners and abortionists. Pliny, who wrote in the first century A.D., claimed that Rome had been without physicians for six hundred years, and that heads of families were expected to minister to their sick kin.

It is not surprising that when Corinth fell to Rome in A.D. 146, men and women who had healing skills brought high prices on the slave market. At this point, Greek practices were quickly adopted, and healing became a Greco–Roman blend. Let us examine the aspects of Roman healing prior to that time.

FEMININE HEALING MYTHOLOGY

For a long time the Romans had solicited and enticed deities from other lands, promising shrines and glory in return for their favors. Asclepius, in fact, was called during a devastating plague around 300 B.C. The healing pantheon, with which Greek deities were later integrated, included many goddesses named for the diseases they healed, such as Scabies, Angina, Genitamana, and Nascia, as well as Fecunditas, who was said to have been present at the delivery of Nero. Diana was also a favorite goddess for pregnancy and birth, and Minerva was revered as a general healer and protector. Mater Matuta was an ancient and long-revered goddess whose task it was to open the uterus to allow babies to come into the world.[1]

Cybele, or Magna Mater, the Great Mother of the Roman Empire, was cast from the same mold as Inanna and Nerthus. Her ascent into Rome came about in the following way: Rome was under perpetual siege around 200

B.C. from both political forces within and armies from without. Frequent showers of stones (hail?) were believed to be attacks of a supernatural nature. The frightened people consulted the ancient body of Rome divination, the Sibylline books, and an oracle advised them to bring in the Magna Mater from Anatolia. The Oracle at Delphi confirmed the advice. The goddess, in the form of a sacred black stone, was imported by ship.

The story is similar to the importation of Nerthus to northern Europe. The goddess, who held power over life and death, was celebrated in rites of spring. Her consort, Attis, was soon himself the focus of a strong cult following. His holiday honored his death and resurrection, and featured activities of spiritual renewal. The worship of Cybele and Attis held forth for over seven centuries and was the target of attack by contemporary Christians.[2]

The figure of Cybele, as well as the entire feminine pantheon of healing, points to the importance of woman in the cosmology of the Roman mind. Worship of these deities was the primary form of medicine until the Greek practices were introduced, and even then they were held with tenacity by the citizens of Rome.

THE HEALING ARTS

Whereas the women of Greece were poorly regarded, Roman women generally enjoyed some prestige and freedom. Prior to the first century A.D. women were allowed to practice in the professions if they desired, but little is known of their work. In the first centuries A.D., many women practiced a full range of therapeutics in addition to the profession of midwifery. Their work seems to have been well regarded, but they were advised, nonetheless, to keep their place of modest servitude. Pliny the Elder noted that women should be as quiet and inconspicuous as possible in their business of healing, "so that after they were dead, no one would know that they had lived."[3]

Soranus (A.D. 98–138), who for centuries was considered an authority on obstetrics and diseases of women, wrote of the ways that women should be trained to deliver babies and treat gynecological complaints. His recommendations for the obstetrix were that she be literate and have good, intact senses; a knowledge of anatomy, hygiene, therapeutics; a love of her work; and discretion. Ideally, she would know a broad range of therapies, dietetics, surgical procedures, and drugs. She would remain cool-headed during emergencies.[4]

Celsus, regarded as the chief scribe of the early Roman era, described women healers as busily involved in their work, examining urine, applying leeches, and administering poppy juice for surgery—all activities at the highest level of professional practice of that time.[5]

Most of the women who studied and practiced the healing arts were from aristocratic families. Some practiced a domestic form of medicine. Octavia, first wife of Mark Antony, wrote a book of prescriptions. For toothache she prescribed barley flour, honey, vinegar, and salt, all baked and pulverized with charcoal and scented with flowers. For ulcerated sore throat she prescribed spikenard and honey with myrrh, saffron, alum, caraway seeds, celery, and anise. A plaster to draw out animal poisons contained orris root, fat of dog's brain, milk of wild figs, dog's blood, turpentine, ammonia, wax, oil, and onions. Her recipe for pain relief included lard or goose grease, wine, cardamom seeds, rose leaves, spikenards, and cinnamon. Salve to sooth the pains of childbirth contained lard and rose leaves, cypress, and wintergreen.

Octavia's remedies were described by Scribonius Largus, physician and traveling companion to Emperor Claudius in the first century A.D.[6] He also mentions potions used by Messalina, the wife of the emperor; Livia, the wife of Augustus; and Antonia, Octavia's daughter. The women are portrayed as "dabbling" in medicine, experimenting on their households. From his observation we might surmise that the efforts of these women were not taken seriously; further, the remedies were likely to have had little effect, for they resemble recipes or cosmetic preparations rather than active pharmaceuticals. Contrast Octavia's pain remedy with Helen of Troy's! On the other hand, Octavia did not include many of the disgusting substances of the folk remedies used by the physicians of her time—dung in every conceivable form, blood, and entrails.

Rome had begun its wretched decline during the years Scribonius was collecting prescriptions from around Europe. The population of the city had grown rapidly at the turn of the century, sanitation was abysmal, and disease was rampant. Because of the surrounding swamp, malaria was ever present.

These were the unhealthy circumstances that Galen, the last of the fathers of medicine, faced in the second century. Galen is credited with writing over five hundred books that remained unchallenged medical dogma until the seventeenth century. Like the work of his Greek predecessors, his was a compilation to which women may have made significant contribution.

Galen praised Origenia's prescriptions for diarrhea as well as Eugerasia's mode of treatment of nephritis, which included squills, bryonia, white pepper, cedar berries, iris root, myrrh, and wine. He mentions a woman named Margareta, who had an unusual appointment as an army surgeon. His celebrated colleague Antiochis was a woman specializing in diseases of the spleen, arthritis, sciatica, and in the preservation of beauty. Galen copied many of her prescriptions, including those for chest pains and gout.[7]

Another woman of this time, Aspasia, was later extensively paraphrased and quoted by Aëtius, a writer in Mesopotamia who lived around the sixth century A.D. His two thousand–page medical treatise, *Tetrabiblion,* contains all that we know of her work.[8] She prescribed these methods of preventing miscarriage: avoid chariot rides, needless worry, and violent exercise. She advised taking simple laxatives such as rhubarb and lettuce. For exceptionally narrow birth canals, she prescribed the application to the vulva of hot lotions of olive oil, mallows, flax seed, and the oil from a swallow's nest. Her method of birth control (to be used only in the case of health problems) was wool tampons soaked in herbs, pine bark, myrrh, wine, and other relatively benign ingredients.

Aspasia gave what were probably exceptionally effective directions for abortions: on the thirteenth day after a missed period, the patient was to be hauled and pulled and jerked about; was to lift heavy burdens; use high douches of strong herbs; take hot baths; and drink a mixture of rue, artemisia, ox gall, eleterium, and absinthe. (Both rue and absinthe are highly toxic in large doses.)

For a displaced uterus, she advised tampons of tar or bitumen, soaked in hot oil. She described operations to remove tumors and create artificial openings into blocked bladders. For uterine hemorrhoids she advised surgery, followed by tampons of mallows, earth, juice of hemlock, and mandragora. She gave instructions for dissecting and replacing herniated intestines, treating varicose hernias by resection, and so forth. Her medicine is quite advanced compared to the ignorant practices that prevailed over the next sixteen hundred years.

Women practiced the art of healing among many other demands and activities, doing the perennial "double duty" at home and at work. The poet Horace observed that "their rewards were good, though gained at the price of fatigue."[9] At the same time, women began to lose ground as professionals when, during Galen's lifetime, more men were attracted to doctoring. As always when this happened, women were edged into less lucrative areas of healing, treating castoffs from the mainstream of medical practice and those who could not afford to pay.

6 *Brilliant Early Christian Flowering*

DURING THE FIRST few centuries after the birth of Christ, the efforts of many women healers found their way into history. One senses in their work a resurgence of power and respectability, of high energy devoted to caring for and curing the sick. Their success can be largely be attributed to the influence and attitude of the early Christians, who respected women for their intellect and contribution to the religious movement.

Jesus himself challenged the religious and social institutions of his day with a frontal assault on patriarchy, shocking his contemporaries with his open consort with and esteem for women.[1] All four gospels of the New Testament note that women were found in the fellowship of Jesus, and that, further, they were the most courageous of his disciples.[2] The leader of the women appears to have been Mary Magdalene, who, according to the secret gospel literature, had a position in the Early Church equal to that of Peter— the "rock" upon which the Church was built. Women were acknowledged to have been given the spirit of prophecy by Luke (Acts 2:17), and were valued in the mission work of the Church. Paul mentions Mary, Tryphena, Tryphosa, and Persis (Rom. 16:6), Apphia (Philem. 2), and many other women who "labored" in the Lord.

Jesus selected the most compassionate, maternal images from the Jewish tradition, creating a Christian god as androgynous in character as any male god in history. In the early years, the feminine-masculine imagery was pronounced. In some of the early sects, God was even seen as a dyadic being (mother-father), rather than the trinity (father–son–holy spirit).

The gospels that offered the most detail on God as mother, which also spoke most completely on the work and role of Christian women, were deliberately omitted from what would become known as the New Testament in a selection process, conducted by various Christian communities, that ended in about A.D. 200. By then virtually all the feminine imagery for God (along with any suggestion of an androgynous human creation) had disappeared from the "orthodox" Christian tradition.[3] The books that were omitted, known as "secret" or "heretical" or "gnostic," present a very different picture of the Christian cosmology. These books include the *Gospel of Mary*, the *Wisdom of Faith*, the *Gospel of Thomas*, the *Gospel of Philip*, and the *Secret Gospel of John*, among others.

From these gospels, three primary characterizations of the feminine attributes of the divine emerge.[4] She is first seen as God, the Mother of All Things—half of the total dyad—in a creative relationship of opposition to a masculine primal source, a metaphor akin to the Eastern notion of yin and yang. Secondly, God the Mother is defined as Holy Spirit—the maternal element of the Trinity. In the *Gospel of Philip*, Spirit is described as both Mother and Virgin, and as counterpart of the Holy Father. The third quality of God the Mother is wisdom, or Sophia ($\sigma o \phi \iota \alpha$). In this context, Sophia is the creative power that gives wisdom to humankind.

Thus, the criterion for full expression of woman as healer—that she be created in divine image—was met in the early Christian beliefs. Under these conditions, the feminine association between spirituality and a healing vocation naturally flourished. Moreover, the work of women healers of this period reflected the early religious teaching of the Church—that the clearest demonstration of love is in caring for the physical and spiritual needs of everyone, rich and poor alike.

The restless spirituality of women found an outlet in Christian service. One of the best-known and most beloved women healers was Fabiola, the lifelong friend, correspondent, and devotee of St. Jerome. This wealthy patrician dedicated her life to charitable missions in order to expatiate some youthful frivolity, and to ease her disappointment in two failed marriages. Fabiola founded the first public civilian hospital—long regarded as the best of its kind—in Europe in 394. She gathered her patients from the gutters, often as they were dying, covered with sores, blind, or mutilated, and reeking with a pestilential stench. Fabiola, who is never referred to as a nurse, functioned as a primary healer or physician. Her friend and Christian colleague, Paula, founded a hospital for the Jews; she bathed them and ministered to their needs while wearing sackcloth herself.

The threat to the lives of the Christian women and men healers in the Roman Empire increased with their numbers and spreading fame. The bloody reign of Diocletian, beginning in A.D. 284, saw the murderers of Theodosia, Nicerato, Theckla, Cosmas, and Damien—healers who are now known as saints—among others. Their healing powers lived on, however, and miracles reportedly took place in the presence of their shrines.

A threat to woman was also emerging from within the Church itself. Jerome, who wrote passionately of his regard for Fabiola and many other women in the healing arts, at the same time could well be seen as the patron saint of misogynists. An often-quoted remark of his is that "woman is the gate of the devil, the path of wickedness, the sting of the serpent, in a word, a perilous object."[5] His words were a harbinger of decreasing tolerance within the general framework of Christianity for the eclectic feminism of the sects.

Still, the first half of the first millennium after the birth of Christ is often regarded as the "calm before the storm," the prelude to the Dark Ages. These were fluid times, when religion was a satisfying and exotic blend of ingredients taken from pre-Christian, pagan, and folk traditions.

7 Medieval Christian Cosmology

THIS CHAPTER DISCUSSES the role of woman healers in Europe during the Middle Ages, beginning with the "dark" time (coincident with the Fall of Rome in A.D. 476) and ending at the termination of the High Middle Ages—around 1300. The Christian cosmology during this time can be seen as a stream that carries woman as healer through her winding course. During the High Middle Ages, the flow grows sluggish, finally becoming a straight and frozen channel. Thus, the latter period is characterized by a gradual hardening of the general framework of Christianity.[1]

THE DARK AGES

The Dark Ages began with devastating disease—bubonic plague—which was spread across Europe by Goths, Huns, and other marauding and migrating tribes. This form of plague, borne by bacilli living in the blood of fleas, caused hemorrhages, dark patches on the skin, a black tongue, and carbuncles in the lymph nodes. Some victims survived, but most died within three days of the first symptoms. Other victims were reported to have broken out with black blisters the size of lentils, leading modern authorities to suspect that smallpox—which, by 500, was also rampant—was occuring simultaneously with the plague.[2]

The specter of horrible disease slowed the invading tribes, and by itself may have turned back the Huns and others. On the war-torn, plague-infested continent of Europe, cities and town disintegrated. As the centuries wore on, in most of the Western world an architect could no longer build a dome, or a shipbuilder a war galley, or a wheelwright a chariot. Since no manuals for the trades were handed down, later artisans would have to begin anew. The vast continent of Europe became primarily rural, with a population composed of over 80 percent peasants, dominated by scattered feudal landholders.[3]

Women, whether nobly born or poor, faced conditions likely to breed poor health. The atmosphere of the feudal castles and the peasant dwellings was rank, with no sanitation to speak of. In the increasingly influential Christian doctrine, a constant war was waged against the flesh. Thus people exalted in not attending to their physical needs–especially cleanliness. They were covered with foul eruptions, exacerbated by rough woolen clothing and the constant presence of dirt, ticks, and fleas. The food supply was undependable and contaminated. Poor nutrition, filth, crowded living conditions, and hard labor took their usual toll, leaving the populace vulnerable to disease, and suffering from perpetual fatigue and mental dullness.

Reasonably healthy, fertile women could expect to be pregnant for most of their married lives, giving birth to about six children, half of whom would die before they reached the age of twenty. As in all declining cultures, females were devalued. Selective infanticide, "exposure," or neglect of female babies (such as shorter nursing periods than for males) were practiced. Manorial and parish records show a disproportionately high ratio of male births during times of pestilence and famine. The poorer the family or conditions, the higher the number of males. In times of relative prosperity, the ratio of males to females born was normal—about 105:100.[4]

Women healers, regardless of social class, spent most of their time tending pregnant women, witnessing the beginning and ending of life, and caring for sickly children. They functioned as herbalists and empiricists, sustaining the healing lore through oral tradition and apprenticeship. They did what women always do—sit at the bedside and work with whatever ingredients and rituals are available to ease pain and suffering.

Most people had access to local wise women, whose medicaments and rites were believed to be exceptionally powerful, to cure where others could not. These women knew something about the potency of herbs, which depended upon the time of day, season, and location of harvest. Since the wise women were usually sought out only in crisis situations that could not be treated by domestic preparations, it can be assumed that they employed the more dangerous plants, such as those containing high levels of alkaloids. They likely had knowledge of other plants and procedures that induce uterine contractions. The nefarious association of wise women with poisoning and abortions is quite understandable. Often, the services of the wise women were sought in secret, so we might assume that their activities were not always of a healing nature. The aura of mystery also enhanced expectancy and hope that a cure or relief would be forthcoming—what is now called the "placebo effect."

It is unlikely that any of the written medical lore known to Fabiola or other competent medical people ever filtered down into the hands of European women of the Dark Ages. The continuity of the earlier medical knowledge was only feebly sustained by copying the tomes from former ages over and over again. Even so, the frequent sacking and burning of the libraries of the great cities—by men who were ignorant, zealous, or both—left scanty information on the healing practices of these years.

What we do know is that following the age of Greek and Roman healing (from about A.D. 340 on), therapies became more complex and imbued with a mixture of pagan and Christian ritual. Contact with the Near East brought interest in exotic ingredients such as mummy dust.

Theriac, or mithridate, is the prime example of fantastic preparations. The number of its ingredients grew from twenty or thirty in Galen's time to well over two hundred before the preparation was finally taken off the shelves less than one hundred years ago. Originally intended as an antidote to poisoning, it was later used as a tonic to ward off pestilence, and as a general panacea. The recipes contained a major portion of the existing pharmacopoeia, in whatever proportions the patient could affort. Wine and opium were usually added, which may have accounted for the drug's long popularity. Many undiagnosed but common ailments did seem to be symptomatic of poisoning—nausea, cramps, delirium, tremors, and so forth—hence, the high regard for theriac or any other antidote that could serve as an emetic or purge.

Healing ingredients found in Europe during the first millennium A.D. included the sexual organs of animals, feces of hedgehogs and dragons, the blood of fledgling swallows, saliva, bones, urine, ambergris from whales, and other organic materials of unknown origin. Pearls dissolved in vinegar were used for skin diseases, sulphur was mixed with human saliva for impetigo, and mercury and clam juice were used for venereal disease.[5] A tongue of an eagle was said to cure cough. For styes it was recommended that one gather several flies, cut off their heads, and rub the afflicted eyelid with their dead bodies. Fifteen frogs impaled on bullrushes would prevent baldness, and if a pregnant woman ate a rat, she would ensure the birth of a black-eyed baby.

Most of these prescriptions are only remotely connected to simple, sensible botanics. They are medicines of desperation. When people are very sick and cures elusive, medicine becomes more aggressive, and ingredients are selected with random and wild abandon in an attempt to stave off disease.

The commonsense domestic treatments and even the professional practice of medicine, which had been present since ancient times, were in decline. The intuitive knowledge that comes from closely watching the seasons, living close to the earth, and carefully listening to the relationships among living things began to disappear from general knowledge. (As mentioned before, we can only guess that some of this knowledge was sustained by the wise women through their oral tradition.) The basis for empiricism—watching the cause and effect of healing ministrations—was obscured. The marriage of reason and intuition—so critical to the advancement of healing—was obliterated. The practices associated with Hygeia such as sanitation and prevention were largely forgotten. Even medical tools buried by the volcano at Pompeii were not reinvented for another six hundred years.

The symbolic and the sacred aspects of healing ingredients changed also. For thousands of years various organic and inorganic items from the earth were believed to contain invisible power to aid the healer in divination or diagnosis and in curing. The medicine bags or "bundles" of the healer often contained rocks, rattles, and parts of animals that had special meaning within the culture. However, it was the pantheistic aspect of the cosmology that empowered the healing ingredients. When gods or spirits are believed to reside, in varying degrees, in all elements of the earth, then those elements can be used to call forth spirit or invisible presence or healing wisdom. When spirit is not immanent within the elements, they cannot serve as a tangible product of the supernatural. As Christianity became the dominant system of religion, the belief in the presence of spirit within the elements of earth was gradually discarded.

Too, amulets representing gods or goddesses who had a healing function have been carried by humans since the Stone Age. They did not symbolize the deity, they *contained* the deity. These figures of the great old religions were almost indestructible in folk memory, and idols (particularly of Diana and Minerva), although forbidden by the Church, were carried by women well into Christian times. Christianity, which dismissed the pagan spirit of the earth, nevertheless maintained the sacred and healing aspect of inanimate objects such as figures of saints, relics, and shrines. They, like the amulets of Diana and Minerva, contained the presence of healing spirits. These became the most highly regarded medicine of the next few centuries, and served as the sacred and tangible projection of the invisible.

THE HIGH MIDDLE AGES (1000–1300)

During the High Middle Ages the feminine aspects of theology and woman's appropriate position in society were also undergoing debate and transformation. During this cultural shift, there was no general agreement on the appropriate role of women in society. Indeed, some women enjoyed relatively rich opportunities in all sectors of society, including the healing arts. Not surprisingly, the culture was in a state of advance rather than decline.

A series of events spurred the transition from the Dark Ages into a more modern era. The sacking and pillage of Europe slackened. Energy and resources necessary for continual defense were released for other purposes. Land clearance made way for larger cities, which engendered competition among tradespeople—millers, smiths, weavers, etc.—who developed more efficient skills than those who had served the old manors. New agricultural technology led to an increased food supply and a healthier population. Mining encouraged a cash economy and trade. The potential for wealth and a semblance of comfort existed among the nobility, the heads of the Church, and the new bourgeoisie, and the rising materialism begat a new spirit of optimism.[6]

THE LIVES OF WOMEN

During these three centuries (about 1000–1300) women of the landed gentry were exceptionally literate and well educated. The elevation of women's status is exemplified in the lives of ruling women like Queen Blanche of France, Empress Matilda of England, Eleanor of Aquitaine, and others who were involved in the political intrigue and other historically significant aspects of medieval times.[7]

Daughters and wives were taught the family trades and worked as brewers, teachers, midwives, weavers, fullers, barbers, carpenters, saddlers, tilers, laundresses, lacemakers, and seamstresses, to mention a few occupations. They went from being unpaid domestic laborers to worthy members of society. Still, they worked for less money than their male counterparts. Advice given in an English book on animal husbandry, for example, was, "If this is a manor where there is no dairy, it is always good to have a woman there at much less cost than a man."[8] They were not equal in any sense, but women were better off than they had been or would be for centuries.

Women began to outnumber men, and it is estimated that by the end of the Middle Ages there were about twelve hundred women to each thousand men. During the height of the Crusades, women were said to outnumber men seven to one in locations that contributed most heavily to the Holy Wars. The excess of women gave them renewed strength by virtue of sheer numbers alone. It also attests to improved survival of the perils of childbirth.

THE STATE OF LIFE AND PUBLIC HEALTH

The Middle Ages saw the beginning of social divisions: nobility, tradespeople, a hierarchical church family, and peasants or serfs. Life for the latter scarcely changed. For the upper classes, daily living was resplendent with new comforts. For the very wealthy—the churchmen and the nobles—unprecedented luxuries adorned their homes and bodies. To be sure, the floors were still strewn with rushes, and the windows were little more than slits filled with crudely blown, thick and uneven glass or oiled parchment. But the walls were hung with tapestries, the great halls were divided into rooms to afford privacy, and the smoking central firepit was replaced by huge fireplaces vented to the outdoors.

Even though most cities could boast only one public bath, tubs were not uncommon in the wealthy households. Bathing itself came into fashion for health and recreational purposes. With many people living in the cities, it was necessary to attend to the removal of wastes and garbage, and to keep the stench at a tolerable level. Homes had outdoor toilets or waterclosets which drained into ditches or were emptied at intervals.

While there was obviously no understanding of the role of germs and pests in disease causation, the people of the Middle Ages began to adopt sanitary measures in order to tolerate living in close proximity to one another. Trenches were dug to facilitate drainage into the rivers; rudimentary sewers were built in the castles.

Infant mortality was abominably high; most babies did not live to celebrate their second birthday. However, if one survived the onslaught of childhood disease, stayed away from the Crusades, and didn't die in childbirth, the odds of living to a ripe old age were not unlike those today.

The problems of gluttony among the nobles and clergy caused a new generation of health problems: tooth decay, digestive disorders, gout, heart disease, hypertension, and obesity. These are among the "diseases of civilization." The remedy for corpulence and coronaries was to be bled five to six times a year.

The peasants suffered, too, but from the usual things the poor and overworked are cursed with: exposure, the effects of backbreaking labor, and crippling deformities. The latter were often a result of poor birthing practices: midwives would dislocate or remove a limb to facilitate a difficult entry into the world. Eye diseases were common, and healing was slow. However, the peasantry consumed a diet low on the food chain, and during times of good harvest their general health and nutritional status may have been better than that of the nobility. Dysentery knew no class boundaries, understandably so in view of the prevalence of polluted water supplies and inadequate means of preserving food. Epilepsy, malaria, influenza, diptheria, and typhoid were reported. "St. Anthony's fire" also occurred during this time. Striking the strongest and healthiest among the people, the disease blistered, gangrened, deformed, and killed. Then it disappeared forever. Ergot fungus (a basis of modern LSD) infected grain and may have killed whole villages. Smallpox periodically raged; lesser skin diseases such as scabies, scrofula, and impetigo were perpetual, facilitated by dirty clothes and harsh fibers.

Leprosy, endemic in the early years of the Middle Ages, left and returned again in full force in the twelfth and thirteenth centuries. There were two thousand leper colonies in France alone during this time—an amazing number, given that the entire population of the country was estimated to be only twenty-two million.[9]

STATE OF THE HEALING ARTS

Women had little help in their healing mission. Virtually all records report that "qualified" physicians and surgeons were scarce and limited their services to those who could pay. The definition of *qualified physician* varied from time to time and country to country, but generally implied a male who had met some official criterion to practice.

Lists of licensed practitioners in various municipalities have emerged over the years. In France and Italy women occasionally appeared on the lists, but their number never approached even a significant minority. In England, medical education was definitely closed to women, and they were not included on lists of approved practitioners during these centuries. Surgeons were virtually always male, of minimal social standing, and associated with the field of barbering. Dental problems were handled mostly by "tooth drawers" at the county fairs, or by a small number of *dentatores* who knew of the advanced Arabic dentistry.

The noble lady became the manor's doctor and pharmacist. Bundles of herbs hung from the rafters of her larder. Domestic healing included some knowledge of antisepsis—wounds were dressed with old wine and the sterile white of eggs—and basic first aid. Midwifery was practiced exclusively by women. During labor the midwife had some skills, but the ability to turn a child in the womb or to perform embryotomy or cesarean section was less widespread than in previous centuries.

During a typical labor and delivery, the midwife rubbed the mother's belly with soothing ointments and evoked the magic of charms—the dried blood of a crane, the gemstone of jasper, the water in which a murderer had washed his hands. There were other incantations that could be done, either Christian or pagan or a mixture of both, but only if there was no likelihood the priest would find out. After the baby was born, the cord would be cut, and the child rubbed with a paste of salt and honey. A bed of salt and crushed rose leaves was prepared for the babe. The midwife dipped her finger in honey and cleaned the infant's palate and gums. She filled her mouth with wine and expelled a few drops into the little mouth. The baby was baptized the same day, if possible, to ensure passage to heaven in the all-too-likely even that its lifespan would be numbered in days.

In England, women who could read had access to the *Leech Book of Bald*. This book, whose author remains unknown, was written in the vernacular and intended as a medical guide for the common people. In general, the book recommended mild, nontoxic botanics and Christian litany. It specified a wide mix of potions, herbs, behaviors, and incantations to be used in the face of illness. For example, the prescription for a large boil was to dig up dock (an herb), jerk it from the ground to the tune of a Pater Noster, take five slices of it and seven peppercorns, mix them thoroughly while singing twelve times the Miserere and Gloria and Pater Noster, then pour it all over with wine, and at midnight drink the dose and wrap up warmly.

So far, all we have discussed is common, domestic healing, which seems to have lost much and gained nothing for about seven hundred years. However, developments were taking place that would allow a small number of women healers to shine, their knowledge and authority absolutely unquestioned by their contemporaries.

TROTULA OF SALERNO

In the Near East during the eleventh century, the Arabs translated Galen and Aristotle and Hippocrates. These medical texts were then introduced back into the West through a circuitous route of scribes. The Jews who could read Arabic and then translate it into Latin became instrumental in this process. Christians then translated the Latin into a form that could be used to broadly communicate the ideas of these texts. As always, scribes had the opportunity to add their own perspective and to delete passages that didn't fit with their worldview.

What happened, though, was that a base for medical practice formed once again. Scholarly interest was piqued, and institutions for training medical practitioners were founded. The most famous was at Salerno, Italy. Founded around the year 1000, it was in existence until shut down by Napoleon's decree in 1811. Salerno was built on a site already famous for its healing baths, one that served as a port of entry for pilgrims returning from Palestine. The early facility included Greeks, Jews, Arabs, and Latins, with both sexes represented among its faculty and student body. It was considered a Christian institution, but the material being taught came from pagan texts.

The most distinguished teacher at this medical university of the Middle Ages was a woman named Trotula. Trotula has been depicted in children's verse as Dame Trot, in art as a goddess of healing, and in history as the author of the world's most enduring treatise on gynecology and obstetrics. She was clearly an unusual woman, although Salerno could boast of having many women of accomplishment as faculty members.

Trotula's life and practice has been well researched. Especially important are the classic texts of Salvatore de Renzi, published in Naples, 1852–59.[10] Parts of Trotula's manuscripts are found in museums throughout Europe.

Her identity was unquestioned until 1566, when a volume of her work was attributed to a man named Eros living at the time of Augustus, but in the seventeenth century her true identity was brought to the fore. Again in 1773 her authorship was disclaimed by another historian, Christian Godfred Gruner, who simply believed that no eleventh-century woman could have exhibited the amount of knowledge in Trotula's books.

Authorities still are not in agreement about Trotula's existence, but the reports of her work as a *magistra medicinae* are persistent and coherent. The outstanding contribution of the materials attributed to her legend was practical information for managing diseases and conditions of women, and basic principles for managing health problems. She obviously had access to the works of Hippocrates and Cleopatra—as well as others—but she appeared less enamored of the mumbo-jumbo of some of the early prescriptions. Nevertheless, elaborate rituals were prescribed for digging and preparing plants. She recommended the use of medicaments that seem strange to us, such as the powdered heart of a stag, and her medicines were administered with obligatory genuflection to the appropriate Christian saints.

Trotula was a skilled diagnostician who used all of her senses in the effort. This was most necessary, since the knowledge of the inner workings of the human body was left to the imagination, dissection never, or rarely, being possible. She discussed pulse and urine diagnosis, as well as the need to make careful note of the patient's features and words.

Some of her therapies were quite advanced. For instance, for vulval abcess she recommended lancing, dilating, draining, and applying medicated oils to soothe and aid healing. For prolapsed uterus she advised that the uterus be restored to its proper position and held in place by sponges or tampons soaked in astringents.

Trotula wrote on a wide variety of issues, including cesarean sections and beauty prescriptions. She was the first to describe the dermatological manifestations of syphillis. She gave opiates for pain, as well as anesthetic inhalations of hyoscyamine, hemlock, and mandrake. Aloes, almond oil, orris root, silver, and mercury were prescribed for skin problems—all agents in common use to this day.

Not all of Trotula's prescriptions seem so modern, however. She was specific on bloodlettings as to when, how, and to whom they should be done. She wrote of a variety of superstitious behaviors for determining the sex of a child and for curing sterility. If a woman was afraid of pregnancy, Trotula advised her to take a stone, wrap it in skin, and wear it with a testicle of a pig and a grain of barley for each month she wishes not to conceive.[11]

Trotula wrote very directly on the need for hygiene, prescribing baths, cleansings, and lotions with antiseptic properties. Surgery, she believed, must be conducted with extreme care for cleanliness and avoidance of contaminants. She described the necessary features of a wet nurse, focusing on health, a clean body, and a good disposition.

Here are her suggestions for counterfeiting virginity, according to de Renzi's translation:

> This remedy will be needed by any girl who has been induced to open her legs and lose her virginity by the follies of passion, secret love, and promises. . . . Let her take ground sugar and the white of an egg and mix them in rainwater in which alum, fleabane, and the dry wood of a vine have been boiled down with other similar herbs. Soaking a soft and porous cloth in this solution, let her keep bathing her private parts with it. The vagina ought to be fully washed. Or let her mix rainwater with well-ground fresh oak bark and make a suppository which she should insert in the vagina shortly before she expects to have intercourse. Or as follows: plantain, sumack, oak galls, large black betony, and alum cooked in rainwater and the private parts fomented with the mixture as above. . . . But best of all is this deception: the day before her marriage, let her put a leech very cautiously on the labia, taking care lest it slip in by mistake; then she should allow blood to trickle out and form a crust on the orifice; the flux of blood will tighten the passage. Thus may a false virgin deceive a man in intercourse.[12]

Trotula's prescription was probably effective. It contains several astringents to tighten up flaccid tissues; boiled rainwater is as sterile a medium as can be found. The latter advice—although not for the cowardly—would surely convince an ardent husband of his young wife's virginity.

In her own way, in her own time, Trotula represented the woman healer of the far-distant future. She personified the balance that is so critical to the advancement of woman as a health-care professional: a knowledge of science, attention to the magic that is embedded in the mind, a mission of service, awareness of suffering, and the gift of compassion. She also had the courage to speak, write, and teach with conviction. But Trotula was the last of these women who most resemble modern-day physicians. A relatively fluid religious belief structure—one that had not hardened quite yet into misogyny—allowed her to practice the way that she did.

Such brilliant flowering of women healers, right before the avenues of healing work are abruptly blocked to them, is notable throughout Western history. Other medical schools were founded by graduates of Salerno, but few permitted women to study. Women who aspired to such a vocation fell into the open arms of the Church, which had great need for able handmaidens during the Crusades.

THE CRUSADES

The mission to reclaim the Holy Land occurred during the High Middle Ages. The adventures were bloody and fraught with incurable disease, but

that seems not to have hindered the masses of people who chose to participate. Women, too, went on the Crusades with high spirits and a keen
anticipation for the exotic lands and customs of the Near East. Some traveled
with children and possessions on a single beast of burden. Others were led
in high style by the "golden-footed queen," who was probably Eleanor of
Aquitaine.

Conservative estimates of Crusade-related deaths are in the millions. The
First Crusade alone claimed some 800,000 lives on both sides; many who
traveled died before reaching their destination. What appears to us as
senseless death and injury was fueled by the pope's promise of absolution for
all who went to the Holy Land.

From the need for people to help the wounded and dying, new medical
orders were formed by the Church. The Order of the Knights of the Hospital
of St. John of Jerusalem (Hospitalers) was founded in 1099. In the twelfth
century, the Order of Lazarus (devoted to the care of lepers) and the Order
of the Knights of the Temple of Solomon (Templars) were founded.

Women's services were welcomed in the improvised infirmaries and clinics
established in Jerusalem and along the Crusaders' route through Europe.
There are many stories about the kindness offered by women through the
orders, such as that of Agnes, a member of the Knights of St. John, and that
of Sister Ubaldina of the Hospitalers. But women were not able to serve in
an authoritative capacity. Rather, their services resembled those of the
modern nurse working under the supervision of a physician.

Hospitals that were established in Europe during this century began a new
model for patient care. Especially well-known was the Hôtel Dieu in Paris,
staffed by the Augustinian Sisters, who were never more than slaves to a
system. Nonetheless, a nursing vocation for women, which required a
dedication to the worse kind of drudgery, was clearly established.

The conditions in the infirmaries, clinics, and hospitals varied greatly. In
some, the sick, dying, and dead could all be found on a single mattress.
Medical knowledge of this time was, as we have said, scant, and under
crowded, wartime circumstances, was probably nonexistent. In some places,
though, funds and energy flowed with religious intensity into the construc-
tion and management of medical facilities. In France, the hospitals built by
St. Louis (the king) and his sister, Marguerite of Bourgogne, were large
Gothic structures with adequate ventilation and drainage. The leprosanitaria
were staffed by the nursing sisters throughout Europe. These hospitals were
so clean and comfortable, and the care therein so gentle, that people were
known to inflict festering lesions on their own skin in order to feign leprosy
and gain admission.

By the end of the thirteenth century, there were an estimated 200,000 women serving as nurses within the orders of the Church. This role was seen by Adelaide Nutting and Lavinia Dock, two early twentieth-century authorities on the history of nursing, as the advance guard of woman's emancipation.[13] From a modern perspective, it appears to be the advance guard of woman's bondage to a male-dominated system of health care.

All healing roles, not just that of woman as nurse, were becoming more defined. Men who were distinguished and recognizable because of the tools of their trade—lancets, pills, saws, and pincers—began to form guilds.

As wars and disasters often result in medical advances, so the Crusades and their aftermath created an environment conducive to the formation of the professions as well as establishing the first major system of hospital care.

HEALING TOOLS: RELICS AND WELLS

The collection of relics was furthered by the Crusades, and through their sale the Church obtained significant wealth. The body parts and exudations of the martyrs of the Crusades and Biblical heroes were the spoils of war. Gallons of Christ's blood and tears, buckets of milk from Mary's breasts, splinters from the cross, dirt upon which sacred feet had trod were sold in promise of miracles. Leg bones, arm bones, skulls, withered hearts, and whole skeletons bedecked with crowns of jewels from a host of saints and near-saints were enshrined.[14]

All relics offered the potential of healing miracles. Some were believed to heal specific disorders, in the tradition of the idols of the ancient pagan world of Greece and Rome. St. Lucy's relics promised cure from eye disease, St. Teresa would be venerated for heart disease, and St. Apollonia was considered especially effective for toothache. Numerous persons would be called upon for problems of fertility and birth and children and leprosy.

The potent drugs of the time also included scrapings from the gravestones of holy men and women, and water from sources near their shrines. Wells and springs have always served as places of worship, dedication, and sacrifice. The very same waters had served many a folk deity, usually feminine, prior to the Christian era. The healing water of Chalice Well in Glastonbury, England, for example, have been drunk and bathed in by Christians, Druids, Celts, and adherents of earlier religions of the Earth Mother that have no name. The water, which flows from a most pregnant belly of a hill, stains all it touches red. The claims for healing from this and other shrines attest to the persistent belief in the connection between healing, the divine, and special places on the earth. When analyzed in a laboratory, the waters typically show no unusual physical properties.

Thus, in the Christian cosmology of the High Middle Ages, the nature of healing is most similar to the days of the diverse Roman mythology, discussed earlier. In both instances, large numbers of deities or sainted mortals, their relics, and pilgrimages to their sacred sites were believed to hold the key to health. Artifacts or relics associated with women were as likely to be associated with general healing as those from men. In the case of women's and children's diseases, and in pregnancy and birth, the feminine worship prevailed. And, in both eras, relics and sites were considered the most powerful of all healing tools.

COURTLY LOVE MYTHS AND MARY IDOLATRY

The romantic ideal of woman as healer was perpetuated by the courtly love stories, epics, and songs characteristic of the High Middle Ages. These tales of adventure were carried throughout the land by the minnesingers and troubadours. In *Gudrun,* the German epic, a wild, wise wife is described who knows all of the healing plants. In *Tristram and Isolde,* Isolde has possession of a chest of poisons and drugs, and knowledge of their use. In *The Canterbury Tales,* Chaucer describes women who raise herbs and care for the sick, and in a many tales of heroism and passion, the lovely lady saves the ebbing life of a knight with compresses, poultices, bandages, baths, lotions, or even gemstones. In the *Edda*—Scandinavian epics in prose and poetry— women who knew the healing powers of the inscribed runestones are mentioned. The *Edda* also tells of women who had received knowledge from spirits on how to care for wounds and where to dig for roots and herbs. Overall, the courtly love and other literature from this period suggests that women were thought of as healers, and that it was a high calling and part of their charm.

The courtly love tradition was correlated with the upsurge in Mary worship during the 1200s. The veneration of the virgin mother of Jesus Christ fulfilled a need to balance out a patriarchal religion with a more accessible human figure. And the longing for the lost goddess, the mother of earth, was satisfied to some extent by the female figure of the human who gave birth to a deity's son.

The image of Mary cast in these times has its shadowy side. As Simone de Beauvoir noted, "For the first time in history the mother kneels before her son; she freely accepts her inferiority. This is the supreme masculine victory, consummated in the cult of the Virgin—it is the rehabilitation of woman through the accomplishment of her defeat."[15]

WOMEN IN RELIGIOUS LIFE

Within this medieval soup, the most obvious healing path for women was through the Church itself. The Church had made virginity and a life of service popular ways to mitigate against the curse of the Original Sin of Eve. Daughters of wealthy landowners were especially welcomed, as they carried a hefty dowry with them into the cloistered walls. The nuns, or "Brides of Christ," were not allowed to pass down any landholdings to future generations. By the end of the Middle Ages, through this and other policies, the Church had garnered over one-third of the land mass of Europe.

The great monasteries and abbeys of Europe had definitely passed their apex of service by the end of the twelfth century. Decadence—insidious at first and then blatant in terms of immorality, greed, and lack of devotion to spirituality—began to set in. Still, there were devoted women who wished to follow the early Christian teachings of healing and service. They gave their lives to the religious life and, in all fairness, enjoyed benefits not available to women outside of the Church. They were unfettered from the reins of domesticity and the strain of repeated pregnancies. They had time for needlework, reading, and travel. The women had books and teachers available, and they often served as scribes themselves. Few of the orders were confined to the convent, so the women could come and go as they pleased.

The breadth of the churchwoman's life extended well into all facets of the healing arts. In addition to the Hospitalers and other defined medical groups, religious life in general was affiliated with caregiving and attention to the ailments of the body.

The names and works of the great abbesses are still with us: St. Petronilla, the first abbess of Fontevrault, for instance, housed in her abbey lepers, prostitutes, and women about to give birth. Matilda, the sixth great abbess of this institution, had more than five thousand people under her jurisdiction. The famed Héloïse taught and practiced the arts of healing at the hermitage of Paraclete for twenty years after her secret and ill-fated marriage to Abelard. Herrade, abbess of Hohenburg in Alsace, wrote a compendium on botany and its medical uses called the "Garden of Delight." St. Hilda at Whitby was supposed to know about the healing power of the runestones. Elizabeth of Schönau, a mystic, founded a Benedictine nunnery in Trier; and Hedwig of Silesia, patron saint of Poland, built monasteries and cared for the sick with her own hands. These, and many more, were remarkable products of the twelfth century.

HILDEGARD OF BINGEN (1098–1179)

Hildegard, the most accomplished abbess of the Middle Ages, the "sibyl of the Rhine," was an unusual phenomenon for any era. Indeed, some modern theologians credit her with being one of the greatest mystics of all time.[16] Her medical writings are considered the most important scientific contribution of the period.[17] Any brief overview risks minimizing her complex character, the exceptional products of her vast intellect, her nerve, and her intuition.[18]

Hildegard displayed gifts of prophesy, claiming visions of the Holy Spirit even as a child. For this reason, or perhaps because she was the youngest of ten children, her parents obligated her to the Church for life when she was about seven years old. She was sent to live with an anchorite—a recluse in a cell adjacent to the church—who fostered her talents. Hildegard's charisma soon drew a following, and she was eventually assigned to head her own convent.

When Hildegard was forty-two years old, she was compelled by her visions to begin writing what had been revealed to her in "lightning daydreams." Thus, the second half of her long life was spent in producing three major works (two theological, one medical), a multitude of plays and songs, and a vast correspondence with admirers who sought her counsel.

Many aspects of Hildegard's work remain puzzling. The fact that she chose to write at all was remarkable since she was unschooled even by the standards of medieval scholarship. She admitted her lack of knowledge of Latin, yet wrote her texts in this, the language of the elite. Furthermore, she must have been acutely aware of the Church's misogynist attitude, as she herself demeaned the female as weak in mind and spirit. Yet she chose to be an outspoken, opinionated public figure who stumped the country preaching to large crowds, and to write on all the scholarly subjects known to the world at that time.

Hildegard drew the attention of the major church authorities who examined her work. They concluded that her theological information was actually dictated by the voice of God, spoken through Hildegard. It was this decision that saved her from serious charges of heresy and, indeed, gave her freedom and power unusual for any church man or woman in the Middle Ages.

Her sources of information for the medical work *Causae et curae* are not known. She did not claim to have received the medical information from her visions, although she did allow that they inspired her to the task. She may have had access to the classic texts, such as those used at Salerno, as well as commonly circulated herbals. Yet her theories and methods are different from any other works. For example, her writings on the four humor theory of health and disease differ from those of Galen or any of the other fathers of medicine. She wrote a surprisingly passionate and factual description of the biological aspects of female orgasm that appears nowhere else in the writings of the Middle Ages. Even Hildegard's reasons for writing on medicine are unclear. Her biographers have found no sound evidence that she actually practiced the type of medicine in her writings. She was credited with cures through prayer, and her abbey probably had an infirmary where common ailments were treated.

Hildegard's practical knowledge of medicaments included the function of 485 plants, each of which she believed to be a God-given remedy. The dosages she recommended were so small as to be near-homeopathic, and she was also likely to prescribe dietary and exercise regimes. She advocated the usual collection of botanics, which probably contained a few active ingredients, and would have some effect, however subtle, on the condition for which they were prescribed. Others (a heart of lion over the umbilicus for difficult labor, wet clay for the paralysis of limbs) seem more like pure imagination. She wrote little of surgery or midwifery; one assumes that convent life offered her little practical opportunity to participate in either.

Many of Hildegard's ideas were far advanced for her time. She recommended treating diabetes by omitting sweets and nuts from the diet. Her discussion of the circulation of blood presaged the model presented by Harvey in the seventeenth century. The breadth and scope of her writings are equal to any produced by the Fathers of Medicine, as well as the Fathers of Science, whom we will discuss shortly.

With characteristic eloquence, Hildegard wrote about the seen and unseen influences of evil spirits in natural history and pharmacy. Devils and dragons and other forms of the supernatural invade healing preparations to a positive or negative degree. The devil is fonder of some than others. For example, she thought the influence of the devil was more present in the mandragora, an herb known to have the power to alter the senses, than in other herbs. She believed that the helm-oak was hostile to the spirits of the air, so that those who slept under its branches or used it to fumigate the house were free from evil spirits and diabolical illusions. Stones and metals, too, had a definite relationship with the dark or the light side of the supernatural. For example, jasper held during childbirth protected against malignant spirits, as did the touch of red-hot steel. According to Hildegard, herbs in the east are full of virtue and have medicinal properties, but those in the west are potent in magic and do not contribute much to the health of the human body.

Hildegard frequently wrote of magic as a source of influence over bodies and souls. As the evil side of all arts, it manifested in images of dragons and of animals having the body of a dog, the head of a wolf, and the tail of a lion, as well as in plants and certain human countenances. The devotees of magic directed their works to impurity and to the pursuit of evil; they named demons as their gods. For Hildegard, there was countermagic, for instance, in places where the fir tree grew. There were powders one could concoct against evil spirits, according to her *Causae et curae*—powders that could confer prosperity and health and courage as well.

Woman as Healer

For such an effect she directed the reader to take a root of geranium, two mallow plants, and seven shoots of the plantagenet, all to be plucked at midday in the middle of April. Lay them on moist earth and sprinkle with water to keep them fresh a while, she advised. Dry them in the setting and rising sun until the third hour, and lay them again on moist earth and sprinkle with water until noon. Then, place them facing south in the full sunshine until the ninth hour, wrap in a cloth, hold them in place until a trifle before midnight. As night begins to incline toward day all the evils of darkness and night begin to flee. Just before midnight, place them above a door or in some garden where the cool air may have access to them. As soon as midnight is passed, remove them once more, pulverize with the middle finger, and put them in a pillbox with a little *bisemum* to keep them from decaying, but not enough to overcome the scent of the herbs. Apply a little of this powder daily to the eyes, ears, nose, and mouth, or bind it to the body as an antiaphrodisiac, or hold it over wine without touching it, but so that its odor can reach the wine, which should then be drunk with a bit of saffron to prevent indigestion, poison, and the powers of magic.

Astrology, gemology, and dream divination also had a place in Hildegard's psychopharmacopeia, despite her protests that such arts were evil. According to Thorndike,

> If Hildegard resorts to a magic of her own in order to counteract the diabolical arts, and if she accepts a certain amount of astrological doctrine for all her censure of it, it is not surprising to find her in the *Causae et curae* saying a word of favor of natural divination in dreams despite her rejection of augury and such arts.[19]

It is easy to applaud works that represent the thinking of modern medicine, and to sneer at the curious and bizarre. That misses the whole point. Hildegard was what she was: the most profound scientist of her time, representing the state of the healer's art. The dichotomy that she so definitely expressed between what was godly and what was of the devil, the division between the sanctioned triple godhead of theology-science-medicine as opposed to magic, would seep into the bones of humanity. At the same time, the definition of magic, and who was practicing it, would shift like the desert sand. It would be the same sort of shift, indeed, often directed at the same sources, that would vicariously decide who would be "inside" and who "outside" in the practice of medicine.

Hildegard's own work was ignored by generations of scholars, while the duplicate efforts of the medieval fathers of science—Bacon, Aquinas, Magnus, et al.—would be heralded. Their dogmas fueled the hue and cry against woman—the ultimate practitioner of the magical realms of healing. Hildegard herself lived in the precarious interface between medieval heresy and divinity. Any one of her works could have gotten her burned or sainted, but she was neither. Although she seems to have been forgotten by her near contemporaries, it was reasoning like hers that sparked the Inquisition and the witch-hunters to destroy the most devout, skilled healers among womankind. Hildegard was the last of her breed. The power the other abbesses wielded was conscripted, as the Church and its holdings begin to topple into the same dark void of stagnant misery—or worse—that was evident during the Dark Ages. Spiritually minded women would always continue to seek a role for themselves in the Church even though cleaning or needlework were the only paths of service permitted. After the twelfth century authority was given to them sparingly and with great reluctance; intense religious interest on the part of any woman was met with suspicion and surveillance.

Epilogue for the High Middle Ages

The eleventh, twelfth, and thirteenth centuries were times of excitement and diversity for women healers. Domestic medicine continued to be practiced, even though the methods that survived the Dark Ages were of questionable value. The sociopolitical developments and the still-fluid religious tone allowed women to practice the healing arts with extraordinary freedom compared to the immediate past and future. The culture allowed an unheard-of emergence of women as physicians and ecclesiastics.

The diversity of the twelfth century was depicted in poetry and philosophy by men who were students at Chartres, the cathedral school that symbolized the intellectual achievements of this time. Here "we find the idea of nature as cosmic power, the goddess Natura (in Goethe's sense), radiant and beguiling, the demonic-divine mother of all things."[20] Such thoughts would soon be punishable by death at the stake.

Abelard, the last of the great itinerent teachers and famed for his literary relationship with Héloïse, was an eloquent spokesman for the "new man," who could be found also in woman. His work has been a resource for humanists who sought to establish values beyond power, war, and violence down through the centuries. He claimed that woman's being was a higher form of manhood, refined in soul and spirit, capable of conversing with God the Spirit in the inner kingdom of the soul, on terms of intimate friendship. He challenged the youth and women of Europe to think boldly and to dare to love with passion, as befitted the new man.

Abelard was declared an archheretic whose ideas were extremely dangerous to the Church, his books were burned, and he was confined to a monastary in isolation for the last years of his life. Despite the efforts of the humanists, by mid-thirteenth century "the time was past when women rulers, abbesses, patrons of courtly society, poets, and mystics could leave a mark on their generation." In the words of F. Heer, "The middle ages had conspicuously failed to solve the problem of woman's place in society; it was left as a heavy mortage on the future."[21]

The next section examines the hardened Church doctrine and the philosophical underpinnings of experimental science. Both lines of thought were used as ammunition against women; the consensus was the mortage on the future of women in the healing arts.

Part Two

*Woman and the Genesis
of Scientific Thought*

8   *The Tapestry*

THE STORY OF woman as healer is woven like a tapestry. It has a continual theme, a warp upon which the color, texture, and change are superimposed by the events of time. The theme is the perceived nature of the universe—the cosmology—that envelops a culture. As this worldview moves through its phases, tones, and polemics, woman as healer alternates between light and shade.

The material in this section is drawn from a time when the cosmological system of Western civilization expanded to include orderly observations of physical systems as well as theology or religious mythology. Science was born not independently of religion but directly from its bowels. Conceived in the minds of ecclesiastics, it was molded by Judeo-Christian dogma and tainted by the imagery of the witch trials.

As always, the new cosmology emerged from human crisis at a time when nature was seen as hostile to life. Unlike the times of similar crises in Sumer and other ancient cultures, the gods did not change. Rather, the intention and nature of God's creations evolved to include a natural order of law that could be revealed to man and, once understood, could be used to harness nature's malevolent and threatening course. God did not become more feminine, nor did woman's position change in the hierarchical structure that places her next to Nature and beneath man.[1] With this reordering of the creation story, the laws governing treatment of disease and healing became scientific and the province of the minds of men. Women could not hope to discern them, or so it was believed.

In this section we will deal with three parts of the story, spanning the thirteenth through eighteenth centuries. First we will discuss the religion, philosophy, and foundations of early scientific thought that blazed the way for the persecution of women healers. Then follows a description of the world events surrounding the "witch" holocaust. Finally, the birth of modern scientific medicine and how it relates to women and the feminine principle in the healing arts will be outlined. We will also show how science emerged as a discipline of study ostensibly separate from religion with different—but no fewer—reasons for placing sanctions on women healers.

The voice of women healers is rarely heard through these centuries, though a few women made lasting contributions to literature: Christine Pisan, an early feminist; Margory Kempe, a self-proclaimed holy woman who dictated one of the first autobiographies in Europe; Dame Julian, an anchorite who wrote poetry about "Mother Jesus." However, firsthand information about women and healing—from women—is scant. Most of the material presented here is gleaned from the documents of the Church, from trials, and from the works of men of science.

Women were much written *about,* as they were under direct attack, primarily for reasons associated with the feminine healing myth. Men feared—and tried to bar from the new scientific worldview—women's intuitive nature, as well as their strong sense of the inherent link between humanity and the earth. In addition, the paranoia of people who were stressed, confused, hungry, frightened, and threatened by a changing world was fueled by the age-old belief that women could more readily lift the veil between the invisible and visible realms.

9   *Women Healers as Heretics: Philosophic Foundation*

IN THE THIRTEENTH CENTURY multiple courses of events created a great nexus that would dictate the future of woman as healer. Here, antecedent and current ideas collided, intertwined, and changed, emerging as a patterned worldview that would keep feminine values silent for about seven hundred years.

By this time, only a faint memory remained of the outstanding women healers of previous generations. Simultaneously, the practices of surgery, obstetrics, and pharmacy (especially anesthetics) were being lost in a vortex of amnesia. The Church, which had offered the healing power of hope and forgiveness, was weakened as vital spiritual energy was sucked out by greed and lust for power. Nevertheless, the men who conceived and built the magnificent Gothic cathedrals of this era had institutions and theology as intricate and powerful as their architecture. The tragedy that befell women was not an incidental by-product of ignorance. It was enforced at all levels of Church and government by creative and sophisticated men whose dogma laid the ground for the heinous crimes deliberately committed against women, beginning in the fourteenth century. Here we will discuss ideas related to the crystallized Church doctrine, as well as the ideas posited by men who are regarded as the forefathers of experimental science.

TRANSITIONS AND TRANSGRESSIONS OF CHRISTIAN COSMOLOGY

In previous chapters I have provided historical correlates for the fact that women could never function as autonomous or independent healers—or without the supervision of a recognized male authority—unless the culture held a religious view that the primary deity was feminine, or had a strongly androgynous or bisexual nature. The instances in which women were recognized as the primary healers were taken from prehistory, from cultures that honored the Earth Mother or Great Goddess.

Women in more recent traditions who functioned as sanctioned healers within the orthodox framework were anomalies, rare exceptions to the dominant male order. Others were working within a religious system, either as abbesses or in nursing orders affiliated with the church. Several notable women through Europe exercised their vocation by establishing infirmaries, clinics, and hospitals, caring for the great numbers of ailing poor. The sizeable majority of women were operating as domestic caregivers, peripheral to any recognized healing tradition. However, after the thirteenth century, even the domestic healers—especially those that had gained notoriety for their skills—were forbidden to practice under penalty of excommunication, imprisonment, or death.

Three major points of theology sealed woman's fate. The first was the alleged masculinity of God and the Son of God, which occurred long before the advent of Christianity, and was previously discussed in conjunction with ancient pagan cosmologies. The second point of theology that seriously affected women was the articulation of the consequences of Original Sin. And finally, charges of dualism or devil worship paved the way for the persecution of heretics, and ultimately for the slaughter of women.

Underlying all of the religious issues were those more insidious, including the development of doctrine promoting women's demeaned position in order to further economic and political regimes.

DOCTRINE OF ORIGINAL SIN

Woman's alleged initiation of Original Sin was the primary ammunition used to subjugate women to the authority of the Church, the state, and men. The idea of Original Sin was an unusual interpretation of creation myths that predate the composition of the book of Genesis by at least seven thousand years, starting in those lands in the Near East that were invaded by the Jewish tribes. Here one finds the symbols of the mythic garden of life: the serpent representing rebirth, the "world tree," the "sun eternal," and "ever-living waters." In all forms of the myth, divinity could be represented by masculine and feminine form. There is no wrath, no evil, no guilt or unpleasantness associated with the garden. "The boon of the knowledge of life is there, in the sanctuary of the world, to be culled. And it is yielded willingly to any mortal, male or female, who reaches for it with the proper will and readiness to receive."[1]

In the Judeo-Christian myth, the serpent (no longer a symbol of wisdom, rebirth, and healing, but of the devil) tempts woman (no longer the human form of the mother of all life, but the incarnation of human frailty) "to eat of the fruit of the tree" (which no longer represented wisdom, but rather an act of disobedience to the one god). And woman, likewise, tempts her mate. Her punishment is to forever bring forth children in pain, and to be subservient to man. The pleasures of living in a paradise on earth give way to shame over nakedness, conception, birth, indeed life itself.

The dogma of the thirteenth century drew on the philosophy of St. Augustine, who held that only the Church could absolve one of this sin. It was an ingenious play of power that kept people chained to the institution with guarantees of forgiveness and eternal life.

Women lost on all counts. In order to maintain the logic underlying the Church's hold on power, women's inherent sinfulness also had to be sustained. If there had been no evil temptress, no sin would exist, and the promised deliverance would wield no control over the masses. The doctrine of Original Sin was critical: any established church dependent on an economic power-base of unquestioned obedience would collapse if it were not considered the gateway to heaven by significant numbers of people.

Later, the doctrine would be used to justify beating women without overt cause except that they were of an evil nature and needed it. Women who dared provide soothing nostrums to others during childbirth would be severely punished, for birth pangs existed to remind woman of her original sinful nature, punishment for Eve's transgression. The Original Sin of Eve became an excuse for torturing and murdering hundreds of thousands of women during the Inquisition and the witch-hunts.

Since Jesus' birth must be uncontaminated by the sin of Eve, theologians performed gyrations of logic. "By a monstrous perversion of ideas, the Middle Ages regarded the flesh in its representative, woman (accursed since Eve) as radically impure. The Virgin, exalted as virgin, and not as Our Lady, far from raising actual womanhood to a higher level, degraded it, starting men on the path of a barren, scholastic ideal of purity that only led to ever greater and greater absurdities of verbal subtlety and false logic."[2] Thus, over the centuries, it was decided that Mary herself was not a real woman, but rather one who was immaculately conceived and ascended bodily into the heavens at death.

In the face of all the pronouncements of popes, monks, priests, and writers of law and doctrine, woman began to regard herself as unclean and impure. She hid her face in shame, especially during menstruation, pregnancy, and childbirth. Lovemaking was no longer hers to enjoy, but rather to endure, in order to conceive children in sin. The feminine role in creation was not blessed but cursed.

Then, as a matter of conscience, perhaps, to justify what was being done to women in order to maintain the power of the Church, it had to be demonstrated that woman was inferior. This proved no great theological problem, especially since woman was a creature made from the rib of man, and not cast in God's image.

St. Thomas Aquinas dismissed woman by stating that one should "only make use of a necessary object, woman, who is needed to preserve the species or to provide food and drink. . . . Woman was created to be man's helpmeet, but her unique role is in conception . . . since for all other purposes men would be better assisted by other men." He even minimized woman's "unique role" in conception. "In the begetting of man, the mother supplies the formless matter of the body; and the latter receives its form through the formative power that is in the semen of the father. And though this power cannot create the rational soul, yet it disposes the matter of the body to receive that form."[3]

These ideas, supposedly proving woman's inferior nature, had appeared in earlier theological writings, but they weren't solidified into doctrine until late in the Middle Ages. However, nothing, not even the Reformation, released woman from Original Sin and from her inferior status. It was a doctrine that worked to accomplish aims that extended far beyond the medieval Catholic Church.

MONOTHEISM VS. DUALISM

The embellished doctrine of Original Sin was sufficient to justify crimes against women. However, the Church was also facing rising opposition within its ranks of clergy and other male members. Accusations of dualism—in the sense of worshipping an evil deity as well as the Christian god—were used to quell the disquieted groups of so-called heretics. First the activities of the Inquisition, and then the witch-hunts, grew directly out of these charges.[4]

Christianity holds to a belief in monotheism, a single reigning and supreme god who has good intentions toward humanity. The existence of evil in the world is therefore problematic. "How is it that God can be all-powerful and all-good, yet create a world in which cancer, famine, and torture are abundant? One answer is that evil is at least in part caused by an evil spirit of great power."[5] In Hebrew the spirit was called Satan, which translated into English as "devil," whose appearance was derived from the older gods of pagan religions such as the horned and cloven-footed Pan.

In the primal earth mother religions, the existence of evil did not cause problems in logic. The Great Goddess embodied the forces of both dark and light; hence, her worship constituted a monistic theology, combining good and evil in a single deity. Most forms of Christianity, but particularly the medieval and modern versions of fundamentalism, are strongly—*but not admittedly*—dualistic in giving the devil a unique character as a fallen angel or deity. In order to sidestep the obvious dualism, Christianity mitigated the devil's powers and limited his domain.

The heretics, and later many women, were accused of worshipping the devil as their primary god. The accusations were probably deliberately falsified. There was no evidence that any of the sects actually did worship or honor the devil instead of the Christian god. On the other hand, the heretics were guilty of seriously questioning points of Catholic dogma and the lifestyle of the clergy. There was widespread and genuine desire for moral reform. From the beginning, most of the splinter groups and the far left and right wings of the Church were much more open to women's active participation than was the main body of Christianity.

THE BEGINNING OF THE END

To protect itself from the disillusioned sects, the Church took the offensive. To advance its interests, the Church revived the Holy Inquisition, a body formed in 1022 when King Robert presided over the trial of heretics at Orleans, France. The charges of devil worship spurred by the Inquisition echoed for seven hundred years across the continent of Europe, through the British Isles, and to North and South America.

The charges scarcely change over time, whether the accused is a Jew, a Catholic, a Gnostic, a woman healer, or whomever else the mainstream deems heretical. They seem to come from the dank and putrid place of the mind that knows what is most offensive to human sensibilities: killing and eating babies, copulating with forces of evil, performing orgiastic and bloody rituals, and possessing occult knowledge that threatens life.

The heretics were identified by their group affiliation: Paulicians, Bogomils, Waldensians, The Order of the Poor Knights of Christ and the Temple of Solomon (or Templars), Cathars, etc. At one time, the Templars were considered integral to the success of the Crusades and were merciless avengers. The popes, in fact, allowed them unprecedented autonomy. As their wealth and power grew, they quickly gained landholdings and built castles. The Templars had monopolies over businesses, and their wealth permitted them to establish the institution of banking. When their fame and power eventually threatened the monarchs of Europe, as well as the ruling powers in Rome, they became targets for the Inquisition. They were accused, as were all heretics, of having knowledge of the occult with the devil as consort. Their mystical traditions supposedly live on in the esoteric practices of Rosicrucianism and in the rituals of the Masonic orders.

The Cathars were strongly dualistic, believing that all physical manifestation was created by the devil to test and tempt humanity. Furthermore, they ascribed to the feminine principle in religion and allowed women to serve as preachers and teachers.

In 1208, Pope Innocent III ordered the Albigensian Crusade against the Cathars. For the twenty years following, the persecutions and executions were relentless. Neither women nor children were spared. By 1235 the Papal Inquisition was firmly established. In 1252, Innocent IV issued the bull *Ad extirpanda,* authorizing the imprisonment, torture, and execution of heretics on minimal evidence, and the seizure of their worldly goods. Heretics could even be tried after they had already died, and the goods of their heirs confiscated. Confiscations were undertaken with such enthusiasm that within less than a century the treasure trove had been mined nearly out. In 1360, Inquisitor Eymeric complained that there were no rich heretics left, and interest in the venture was waning. "It is a pity that so salutary an institution as ours should be so uncertain of its future."[6]

The legal system became increasingly harsh, fueled by each new conviction; soon, the distinction between sorcery and heresy blurred—all the accused (including those accused of witchcraft) were guilty of worshipping the devil.

The arm of the Inquisition reached out primarily to the members of the aberrant religious sects. The paranoia about "woman as sorcerer"—and, hence, "woman as witch and healer"—spread slowly at first. It did not fully ripen until the fifteenth century, fostered by the events of the Renaissance and Reformation.

THE GENESIS OF EXPERIMENTAL SCIENCE

The forefathers of science established a philosophic basis for the persecution of women that expanded upon the concepts of dualism and Original Sin. Who were these men? Chiefly, Roger Bacon, St. Thomas Aquinas, Arnald of Villanova, Albertus Magnus, and Michael Scot. Since scholarship was not allowed to exist independently of the Church, science could not be derived from any body of knowledge other than theology. Scientific theorists were ecclesiastics: Roger Bacon was a Franciscan, Aquinas and Magnus were Dominicans. Michael Scot was a high-ranking clergyman, physician, and court astrologer; Arnald was a physician and alchemist, and counsel for the Spiritual Franciscans and popes.[7]

These men were not necessarily laboring under a burden of intent to facilitate the holocaust against women. It would gain its momentum with their words years after they were dead. In their writings, each mentioned women colleagues who practiced healing in a fashion they approved. Arnald notes his indebtedness to women for teaching him about the appropriate time for gathering herbs, and about charms and magic stones. He wrote of their marvelous remedies: the use of the color red for smallpox, potions for hemorrhages, and secret poultices for sore throats. Albertus Magnus championed education for women, believing that the Virgin Mary herself must have known the seven liberal arts! Michael Scot taught midwives the practices of astrology having to do with the moments of conception and birth.

These men took it upon themselves to describe all extant knowledge of the seen and unseen and felt qualified to hold forth on any subject imaginable. St. Thomas Aquinas wrote as though he had been commissioned to summarize the doctrines of the Church. It was largely due to his efforts that the fluidity of thought that characterized the evolving medieval intellect crystallized into dogma.

While each man expressed many subtleties of thought, there is a stream of medieval consciousness that can be captured as it rises like a vapor from their collective work. All wrote of healing nostrums, even though only Michael Scot and Arnald of Villanova seem to have functioned primarily as physicians. Their prescription involved pages and pages of ritualistic preparation, including a wide mixture of medicine, botanics, magic or sorcery, astrology, gemology, religion, alchemy, dream interpretation, geomancy, necromancy, and divination.

In order to advance knowledge and protect humankind, these men thought it necessary to sort out which practices involved natural science and which involved the supernatural, as well as those that involved experimental science versus magic. Since either godlike or demonlike forces were seen as capable of penetrating the manifestations of natural science, supernatural events, experimental science, and magic, they needed to be identified somehow. Furthermore, there was a kind of covert continuum of practice and observation, which extended over three levels: (1) that which was of God, filled with God, and therefore correct; (2) magic or sorcery, which was probably not of God, but there was not vast agreement on whether it was of the devil; and (3) heresy which was, in no uncertain terms, the work of the devil. What all this boiled down to was that if practices were heretical, they were justifiably punishable and eventually would fall within the jurisdiction of the Inquisition.

After the Middle Ages, the category of magic or sorcery—always difficult to assess—was simply collapsed into the category of heresy. Only two categories remained: that which was of God and that which was of the devil. The selected passages below demonstrate the twisted logic required to categorize healing prescription or ritual. We also gain a sense of how hard these men tried to establish what was good medicine and what was not. Their decisions held sway for centuries. Their efforts led their successors to arrive at what they considered to be the best possible solution for the problems of the day: women and their medicine must be condemned.

A passage from Arnald of Villanova's *Antidotarium* imparts the flavor of the mainstream medicine of his time.

> In the name of the living Father of our Lord Jesus Christ, take the purest gold and melt it as the sun enters Aries. Later form a round seal from it and say while so doing, "Arise Jesus, light of the world, thou who art in truth the lamb that taketh away the sins of the world and enlighteneth our darkness." And repeat the Psalm, *Domine dominus noster*. After doing this much, put the seal away, and later, when the moon is in Cancer or Leo and while the sun is in Aries, engrave on one side the figure of a ram and on the circumference *arahel tribus juda v et vii*, and elsewhere on the circumference let these sacred words be engraved, "The Word was made flesh and dwelt among us." and in the center, "Alpha and Omega and Saint Peter."

He claims that the power of the seal includes

> works against all demons and capital enemies and against witchcraft, and is efficacious in winning gain and favor, and aids in all dangers and financial difficulties *(vectigalibus)*, and against thunderbolts and storms and inundations, and against the force of the winds and the pestilences of the air. Its bearer is honored and feared in all his affairs. No harm can befall the building or occupants of the house where it is. It benefits demoniacs, those suffering from inflammation of the brain, maniacs, quinsy, sore throat, and all diseases of the head and eyes, and those in which rheum descends from the head. And in general I say that it wards off all evils and confers good; and let its bearer abstain as far as possible from impurity and luxury and other mortal sins, and let him wear it on his head with reverence and honor.[8]

The inconsistencies in this mode of scholarship also appear in his work *Those Things Whose Use Is Permitted in the Cure of Epilepsy*. He expresses his disapproval of the use of characters and superstititions in medicine, and forbids even the use of the sign of the cross or Lord's Prayer in collecting medicinal ingredients. He also rails against the enchanters, conjurers, and invokers of spirits, diviners and augurers who practiced the healing arts, finding them a godless crew who served the devil.

Another instance of inconsistency appears in Arnald's *Breviarium*. Arnald condemns the incantations used in childbirth by the "old wives" of Salerno. (One might question who the "old wives" were, and whether, indeed, they might not have been the brilliant women of Trotula's time.) They would take three grains of pepper; the "enchantress" would say over each a Lord's Prayer, "Deliver us from evil," and the request "Deliver this woman from the pangs of childbirth." Then the grains would be administered, one after another, in wine or water so that they should not touch the patient's teeth. Finally, the "old wife" would repeat the incantation three times, each time accompanied by a Pater Noster.[9]

Arnald calls these "diabolical practices." Yet in the same work, he discusses a similar practice that cured him of over one hundred warts within ten days. The warts were touched, the sign of the cross was made, and the healer turned to a bush. Kneeling, he repeated the Lord's Prayer, substituting for the words "Deliver us from evil" the request "Deliver Master Arnald from the wens and warts on his hands." The tips of three of the stalks of the bush were plucked to the tune of three Pater Nosters, and then placed in the ground in a damp and secluded spot. The warts, declared Arnald, disappeared as the stalks withered. The difference? In the latter instance, the practitioner was a priest. We can see from this example that it was not what was being performed, but *who* was doing it that determined whether the healing fell into the realm of the diabolical or the divine.

Michael Scot had little sympathy for magicians or sorcerers. He considered them evil tricksters, but wise nevertheless in understanding the secrets of nature and in predicting the future. He listed twenty-eight varieties of divination, all powerful tools to predict the future, all evil. He then goes on to describe in great detail in his work *Physionomia* how dreams might be interpreted, how one should sleep to have dreams of prophesy, and so forth.[10] He emphasized dreams as diagnostic tools for the state of health—in particular, the condition of bodily humors. In the *Liber introductorius,* he describes medicines as he knew them—herbs, stones, words, astrological influences—and says if none of them work, the patient should be sent to an enchantress or a diviner.[11]

Albertus Magnus, considered the greatest intellect of the century and an early proponent of scientific experimentation, believed that dreams were especially the affair of magic. But he thought magic could be either good or bad, and in any event, it was a branch of science. He said in *On Sleep and Waking* that the defect was not in the science, but in the men who were unable to distinguish what was contingent from what was necessary.[12]

Of all of the nostrums and divinations and incantations that constituted the questionable field of medicine, only alchemy and astrology survived without being tainted significantly by association with magic or demons; their practice continued to be supported by the Church. Women were rarely associated with either, and they remained the exclusive territory of licensed physicians for about five hundred years.

Other healing modalities were not so well defined. Plants, animal parts, and gems were used by all healers—how could their use incriminate one as practicing demonlike medicine? Certain substances had medicinal effects but may or may not have "magic" effects (or divine effects, as Albertus Magnus called them). Magnus believed that betony conferred the power of divination, verbena was a love charm, still other herbs extinguished lust, while others invoked demons. In other contexts, these same herbs have medicinal virtue. Therefore, we must distinguish *godlike* from *demonlike* in terms of intent, not content. According to the literature, stones and animals parts, too, could variously kill or cure, hex or bless. The delineation between medicine as a natural science impregnated with the breath of God and magic as a diabolical art becomes even muddier.[13]

Roger Bacon, whose work laid the foundation for the careful observational methods of science, felt that magic and science were so similar that they could not be distinguished from each other. He knew of the occult literature and magical practices of his time, characterizing much of the latter as false, fraudulent, and futile. At the same time, in *Opus tertium* he admits to the power of magic and says that it can perform marvels with the aid of demons.[14]

Who were the practitioners of magic, if indeed the practices themselves were so difficult to separate out from the medicine and science of the time? Bacon refers to them as magicians, witches, "old wives," and wizards. What they were not, he asserts, were astronomers or philosophers.

He associates magic and "old wives" with the idea of fascination—the ability of one person to effect another's mind with words or charms—a concept similar to that of the evil eye in many cultures. Words, formulas, or incantations employed to "fascinate" possess no transforming power in and of themselves, according to him. If they work, it is because of demons. The belief in any intrinsic power of the charms was a simple notion of philosophers, he asserts. Note that he doesn't say they don't work, but he says that they don't work for the reasons people might think.

Aquinas, unlike Bacon and Magnus and other more moderate thinkers, held that the methods of magic were immoral and evil, and—except in order to offer a refutation—should under no circumstances be studied.

Aquinas proclaimed the reality and danger of magic or sorcery. He condemned divination, carefully distinguishing it from divine prophesy. Again, the criteria for discrimination were not directed toward the method itself but toward who was involved and what their intentions were. He avowed the reality of witchcraft, stating that if men deny witches, they are also denying demons, in violation of Church precepts. He gave witches their due by claiming that they had the ability to interrupt the act of sexual union—a charge that would be remembered by impotent men for centuries.[15]

Aquinas, too, believed in the factual power of fascination, or evil eye. He thought the eye was affected by the strong imagination of the soul. It was capable of corrupting the atmosphere and injuring tender bodies that come in contact with it. This is how malicious old women injure children.[16]

Like the other forefathers of science, Aquinas could find no fault with alchemy or astrology. But herbs and words could be found in the armamentarium of both magic and medicine, and therefore were always suspect.[17]

SUMMARY

The case against women practicing the healing arts was strongly made on acceptable theological and scientific grounds. It was never insinuated that women lacked the knowledge or the wisdom to ply the healing arts—indeed, quite the opposite: women were credited with knowing their business, with having powerful secret remedies, and with the ability to intervene on the planes of the physical and the supernatural. However, because they were women—not men, nor philosophers, nor priests, nor physicians—any manifestation of their healing practices was deemed the work of demons.

The importance of the Church's position and the writings of the learned men of the time cannot be underestimated. They provided the populace with what seemed to be rational and necessary justification for oppression and murder. Women were ensnared by the decisions of the forefathers of science and the doctrines of the Church concerning what was of God and what was of the devil, in terms of healing practices. The upshot was that, regardless of the type of healing practice, if it was part of women's repertoire, it, and they, were in communion with evil forces. So the thirteenth century closed with what appeared to be a satisfactory and final answer to the persistent problem of women who chose to be healers.

10   Fate of the Wise Women

As THE MIDDLE AGES waned, life lost its gentle shadings. Passion and violence, decadence and piety, the throes of death amidst the dance characterized these times.[1] Calamity struck Europe. The ecology was under stress; plagues and wars raged. This chapter examines how these stresses led to the brutalization of women, severe sanctions on women healers, and murder of those who plied the healing arts. The chapter begins around A.D. 1300 and ends with the seventeenth century.

In the fourteenth century, there was a general cooling down of the northern hemisphere. Glaciers advanced and winters took on a new severity. Once again, the seas rose, and the delicate balance of humans and their environment was off center. All of Europe was touched in one way or another. The continent consisted of a vast peasantry who were greatly affected by the failure of their efforts to produce meager sustenance. However, environmental conditions affect everyone—peasants, burghers, and kings alike. Changes in barometric pressure, in temperature, and in rainfall affect the growth of trees and babies. In an era that had seen little change, that knew of no alternatives to its own traditions, the potential for chaos when the balance between humans and the environment was disturbed was especially great.[2]

Between 1308 and 1317, the unusual climate created a devastating situation, beginning in the far north and spreading throughout Europe. There was no system for relief—millers hoarded grain to obtain high prices, and starvation was rampant. In three hundred years the population of Europe had tripled. The equation of more people plus less food was deadly.

PLAGUES, POX, AND WAR

The crop failures of several years, coupled with filthy conditions in overcrowded towns and cities, opened the floodgates to diseases that would lay waste like no others before or since.

In October of 1347 twelve Genoese galleys, thought to have come from the Crimea, were guided by dying men into the harbor of Messina. One observer reported that "in their bones they bore so virulent a disease that anyone who only spoke to them was seized by a mortal illness and in no manner could evade death."[3] The ships were ordered out of the harbor, but not before the men had come into contact with enough people to start the disease spreading first through Sicily, then France, and through the rest of Europe.

The pandemic was known as the Black Death. Infection from the disease occurred in three forms: bubonic, pneumonic, or septicemic. Most victims died within three days. From one-third to one-half of Europe's population perished. According to Church records, fifteen hundred people died in three days in Avignon. The Franciscan order alone claimed 124,434 losses. Total villages were wiped out; in 1350 the population of London was only half of what it had been ten years earlier.

Women were far more likely to survive the plague than men, and in some areas their recovery rate was about seven times as high. Many people believed that women were using magic to ensure their survival, and even to cause the death of men.[4]

The only recognized treatment for the plague was to lance the buboes in the lymph nodes, which gave some relief and seemed, in a few cases, to have a positive effect on recovery. John of Burgundy, a physician of Liège, advised that, to prevent the disease, one should stay in the house with the windows closed to keep out the corrupt air and burn juniper continuously on the hearth. He admonished all to keep their hands clean, but to avoid baths because they opened the pores. Blood should be let once a month. If these measures failed, the plague should be treated with teas of dictamnus, scabious, roses, and violets; he recommended that the abscesses be lanced.

At the first sign of plague, those who could left for the country or someplace as yet untouched by the disease. The few physicians there were seldom stayed behind to treat the victims. It was just as well—since most were astrologers or specialists in urine diagnosis, their skills would not have been very useful to care for the dying.

Most accounts of the time observed that the ill and dying were left in the hands of "quacks," barbers, and "ignorant" women. No record remains of the type of treatment that women used, but we can speculate that the usual mixtures of soporifics and sedatives were available, and that they were able to provide more relief than the flower teas prescribed by John of Burgundy.

The Black Death returned again and again to Europe. In 1478 it was particularly devastating, killing one-third of the remaining population. Those who remained alive had probably developed some immunity. However, the plague was only one of the pestilences that would take their toll. In the same year, that the Black Death began its major rampage, a mortal form of syphilis broke out after a relative quiescence of seven hundred years. Other diseases of the times included erysipelas, leprosy, smallpox, measles, and Saint Vitus' dance. A disease called the sweating sickness ravaged England from 1486 to 1551, crossed the channel to Europe, and then disappeared. It affected the heart and lungs, was accompanied by fits of shivering and profuse sweating, and often left its victims dead within hours.

In addition to the plague, there was war. The Hundred Years' War between France and England began when ravaging bands attacked French towns in 1346, coincident with the Black Death. Within the century, Italy was in turmoil; contenders for lands of the state and Church fought themselves and each other; France fought Italy, and England fought first the internal War of Roses and then Scotland. The plague years scarcely dampened the fighting. "One might have thought that universal destruction would have sickened rulers with blood. But if death is invited to the dance, he is the last to leave."[5]

To the countries of Europe and to the Church, the cost of sustaining perpetual war over several hundred years was enormous. Monies were extracted mercilessly from a disgruntled peasantry, who rebelled, fought, and made demands as never before. The clergy became a laughingstock; the pope and cardinals were burned in effigy. In a fairly short time the properties of the Church fell to rubble, the land lay fallow, and the tithes went uncollected.

LEGISLATION AND THE HEALING PROFESSIONS

Women healers had to function in the midst of overwhelming devastation and tragedy, under perpetual scrutiny by Church and state. Several French women in the early 1300s were reported to have been excommunicated under a ban by the prior of Saint Genevieve for practicing without appropriate licensure. How many more were excommunicated and how many were overlooked and allowed to practice is uncertain. A license in France, as well as in other countries, usually required an examination by self-declared masters of surgery or medicine. Most often the licensure requirements were simply ignored by both men and women. Paris, with 200,000 inhabitants at the end of the fourteenth century, had only ten licensed doctors. Thirty-eight (including five women) practiced "irregularly," and were taxed heavily, indicating that their earnings must have been substantial.

In the late 1300s, in France and England, women were rarely allowed to sit for licensing examinations. Guy de Chauliac, the most respected surgeon of the Middle Ages, argued against their presence among the ranks of medical practitioners, calling women idiots who gathered herbs and practiced religious nonsense. (Guy's own medicine was based upon unusual concoctions such as dragon's blood and mummy dust.)

Guilds were being formed in England and elsewhere. These served as the basis for determining who could do what to whom, and from the guilds grew the modern professions of medicine. Executioners could set bones; barbers could cup, bleed, and give enemas. Surgeons formed their own guild in 1435, to be joined by the barbers in 1493—a motley, unsavory lot.

Women could practice midwifery, although it too was a profession in poor repute. The midwives were frequently fined, imprisoned, or even sentenced to death if they displeased an influential patient or assisted at the birth of a stillborn or deformed child.

In spite of sanctions against them, some women continued to practice. The most famous case is a woman named Jacoba (or Jacobina) Felicie who was fined time and again for practicing medicine in Paris without appropriate credentials. Jacoba had received her training with a mentor. (This was not an unusual practice, especially for married men, who were not allowed to attend the universities.) Nevertheless, in 1322 she was arraigned before the Court of Justice by the dean and masters of the Faculty of Medicine. The charges against her read:

> (1) That the said Jacoba visited many sick folk labouring under severe illness in Paris and the suburbs, examining their urine, touching, feeling and holding their pulse, body and limbs, (2) that after this examination she was wont to say to the said sick folk "I will cure you, by God's will, if you will trust me," making a compact with them and receiving money therefrom, (3) that after the said compact was made between the said party and the sick folk or their friends that she would cure them of their internal sickness or of wounds upon their outward body, the aforesaid party used to visit them several times assiduously and continually inspecting their urine and feeling and touching their limbs, (4) and that after this she gave and gives to the aforesaid folk sirups to drink conformative, laxative and digestive, as well liquid as not liquid, and aromatic and other potions, which they often drink and have drunk in her presence and at her order, (5) and that she continues so to practice though unqualified in the schools of Paris and unlicensed by the Chancellor of Paris and the Dean of Magistrates, (6) that she has been warned and inhibited but (7) goes on as before.[6]

The prosecution called witnesses to testify against Jacoba. They all agreed that the charges were mostly accurate, but they also said she was a wise and practiced physician who had cured them. Some even mentioned the names of other physicians who had failed to offer relief or cure, much to the embarassment of the Faculty of Medicine. According to the witnesses, Jacoba had made no financial arrangements with them, suggesting that they give her what they thought appropriate after they were cured.

Jacoba argued that she should be judged by her results. Then she went on to speak of the need for women physicians:

It is better and more seemly that a wise woman learned in the art should visit a sick woman and inquire into the secrets of her nature and her hidden parts, than that a man should do so, for whom it is not lawful to see and seek out the aforesaid parts, nor to feel with his hands the breasts, belly and feet. . . . And a woman before now would allow herself to die rather than to reveal the secrets of her infirmity to a man, on account of the honour of the female sex and of the shame which she would feel. And for these reasons many women and also men have perished of their infirmities, not being willing to have doctors, lest these should see their secret parts.[7]

Jacoba's testimony was ignored. The prosecution argued that since she had not been "approved" by the faculty, she must be ignorant of the practices of medicine. They discounted her patients' cures, stating that they were "certain that a man approved in the aforesaid art could cure the sick better than a woman."[8] Finally, they decided that since women had no status as adults in a court of law, they shouldn't be practicing medicine either.

Jacoba was reprimanded and allowed a limited practice, but she could not receive remuneration for her services. Jacoba may also have been a Jew, which is another issue. Jews were banned by the Church from practicing the healing arts. However, they were reputedly so skillful that they were hired at high cost and some risk by nobles and ecclesiastics. Of the few women listed as physicians on the rolls of the major cities of Europe, a surprising number were Jewish, often members of medical families who specialized in the treatment of eye diseases. In Frankfurt, for instance, fifteen women practitioners were listed between 1389 and 1497, four of whom were Jewish.[9] The Jewish women were likely trained through mentorship or at Salerno, the only medical school that continued to accept women as students.

By the sixteenth century, civil authorities and private enterprise had entered the licensing fray. In England, the College of Physicians incorporated itself in 1518, making it clear that only they would practice the arts of healing. "Quackery," stated the Acts of Incorporation, was composed of "ignorant persons of whom the great part have no manner of insight nor any kind of learning, some also can no lettres in the boke so far forth that common artificers as smyths, wevers, and women boldly and continually take upon them great cures and things of great difficulty in which they partly use sorcery and witchcraft, partly apply such medicines unto the disease as be very noyous and nothing metely therefore, to the high displeasure of God."[10] Note that women are singled out. This was "in effect a *carte blanche* defamation devoid of natural justice and representing the intolerance of a priestly caste towards a heretical sect."[11]

The barber-surgeons had no intention of treating nonpaying patients, who were plentiful, and furthermore, they harassed the women and other folk

Woman as Healer

healers who were doing charitable work. The king of England enacted the "Quack's Charter," withdrawing some of the previous monopoly granted to the barber-surgeons in order that the poor receive some care. The folk healers, by virtue of their knowledge of "plant rootes and waters" were allowed to cure surface or skin maladies with plaster, poultices, and ointments.

The newly established medical professionals were irate over the reversal by the king's charter. They did not want to care for the suffering poor, and they didn't want anyone else to either. Thomas Gale, Queen Elizabeth's surgeon, complained bitterly:

> I did see in the two hospitals of London, called St. Thomas and St. Bartholomew's to the number 300 and odd poore people were diseased of sore arms and legs feet and hands with other parts of the body so grievously affected that 120 of them could never be recovered without the loss of a limb. All these were brought to that mischief by witches, by women, by counterfeit worthless fellows that take upon themselves the use of an art not only by robbing them of their money but of their limbs and perpetual health.[12]

In these centuries, the waning of the Middle Ages, the searchlight was homing in on women. The blame for all of humankind's failures and the disgruntled moods of the earth was once again focused on woman: it was witchcraft. This charge became the single most effective means of controlling the monopoly of the healing professions. How deliberate was it? "Given the number of instances in which the Church combined with various economic groups from doctors to lawyers to merchant guilds, not only to make pronouncements about the incapacities of women, but often to accomplish the physical liquidation of women through witchcraft and heresy trials, one can hardly say that it all happened without anyone intending it."[13]

WITCH-HUNT/WOMAN-HUNT

Women's skill in the healing arts was generally not discounted. But, since women were not officially allowed to study medicine, it was widely accepted that their information could only have come from the devil. The position of the Church was "that if a woman dare to cure without having studied, she is a witch and must die."[14] The machinery of Church and state had conspired to create "the shocking nightmare, the foulest crime and deepest shame of Western civilization, the blackout of everything that *homo sapiens,* the reasoning man, has ever upheld."[15]

The women who were accused of witchcraft bore no resemblance to the witches of fairy tales. The misconception that they did has inhibited, until the past hundred years or so, serious study of Western civilization's greatest crime. Yet now, as then, the "witch" is the shadow of the darkest thoughts within the human psyche.

The moral and ethical crux of the persecutions was that "witch hunting *is* woman hunting or at least it is the hunting of women who do not fulfill the male view of how women ought to conduct themselves."[16] Most studies of the era have assiduously avoided this larger issue, concentrating instead on select details of the trials, persecutions, and sociopolitical conditions. Only recently, with the probe of serious feminist historians, anthropologists, and writers—Christine Larner, Barbara Walker, Barbara Ehrenreich and Deidre English, and Mary Daly, among others—has the impact of this tragedy come to light.[17]

In some areas, women were burned by a ratio of ten women to one man. In Scotland, where the number of men burned was exceptionally high, the ratio was still five women to one man. In twelfth-century Russia, when the authorities were looking for witches, they simply rounded up all the women in a given area. The stereotypic witch is not, and has not ever been, a male. To say that the witch-hunts were crimes against humanity misses the point. These were crimes against one-half of humanity that guaranteed that all women who chose healing as a vocation would be placed in the limelight of suspicion. The church fathers had predetermined much earlier that witchcraft was a woman's crime.

Men *were* also accused, but in spurts, in circumscribed locations where witchcraft and heresy had not been well delineated. There was a run on politicians during the reign of Queen Elizabeth I, and on high-ranking German clerics during several eras. Men who dared to think independently, such as Giordino Bruno and Galileo, were always at risk for heresy charges, but more often men were burned or hanged for pure political expediency. Men healers (i.e., those who practiced without having "studied") were not subject to blanket accusations, even when "quackery" was the issue in the seventeenth and eighteenth centuries.

ACCUSATIONS, TRIALS, AND BURNINGS

The details of the witch accusations, trials, and burnings—often recorded at the time of the crimes—have been reported by numerous authors for the last hundred years. Women healers were one of the most contentious groups, and for that reason I recite their involvement here.

The position held by the Church and enforced by civic bodies—that women who practiced without appropriate study must die—had a catch, of course. Women, except for a dwindling enrollment at Salerno, were not allowed access to education. All women healers, therefore, were suspect. Any woman with exceptional talent was suspect; any woman who had acquired her knowledge through the oral tradition of woman's domestic healing was suspect; any woman who had studied independently with a master healer (even a man) was suspect. Any woman who had the bad luck to be associated, by proximity or reputation, with a physician's failure to cure his patient was suspect.

By no means were all the women accused of witchcraft engaged in the practice of the healing arts. Healing was a *sufficient,* but not a *necessary* condition for condemnation. And, by the time women reached trial, the original ground for accusation would take a diminished role in a trial format that remained standardized for approximately three hundred years. When the accusation was "healing," it was not healing, per se, that was the crime. The logic went that if a woman was practicing an art for which she could not have studied, she had made a pact with the devil.

From the beginning, the Holy Inquisition (first Dominican, later Jesuit orders) found the suspects, tortured them, and then judged them in trials. It owned or leased the appropriate equipment and torture chambers. The sentencing and prosecutions were in the hands of civic authorities. They followed the Church's precepts with holy zeal, as did the Protestants, who owed no allegiance to Catholicism.

A woman could be arrested on the most minimal evidence. It was not even necessary to inform her of her crimes, or bring evidence in support of her character. She might even be tried and found guilty without her knowledge or testimony, and then burned.

Once a woman was arrested, the brutal torture accompanying her "confessions" assured that almost no one was found innocent. Arrest, then, was tantamount to death. Transcripts of the trials have been published in a number of places, each a testimony to the insanity and sadism of the accusers.

The following scenario is adapted from a report of the first day's torture of a woman accused of witchcraft in Prossneck, Germany, in 1629.[18] First, she was put on the "ladder," alcohol was thrown over her head and her hair was set afire. Strips of sulfur were placed under her arms and ignited. Then the torturer tied her hands behind her back and hoisted her to the ceiling, where she hung for four hours while he went to breakfast. On his return, he threw alcohol over her back and set fire to it. Placing heavy weights on her body, he jerked her up to the ceiling again. Then he squeezed her thumbs and big toes in a vise, trussed her arms with a stick, and kept her hanging until she fainted. Then he whipped her with rawhide. Once more to the vises, and he went to lunch. After his lunch she was whipped until blood ran though her shift. The next day, it was reported, they started all over again, but without pushing things quite as far as before.

The above is a relatively typical case, except that some torturers used more ingenious and cruel devices. In England, however, torture was attenuated, and women were usually hanged instead of burned. Sometimes the women were mercifully strangled before they were burned in a tar barrel. On the Continent, they were more often burned "quick" (alive). In most cases, the woman was required to pay for her confinement, for the activities of the torturers, fees for the torture equipment, and for the beer, meals, and banquets of the torturers, judges, clerics, and others involved in her arrest. Complete lists of official fees were published.[19] The accused woman's estates were confiscated. (In a few areas, such as Venice, where the citizens forbade such practices, the witch-hunts were relatively minimal.) Finally, all costs of her murder were charged to her heirs. If she should be boiled in oil—a favorite in certain parts of France—the fees were especially high.

Torture and execution were lucrative businesses that supported large numbers of townsfolk. The witch finders were also well remunerated. In every country, finding a "witch's mark" was sufficient evidence to convict a person. The mark was any mole, wen, or other skin mark, or any place that didn't bleed when pricked or that didn't hurt when a needle was plunged in. ("Needles" still in existence show that many were fake and simply retracted under pressure.) The women were stripped and shaved, and genitals probed for any peculiarity, any tab of skin that the demons might suck upon. When the witch's mark was found (as, of course, it invariably was) the proceedings against the woman were validated.

At this point the woman would be asked to confess and, prior to significant torture, would declare her innocence. Then she would be sent to the dungeon and tortured with whatever ingenuity could be mustered. Finally, most would confess something, knowing full well that it meant death—preferable to life, at this stage. The woman would have to second-guess the confessor, however, concocting just the sort of filth he wanted to hear. The accused would be asked to name accomplices, and the torture would continue until she had named enough suspects to satisfy the warped needs of the Inquisitional body. After confessing, a good Christian woman would usually have pangs of conscience and retract her statements, only to be sent back to the torture chamber. If the woman didn't confess, she would be brutalized until she died. Her death justified the process, because it demonstrated that she truly was guilty of the accused crimes.

Hundreds of children pointed the accusing finger at adults who they claimed had bewitched or abused them, or damaged their property. These were not necessarily children who were being accused of witchcraft, although that happened, too.[20] Some of the physical and sexual abuse these children describe is conceivable. Other accusations, such as witches flying through the air and changing into animals, don't fit a current model of the possible.

The most common elements that the accusers wanted in a confession were (1) a pact with the devil, (2) riding by night, (3) the formal repudiation of Christianity, (4) secret nocturnal meetings, (5) the desecration of the Eucharist and the crucifix, (6) an orgy, (7) sacrificial infanticide, (8) cannibalism, and (9) the raising of tempests or storms.[21] The accused woman would ultimately confess to as many of these points as her accusers demanded. An additional accusation, often used to incriminate the healers, was the alleged possession of ointments or poisons.

BREADTH OF THE CRIMES

The actual number of women murdered will never be known, even though many reports are accessible, particularly ones written after 1600. The Inquisition and the civil authorities occasionally kept records, but in a prebureaucratic age, accuracy is questionable. However, there was likely no cover-up. The numbers burned were a source of ecclesiastic pride, and the proceedings were nothing to be ashamed of as far as both church and civic bodies were concerned. Most records would simply state that "many" witches were burned. Authoritative estimates range from two hundred thousand to nine million. In Germany alone, one hundred thousand witch burnings have been carefully documented.[22]

Fires burned throughout Europe. In about 1600, a contemporary observer noted that "Germany is almost entirely occupied with building fires for the witches. Switzerland has been compelled to wipe out many of her villages on their account. Travelers in Lorraine may see thousands and thousands of the stakes to which witches are bound."[23] The Inquisition acknowledged burning 30,000 witches in 150 years. Records from Osnabruck in Germany show 121 witches were burned in 1583, and 133 in 1589. At Como a Vatican official reported that 1,000 witches were burned in 1523. In three little German villages—Rheinback, Meckenheim, and Flerzheim—from 300 households, 125 to 150 persons were executed within five years. Another small village, Riezler, Germany, could claim between 1,000 and 2,000 burnings. In Lorraine, the attorney general boasted that he had burned 900 witches from 1581 to 1591. Authorities guess that about 1,000 witches were hanged during the entire witch craze in England. In Treves, 7,000 were reported to have lost their lives, and in Geneva, 500 were executed in a single month. Some small towns were left with one woman or no women at all.[24]

By far the greatest crimes were committed in Germany. Würzburg and Bamberg, controlled by cousins who served as prince-bishops, were heavily involved in witch-burning activities. The inquisitors had ovens built to handle the mass murders, of much the same design as those built during Hitler's time.

The prince-bishop of Würzburg stated that man's great misfortune was to have been born from woman's stinking private parts. In Würzburg, indeed in many parts of Germany, it was reported that the most virtuous, most beautiful, and most modest girls were burned. Three hundred children were burned, many accused of having intercourse with the devil. The murders in this part of Germany cut a swath through all social strata and all ages.

We are dealing here with an evil that surpasses rational understanding. Here was, indeed, the worst aberration of humanity, and it trickled down the hierarchy of authority.

Pope Innocent VIII, who issued the key document that allowed the persecution to take form, was of a most macabre mentality. He was concerned that the Inquisition lacked popular support, and indeed it did in many sectors. Upon those who failed to see the light, he said, "will fall the wrath of God Almighty." His bull was affixed to the *Malleus maleficarum* (the "Hammer of Witches"), which became the step-by-step how-to manual for dealing with the "witch problem."[25] As he was dying, he attempted to revive himself by taking nourishment from a woman's breasts. He also demanded blood from three young boys, who subsequently bled to death.

THE MALLEUS MALEFICARUM (HAMMER OF WITCHES)

Published in 1486, the *Malleus maleficarum,* used to incriminate women and to detail the means of torture, was created by two Dominican inquisitors, Heinrich Institor (Kraemer) and Jacob Sprenger. It was the most influential of all early books, with at least thirty editions appearing before 1669. Available in English, German, French, and Italian, the *Malleus maleficarum* was accepted even by the Protestants, who otherwise opposed the Inquisition.

The authors of *Malleus maleficarum* sacrificed all rational arguments, all common sense, to meet their theological purpose. Rational, humanist objections were inevitably put forth by members of the clergy, who were ignored or threatened with loss of their own lives.

The sinister book is explicitly sexist. Women were more likely to be witches, it charged, because they were more stupid, weak, superstitious, and fickle than men. Further, they were sensual and hopelessly, insatiably carnal. The Dominicans claimed that the word *female* itself proved that, because it was taken from *fe* (faith) and *minus* (less). It is "an unsurpassed revelation of the primal anxiety about women that lurks in the heart of every man. The only comparable documents we have are the great Greek myths that preserve traces of male fear of the power and evil of women."[26]

Woman as keeper of the mysteries of generation was expressly indicted:

Now there are, as it is said in the Papal Bull, seven methods by which they infect with witchcraft the venereal act and the conception of the womb: first, by inclining the minds of men to inordinate passion; second, by obstructing their generative force; third, by removing the members accommodated to that act; fourth, by changing men into beasts with their magic act; fifth, by destroying the generative force in women; sixth, by procuring abortion; seventh, by offering children to the devils, besides other animals and fruits of the earth with which they work much hard.[27]

In a recitation of how a devil might produce various calamities, they include "to cause some disease in any of the human organs, to take away life, and to deprive men of reason."[28]

Midwives were feared above all and accused of offering the babies they delivered to devils. Midwives surpass all others in wickedness, noted the inquisitors in their diatribe against midwifery.

Concerning just how women impeded procreation, the inquisitors claimed, "Extrinsically they cause it at times by means of images, or by the eating of herbs; sometimes by other external means, such as cocks' testicles."[29] Again, woman's botanical lore formed a basis for suspicion.

Amidst the sadistic comments lurks the ludicrous. The following passage is included for the sake of levity:

And what, then, is to be thought of those witches who in this way sometimes collect male organs in great numbers, as many as twenty or thirty members together, and put them in a bird's nest, or shut them up in a box, where they move themselves like living members, and eat oats and corn, as has been seen by many and is a matter of common report? It is to be said that it is all done by devil's work and illusion, for the senses of those who see them are deluded in the way we have said. For a certain man tells that, when he had lost his member, he approached a known witch to ask her to restore it to him. She told the afflicted man to climb a tree, and that he might take which he like out of a nest in which there were several members. And when he tried to take a big one, the witch said: You must not take that one; adding, because it belonged to a parish priest.[30]

The sentiments behind the most sinister book in history extended into the twentieth century. The Reverend Montague Summers, responsible for translating the *Malleus* into English in 1928, wrote in his preface, concerning the Inquisition: "There can be no doubt that had this most excellent tribunal continued to enjoy its full prerogative and the full exercise of its salutary powers, the world at large would be in a far happier and far more orderly position to-day."[31] He then likens the witches and heretics to the Anarchists, the Nihilists, and the Bolsheviks.

WHO WERE THESE WOMEN AND WHAT WERE THEY REALLY DOING?

In the turmoil and uncertainty of the last few years of the Middle Ages and during the Renaissance, women became scapegoats for misfortune everywhere. Assigning blame to others gives a sense of prediction and control over one's own life. Therefore, when a cow failed to give milk, it was easy to blame a witch. Who was the witch? Someone either distrusted or disliked, or who looked unusual, or had been seen near the cow. Identification and conviction or destruction of the witch were believed to reverse the unwanted conditions.

Man's impotency could also be cured, it was believed, if the person suspected of causing the problem was found and punished or killed. Thomas Aquinas had earlier written into Church records that a witch was likely to blame if a man's penis wilted.[32] Such accusations proved to be a way of getting rid of a tiresome wife, or a meddling mother-in-law.

Wealthy women and those with enviable healing skills were likely targets for suspicion of witchcraft. Still other women were accused because they were obnoxious, or needy, or simply old, deformed, or mentally handicapped.

In several sociological analyses of localized witch phenomena in England, it was found that accusations most frequently occurred when a woman had been rebuked or insulted, or refused food or a favor. The person who had rejected her needs would accuse her of being a witch.[33] This meant that any woman low on the resources of living could be a target, an example of "blaming the victim."

Older women who had no supportive network or were on the margins of society had to find some way to provide for themselves. They were unable to rally protection in a male-dominated society that viewed them as a surplus commodity. Midwifery and folk healing—risky occupations in which the practitioner was doubly damned—were alternatives to starvation. If the healer failed (or even if she was most skillful) she could be readily labeled as "witch." Many of the babies born were already dead or would die soon. The mothers, too, often died from the raging fevers of childbed. The midwife would be blamed for these consequenses.

GOOD WITCH/HEALING WOMAN

Women healers who worked out of deep commitment to a healing vocation and with exceptional skill—even though they were called "good" or "blessing" witches and practiced what authorities considered "white magic"—were also embraced in the paranoid delusions of the persecutors. Also known as wise women (*femina saga*), they were accused of the "crimes" of aiding the sick, birthing babies, and caring for the dying. In areas where the emergent male professionals had their greatest strength, many of these women were accused of witchcraft.

The Dominican Johann Herolt said that "most women belie their Catholic faith with charms and spells, after the fashion of Eve. . . . Any woman by herself knows more of such superstitions and charms than a hundred men."[34] Superstitions, charms, and spells, of course, constituted the practical medicine of the day.

Not only were wise women accused of healing without having studied, they were also charged with the ability of "laying on cures and laying them off"—transferring ailments from one person to another, or from a person to an animal.

William Perkins, a Scottish minister and leading witch-hunter, voiced the prevalent Protestant position on the healing arts of the wise women: the "good witch was more a monster than the bad. . . . If death be due to any . . . then a thousand deaths of right belong to the good witch." He went on to say that it would be better if all witches, but especially the blessing witch, were to die. For, he said, "though the witch were in many respects profitable, and did not hurt, but procured much good, yet because he hath renounced God, his king and governor, and hath bound himself by other laws to the service of the enemies of God and his Church, death is his portion justly assigned him by God: he may not live."[35] The opinion of Protestant minister George Gifford was that a woman healer should be condemned not because of what she does, but because "she dealeth with the devil."[36]

The English authorities were unanimous in their condemnation. At the same time, they admitted that "good" witches existed, and that they should be consulted if the physician failed to cure an illness.

The public, likewise, believed that the wise women were specially skilled. However, their attitude toward prosecution may have differed, since they stood to benefit from their healing. One story has it that a jailer at Canterbury Castle in 1570 released a witch because he believed she did more good for the sick than all the priests' prayers and exorcisms.[37]

The wise woman's use of herbs was problematic, because it was widely believed that those who used herbs for cures did so only through a pact with the devil, whether it be implicit or explicit. In the previous chapter, we saw how the great minds of the Middle Ages wrestled with the issue of botanics. As will be discussed later, the major problem was that the plants in and of themselves could not be credited with any potent effects. Their effects, like those of chants, spells, or prayers, therefore, had to come from either God or the devil. The strongest plants, such as the mood-altering alkaloids, were mostly the devil's doing.

In Germany women could be accused of witchcraft for owning oil, ointment, pots of vermin, or human bones. All of these, of course, were common medicaments of the time—on any pharmacist's shelf, in any woman's pharmacopoeia. The oil and ointment may have had other connotations, to be discussed on p. 92.

Any problem that eluded cure was readily attributed by the licensed doctors to witchcraft. In some instances of failure, there might be some question by the prosecuting authorities. In cases in which the prosecuting authorities had any question, the *Malleus mallifaricum* advised: "And if it is asked how it is possible to distinguish whether an illness is caused by witchcraft or by some natural physical defect, we answer that the first is by means of the judgement of doctors."[38]

Many instances of wise women being accused of witchcraft are reported. For instance, Alison Peirsoun of Byrehill had established her reputation as a gifted healer. Consequently, the archbishop of St. Andrews sent for her. Afflicted with several disorders that we might call "psychosomatic," he had been treated by many practitioners without relief. Alison, by whatever means, cured him. Later, he not only refused to pay her bill, he also had her arrested. She was charged and executed for witchcraft.

A wise woman whose life created a vivid stir was Gilly Duncan. Gilly was a young servant woman in the employ of David Seaton, deputy bailiff of a small town near Edinburgh. Gilly had established a reputation as a healer and cured those who were troubled or grieved with any kind of sickness or infirmity. Seaton felt her exceptional skill was unnatural. He also claimed to have seen her going to unexplained places at night. He obtained torture devices and began to question her. He jerked her head around with a rope, applied the thumbscrews, and examined her for the devil's mark. She finally confessed to the wicked allurements and enticements of the devil. Satisfied with his work, Seaton turned her over to the authorities. They forced her, with their own means, to name her accomplices. Those accused, the so-called witches of North Berwick, were tried and hanged in about 1592.

These witch activities added to the fears of King James IV (James I of England), who believed that plots and supernatural forces threatened his life. It was he who commissioned the first translation of the Bible (The King James version) in which the word *witch* appeared, the most-quoted instance being Exodus 22:18: "Thou shalt not suffer a witch to live." As early as 1584, Reginald Scot pointed out that the word *Kashaph*, which appears in several places in the Old Testament, is best translated as "poisoner," and not

Woman as Healer

"witch."[39] His protests were ignored, and use of the word *witch* in the Book of God was further justification for murdering hundreds of thousands of women.

WOMEN ACCUSED FOR SHAMANIC PRACTICES

As related in Chapter 2, virtually every tribal culture bears evidence of having, or having had, a shaman who seeks knowledge and power through communication with the supernatural. The information gained from these deliberate forays into the spirit world is used to heal, as well as to forecast and influence the elements of nature, and generally serve as an information basis for the well-being of the community. Moreover, the voyages are taken with the presence and counsel of a guardian (or power) animal.

The trial documents and other writings of the late medieval period and Renaissance indicate that the women healers were *accused* of having the traditional attributes of the shaman. No clear evidence that they were actually *practicing* shamanism has come to light, but the documents are of interest in that they indicate a latent fear and persistent concern over the existence of such practices.

For example, a woman's attachment to a pet or a "familiar" was a clear indication to the witch-hunters that she was in league with the devil. In fact, the animal was believed to be a demon in disguise—a creature from the supernatural realm who communed with her, was nourished by her body, and traveled on her nocturnal journeys. Two of the seven ways of identifying witches, according to Michal Dalton's *Country Justice* (written in 1618), involved animals. "They have ordinarily a familiar or spirit which appeareth to them," and secondly, "The said familiar hath some . . . place upon their body where he sucketh them."[40] The later statement referred to the damning witch's mark. Supernumerary nipples (which occur with some frequency in men and women) were an especially telling sign.

Certainly, it is not at all unnatural for a woman to develop a special bond with an animal, particularly old, lonely, and childless women, who were a prime target for witch accusation anyway. Cats were viewed as particularly suspect and were often tortured during the trial proceedings and killed along with the women. In the reign of King Louis XV, sacks of condemned cats were burned on the public square with the witches. Since the cats were the natural enemy of rats, who hosted the plague-infested fleas, destroying them might have helped facilitate the spread of the plagues.

We cannot know whether the women were actually using the animals in the shamanic way. A few probably were, given the universal continuity of the practice across the planet. Surely, though, for most, the animals were pets and nothing more. What is important is that the memory of these archetypal practices, that is, that an animal could serve as a basis for information or power, remained to serve the motives of civic and ecclesiastic authorities in condemning women.

Knowing and influencing weather conditions is a common province of shamanism. Planting and harvests, hunting, defense and attack, and all other activities of a nature-dependent society were intimately involved in the wisdom and foresight of the shaman. During the several centuries of the witch-hunts, woman's spurious proximity to wind, rain, hail, or drought was tantamount to an accusation of witchcraft, reflecting perhaps another subconscious connection to a fear of the shaman.

The "night flight" theme runs through virtually every witchcraft trial. Witches were believed to be able to fly through the air at will to join with others and engage in grisly activities and sexual orgies. That such flights could take place was not just an invention of the peasantry but also a belief of the learned that until recent centuries was embedded in scientific thought.

In shamanism, the travels are made in an altered state of consciousness, which is willfully and deliberately attained either by sensory deprivation, fasting, drums or chant, or specific plants. The witches were accused of using "flying oyle," which is discussed in more detail below.

"FLYING OYLE" AND WOMAN'S BOTANIC LORE

While the specific nature of the plants the witches were accused of using is not addressed in the trial documents, the possession of oils or ointments was grounds for accusation.[41] The discussion of the drugs may have been minimized because of the logical problems it would pose: if the night flights were a function of drug-induced illusion, it would create an inadmissible diminution of the devil's power. Since the Church in the thirteenth century had no problem in specifying which plants were of the devil and which were of God, it is possible that by the time of the witch trials, the Holy Inquisition was simply not interested in pharmacy. There was more concern, it seems, about whether the witch rode on the front or back of a broom, whom she met, and so forth.

The details on the ingredients and use of oils and ointments come from the writings of the scientists, physicians, astrologers, and philosophers who were interested in *magia licita* (natural magic). These men included Agrippa of Nettesheim, Johannes Weyer, and Francis Bacon, who attribute their information to old women, wise women, or witches. If they themselves used the potions, they do not admit it.

Weyer, particularly, was sympathetic to the plight of women and attempted to prove that their alleged flying experiences might be due to the plants rather than demons. On the other hand, he did not rule out demons entirely, believing that they might well influence some helpless women through plants.[42]

According to reports, the women supposedly combined concoctions of plants with a fatty substance for skin absorption. (Witches were frequently accused of using the fat of dead babies for this purpose.) They would then anoint some object—brooms, pitchforks, benches, and large kneading troughs have all been mentioned—or rub the mixture directly into their "hairy parts." Sensitive vaginal tissues absorbed the mixtures especially well. Observers say the women were convinced they were flying. They remained visible, if oblivious to shovings, beatings, and the passage of time.

Reports of the exact ingredients of the oils varied, but most of the botanics listed were highly alkaloid in content. Minimally, they would cause agitation, and in large doses could induce coma or cause death. Francis Bacon offers his speculation:

> The ointment that witches use is reported to be made of the fat of children digged out of their graves; of the juices of smallage, wolf-bane, and cinque-foil, mingled with the meal of fine wheat. But I suppose that the soporiferous medicines are likest to do it; which are henbane, hemlock, mandrake, moon-shade tobacco, opium, saffron, poplar leaves, etc.[43]

In 1561, Porta, in *Magiae naturalis,* wrote that the ointment contained the juice of celery, poplar leaves, calamus, nightshade (belladonna), jimson weed, and aconite. Rübel mentions mandrake root, henbane seed, gray barley, hemlock, nightshade berries, and badger and fox grease, mixed with the juice of poppy seeds.[44] Weyer suggests cannabis; several others cite preparations of toad (which would contain bufotenin, a mild hallucinogenic). Rock crystal, fern, and rue are listed by various sources.

The ingredients, like the medicaments of the day, were often from sources like bats, snakes, dung, parts of human cadavers, and so forth. Ritual was as important as substance.

> For such travelling, both men and women, that is, the witches, use a salve called *ungentum pharelis* or "lighthouse ointment." It is prepared from seven herbs, each one of which is picked on a certain day. Thus on Sunday they pick and dig heliotrope, on Monday crescent-shaped fern, on Tuesday verbena, on Wednesday spurge, on Thursday houseleek, and on Friday maidenhair, and all this they use to make the ointment; they also add bird's gall and the fat of various animals, which I will not describe lest someone should take offense. When they feel the urge, they rub their bench, their rake or loading fork, and off they fly.[45]

With the exception of the last recipe, most of the concoctions described are powerful psychoactive drugs. Harner, an authority on shamanic practices, believes for this reason the women were not actually practicing shamanism.[46] The drugs preferred by shamans in most cultures allow them to maintain a sense of the ordinary state of consciousness while journeying to the spirit world. Such communion at more than one state of consciousness would be impossible if the person were comatose.

However, our information on these plants is largely based on oral ingestion. A gradual diffusion through the skin may have resulted in a state more like that of the shaman's. Women who used these plants in healing probably knew how much to use to alter consciousness for pain relief, as well as how much to use to travel through landscapes of the mind, or to poison. The ingredients for each of these purposes—especially hemlock, aconite, and belladonna—are the same.

What were the putative effects of these plants and how do they fit into a modern pharmacopoeia? Most are alkaloids with medicinal and hallucinogenic properties. Bufotenin, a chemical isolated from the glands of toad skin, has a synergistic effect when used with plants, although it is debatable whether it has hallucinogenic properties itself.

Aconite (buttercup) is usually regarded as a poison, although it may be used in homeopathic doses for epilepsy and tremors. It is known to cause numbness, followed by paralysis of the lower extremities, leaving the mind clear. This particular action may have caused the women's reported long periods of immobility with their eyes wide open. They may not have been comatose at all, just temporarily paralyzed. In ancient times, aconite was used to kill criminals, and also as a euthanasia for infirm old men. In Chinese medicine, it is used as a narcotic.

Henbane, belladonna, and mandrake all contain scopolamine, hyoscyamine, and atropine. Although all are toxic in large amounts, each chemical has a host of medical uses. Henbanes have been used in domestic medicine for toothache, as sleeping aids, and nervines. Mandrake (mandragora) has long been used as a sleeping potion, a nerve medicine, and an anesthestic during surgery. From the time of Trotula, mandrake, opium, and other sedatives were soaked into a sponge, which was placed over the patient's face. It was an uncertain anesthetic, at best. Sometimes it worked well, sometimes not at all, and sometimes it was deadly. Mandrake also has a long and magical history as an aphrodisiac. The roots of the plant resemble a penis; thus, the widely accepted "doctrine of signatures" would hold that it be used for disorders of the male. The more delicate parts of the plant were used for female-oriented problems.

Belladonna has been used for a broad range of disorders, including asthma and cardiac arrhythmia. The symptoms of overdose include flushed skin, dilated pupils, dry mouth, and delirium. Death can occur as a result of respiratory failure.

Henbane has been related to divination. It is also sometimes regarded as a "truth" drug.

Scopolamine, hyoscyamine, and atropine are all important antispasmodics. Scopolamine is also a popular treatment for dizziness and motion sickness. Interestingly, after decades of arguing that nothing of medical value could be absorbed through the skin, medical science has developed infusion patches containing scopolamine (for motion sickness) and nitroglycerine (for angina). The patches deliver medication more effectively and with greater consistency than oral administration.

The effects of the narcotics mentioned are well known. Too, if Weyer is correct and cannabis was an available ingredient, one might expect the usual relaxed and moderately euphoric state experienced with marijuana ingestion.

Some of the ingredients have mild, or uncertain, pharmacologic effects. Cinquefoil, for instance, was used in domestic medicine as a toothache remedy, but otherwise is rarely mentioned as a specific for any other condition. The frequent mention of fern, or "fern seed," in the ointments is also questionable, since it remains unclear what this might be.

The significance of this is that the plants the women were accused of using were known to be more potent than the physician's astrological diagnoses, bleedings, and purgings, and his pharmacy of hundreds of benign ingredients, plucked and stirred together with superstition.

EXPLANATIONS FOR THE WITCH CRAZE

The murders of women, particularly women healers, reflect the deepest human fear of power. The women's supposed jaunts into the supernatural— where the shaman seeks power—were targeted as special threats to Church and state. Women who offered remedies or who promised magic in times of stress possessed an awesome power, because healing, even the simple domestic kind, is power of a very basic nature.

The belief systems that create witchcraft, magic, and religion concern power. They supply relief of anxiety in troubled times, a sense of control over what may or may not be controlled, and scapegoats in case of failure. Christine Larner, in her contribution to the growing body of information on the sociopolitical aspects of witchcraft, notes:

> The healer is a source of hope in the community. But his power is two-edged. If he should fail, demand extortionate and uneconomic returns for his services, or become hostile, then he becomes a source of menace and focus for

anxiety. The refusal of Canon Law to distinguish between black and white magic, while based on the idea that all power not sanctioned by the church is either ineffectual or demonic, regardless of whether it is intended to heal or harm, in fact reflects a peasant reality: that the healer can be dangerous.[47]

Larner has also observed that the healer represents power at the most local level of a continuum that ends with the most abstract and social level: God and the devil.

Given the fear of power in anxious times, the mantle of power worn by healers in all times, and the primal fear of women and their mysteries, the reasons behind the murders of women healers are comprehensible, if unforgivable. Why women not involved in the healing arts were killed requires more explanation.

An extreme explanation for the persecutions is that the entire witch craze was invented by the ruling classes to quell peasant uprisings against the nobles and clergy. The attention of the peasants was thereby focused on their neighbors and distracted from the nobility, whom they blamed for their poverty and the perpetual warfare of the times.[48] According to this line of thought, there never were any witches nor anyone who practiced anything resembling witchcraft. This thesis does little to address why most of those murdered were women and why healers were singled out. Nor is it convincing in view of the theological underpinnings of the persecutions.

Another explanation is that women were not actually practicing witchcraft, but honoring the old pagan religions, worshipping old gods who had assumed the persona of the devil in Christianity. Margaret Murray, whose ideas followed the classic path set by Frazier's *Golden Bough,* held that many of the accused women were engaged in a fertility cult, worshipping a horned god (Dianus) of an earlier religion.[49] A similar proposal was made by Anton Meyer, who believed that the women were involved in an ancient fertility cult that worshipped the earth goddess.[50] Jules Michelet, a medieval scholar of the nineteenth century, believed that many women chose to become "Satan's bride." Women, out of despair, he said, sought other gods, including her "ally of old and her confidant in the Garden." He also asserted that the women may have abused their power. "Great and irresponsible power is always liable to abuse; and in this case she queened it in a very true sense for three long centuries during the interregnum between two worlds, the old dying world and the new one whose dawn was still faint on the horizon.[51]

The ideas of Murray, Meyer, and Michelet are appealing but poorly documented. Yet the old religions empowered women to a far greater extent than Christianity. We know that women carried amulets representing the Roman goddesses long after Europe was Christianized. How widespread,

Woman as Healer

and how open, the practices of the old religion were will never be known. It is unlikely, though, that the Church saw the old religions as much of a threat compared to the splinter sects of heretics within its own ranks.

A balanced perspective is that women are attracted to witchcraft in both its light and dark guises. Witchcraft—the generation of supernatural power—is an outlet for the spiritually unrewarded, a means of gaining status for the culturally deprived. Women, particularly those living at the edge of society, sought it as a means of control, stature, and economic survival in a world that promised none of these. The women may well have met in a group—more or less organized—to discuss their activities and share the fantasies that colored their otherwise drab and desperate lives. The group meetings of women—for whatever purpose—continued to add fuel to the inquisitors' great fear that women were becoming organized.

However, there is one other position used by the Christian church to defend its actions that unfortunately has not died a justly deserved death, one that deeply affects all women in the health-care system—healers and healees alike. It is that the millions of women accused of being witches were actually heretical, engaged in satanic practices. However, in the current theory their activities are seen as psychotic or neurotic, rather than demonic. Gregory Zilboorg, a psychiatrist, presents this position in an attempt to show that the development of modern psychiatry had its origins in the problem of witchcraft.[52]

Dr. Zilboorg states: "In brief, the *Malleus Maleficarum* might with a little editing serve as an excellent modern textbook of descriptive clinical psychiatry of the fifteenth century, if the word *witch* were substituted by the word *patient,* and the devil eliminated."[53] Zilboorg continues, "Moreover, the medical literature of the nineteenth century collected a number of data which it subjected to such careful clinical scrutiny that no doubt is left in our mind that the millions of witches, sorcerers, possessed and obsessed, were an enormous mass of severe neurotics, psychotics, and considerably deteriorated organic deliria."[54]

He asserts that after reading the confessions of the witches, he saw that "they were actually *heretical,* they actually sinned against the Sacraments, they actually murmured profanities in the churches, and they actually either rebelled against or were afraid of the sign of the Cross all this while mentally sick, of course. In the light of present-day psychopathology it is not very difficult to see that we are dealing here mostly, not with hysterias, but with compulsion neuroses and schizophrenic psychoses."[55]

Nowhere does Zilboorg discuss or consider the psychopathology of the Church and state officials in the tribunals and torture chambers who devised the murders of these "neurotics and psychotics." Nor does he address the

---

fact that fear, wrought by the techniques of the Inquisition, in and of itself created pathological behavior, as well as structuring the contents of confessions. Nor does he consider the sanity of the physicians who were called in to decide whether a cure or a disease was "natural" or not.

FINALE: THE END OF THE WOMAN-HUNTS

Gradually, first in the cities, then in the countryside, women ceased to be burned. In England, the last witch was officially hanged in 1684, in America in 1692, and finally in Germany in 1775. The madness wound down only when Christianity lost its strong hold on the governments of Europe. The woman-hunt "could not become rampant until personal religion had become political. It could not survive the advent of secular ideologies."[56] When religious affairs were separated from politics, women were no longer murdered for crimes they did not commit. The witch-hunts had always been most severe in the regions ruled by Roman law and in the countries where Protestantism was most integrated into government. Through the Reformation, the Counter-Reformation, and the increasing heterogeneity of religious expression, dissent became stronger. The trials came under increasing scrutiny and mistrust. It was suggested that they too might be the work of the devil and had best be stopped.

In 1736, a law was enacted in England that denied the reality of the witch accusations. The law stayed in effect until 1951, providing for the prosecution of those who *pretended* to have magical powers. The actual existence of magic (or sorcery, or witchcraft) was thereby discounted.

Despite the cessation of the crimes against women, they were not given full citizenship in any country, nor was their role in the healing professions reinstated. Rather the hunts served to lower women's status and increase the level of misogyny and distrust. The persecutions halted not because the attitude toward women changed, but because the power base of governments shifted. Nor, as will be discussed in the next chapter, can the dawning of the scientific age be credited with stopping the madness. Most early scientists acknowledged and feared the witches. Samuel Johnson and others believed that the decrease in the number of trials was a result of women ceasing to practice the black arts.[57]

During the years of the witch-hunts, women healers had been edged out by guilds, and then by the incorporations of physicians, surgeons, and apothecaries. Their work was prohibited by law in every country in Europe. The Inquisition and Christian theology had been used to exclude women from the ranks of independent practitioners. In the new worldview, science and the laws of nature would be invoked for the same purpose.

"Venus of Willendorf," c. 30,000–25,000 B.C., the Great Goddess or Mother Goddess. She was a composite image of the giver of all life and the wielder of the destructive powers of nature. Courtesy of Naturhistorisches Museum, Vienna.

Snake Goddess, in faience, from the Palace at Cnossus, c. 1600 B.C. Woman holding the sacred snakes is a common theme throughout the ancient Western world and is associated with the healing arts. Courtesy of the Archaeological Museum, Iráklion, Greece.

Radiant Inanna, Queen of Heaven and Earth. Sumerian goddess, Akkadian period, c. 2300 B.C. Courtesy of the Oriental Institute, The University of Chicago.

Marble statue of Athena, goddess of wisdom, especially honored for her ability to cure eye diseases. Courtesy of Städtische Galerie, Liebighaus Museum, Frankfurt am Main, West Germany.

Hygeia, Greek goddess of healing, c. 4th century B.C. Courtesy of National Archaeological Musuem, Athens.

Mosiac of the 5th–6th century portraying St. Felicity of Carthage, patron saint of sick children. Archepiscopal Chapel, Archbishop's Palace, Ravenna, Italy.

St. Lucy by Francesco del Cossa, 15th century, invoked for
diseases of eyes. Courtesy of National Gallery of Art, Samuel
H. Kress collection, Washington, D.C.

Birth scene from the Uttenheimer Altar, 1480, with midwives swaddling the Christ child and warming the receiving blanket, indicating role of women in obstetrics during the period. Courtesy of Germanisches Nationalmuseum, Nüremberg.

Medieval childbirth scene, woodcut by Jost Amman. Note the physicians casting horoscope, and women tending to labor. Courtesy of Smith Kline Corporation Collection, Philadelphia Museum of Art.

a. Lady Mary Wortley Montagu, who introduced into England the Turkish technique of inoculating for small pox about eighty years before Jenner announced his vaccination method. Courtesy of The New York Academy of Medicine.

b. Dr. Elizabeth Blackwell, 1821–1910, first woman graduate of an American medical school. Courtesy of New York Infirmary.

c. Dr. Harriot K. Hunt, 1805–1875, devoted her life to medicine and symbolizes woman's entry into the field. She was repeatedly rejected by Harvard University on the basis of her sex, and was never formally awarded a medical degree, although it was common to confer degrees on men who were trained in the same apprenticeship system as she was. Courtesy of Schlesinger Library, Radcliffe College.

d. Dr. Marie Zakrzewska, 1829–1902, physician, tireless professor of medicine, and fundraiser. She established the New York Infirmary for Women and Children and the New England Hospital for Women and Children. Courtesy of Sophia Smith Collection, Smith College.

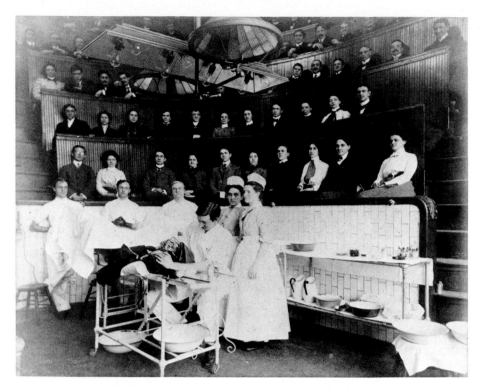

Surgical clinic at Cornell University, conducted by Dr. William Polk. From its start in 1898, Cornell accepted women as students, and it has a history of distinguished graduates. Courtesy of the Medical Archives, New York Hospital–Cornell Medical Center.

Dr. Mary Putnam Jacobi, 1842–1906, physician, professor, scientist, winner of Harvard's Boylston Medical Prize for research. Courtesy of the National Library of Medicine, Bethesda, Md.

Florence Nightingale, 1820–1910, founder of the modern profession of nursing. Courtesy of the National Library of Medicine, Bethesda, Md.

Hannah Maria Young, 1832–1903, author's great-great-grandmother. In her obituary she was called "the noblest woman in the Missouri Valley." Riding her horse ("Old Dave"—who always got her home) and buggy, she went out on frequent errands of mercy, tending the sick. Courtesy of Louise Flynn.

The Visiting Nurse, taking a shortcut over tenement roofs, 1908. Courtesy of the Museum of the City of New York.

II *Absent at the Birth of Modern Medicine*

THE CRIMES AGAINST women healers were committed during a period of otherwise remarkable discovery and enlightenment in the arts, the humanities, and fledgling science and technology. The witch-hunt era includes the Renaissance, which began at different times in various parts of Europe, but is roughly coincident with the fourteenth to seventeenth centuries. Normally, the status of women mirrors cultural advancement and, in fact, is often a gauge of civilization. During the Renaissance, this was not the case; none of the achievements reflected the rebirth of feminine values.

These three centuries included the Scientific Revolution, considered to have begun in the sixteenth century when Copernicus concluded that the earth was not the center of the universe. Kepler and Galileo established the scientific validity of Copernicus's new cosmology. These early scientists, like the women who did not fit the prescribed role model, were always at risk for charges of heresy.

At risk or not, men of medicine saw the potential empowerment of scientific thought, and gratefully and quickly hitched themselves to the rising star. Defining the sticky connection between healing, magic, and religion had become an onerous task. Science, disassociated from both magic and religion, provided a refuge for those weary of deciding what medicine was of God and what was not. After the Scientific Revolution, whether woman's medicine was of God or not was a moot point. The early scientists were an extraordinarily devout group who did not separate God out of their discoveries. Many, too, such as Isaac Newton, dabbled in the occult. Nevertheless, medicine and science, soon to be inseparable, were framed by a new and essentially godless dogma.

Some changes in Western healing took place during these centuries—particularly the seventeenth—not within the therapeutic framework, but within the theoretical structure that has dominated healing arts until the present day. This structure omitted women completely. Their presence was seen as irrelevant, even antagonistic, to the pursuit of science. Woman and

nature were explicitly bound in the emerging metaphor that proclaimed the
need to dominate and control the feminine forces.

As the centuries progressed, women's roles in medicine became even more
stratified and delineated. Any opportunities available to women beyond the
domestic sphere vanished rapidly. The contributions made by women to
medicine and science were ignored or trivialized.

This chapter treats the turning points of medical science, and the state of
the art of healing during those years.

THE SEPARATION OF MIND AND BODY

No event in history has so quickly altered an institutional belief system as the
philosophic separation of mind from body. The credit for formulating this
theory goes primarily to René Descartes, although his own life and writings
scarcely bear witness to the stringent dichotomy.

Descartes, in a visionary experience, saw the *sequelae* of the universe unfold
in mathematical formulations. The enormous nature of the revelations and
their seemingly divine source are reminiscent of the experiences of Hildegard
and other early scientists.

For our purposes, the essence of Descartes's work can be summarized as
follows: (1) there is a certainty and knowability of scientific truth; (2)
mathematics is the key to understanding these truths; (3) the process of
analytical reasoning—breaking something down into its smallest parts—will
lead to ultimate understanding; (4) the universe is a physical thing, and it
and all that it contains can be analogized to machines; and (5) the mind and
body are separate entities.[1]

For the healing arts, the direction given by Descartes's work was a turning
point. Mind and body were to be conceived as having no relationship to one
another. According to Descartes, there was nothing included in the concept
of body that belonged to the mind; nothing in that of mind that belonged
to the body. Thus, the invisible, nonmaterial realm was separated from the
visible, the material. The disciplines of medicine and science became the
study of what could be physically realized; what could not be seen became
the province of other disciplines.

The theoretical separation between mind and body permitted autopsy,
biopsy, and other invasions of the body to take place without fear of
damaging the immortal soul. The great progress that was then made in terms
of understanding the morphology and function of the human body cannot
be discounted. When the Cartesian presentation became generally known to
the men of science and medicine, the grip of the ancient Galenic dogma—
before considered the absolute truth—began to loosen.

One unfortunate result of the Cartesian notion was the separation of caring and curing in the healing arts. Compassion and intuition, because they are also invisible, were subtracted from science and medicine. The function of caring continued to be recognized in the healing arts, but as a nonscientific necessity, a second-order need largely performed by women under the direction of male physicians.

Healing was further dehumanized by the belief that all living things, including human beings, could be known and controlled if they were conceived of as machines. Since the most sophisticated machine was then the clock, the "clockwork universe" became an important metaphor. People, like clocks, could be understood if they were broken down into small components that could be studied. This process of analysis moved Western medical science progressively and reductionistically through the centuries. Today, the hope for understanding the human condition, its health and disease, has been pinned on molecular biology—dealing with the smallest identifiable particles of human life.

Finally, Descartes's notion that there exist knowable laws of nature that are expressible through numbers has kept medicine connected to the basic sciences. The promise of this theory, as yet unfulfilled, was most seductive: if man can ascertain the immutable formulae, he can predict and control all universal events. So, on the one hand, the egocentricism of the old cosmology—that the earth was the center of the universe—was revoked. On the other hand, the new cosmology of scientism bestowed on man the control of the universe. Man began to realize the powers of being human, of having a mind that could divine the nature of all things. The irony is that the powers of the mind were, themselves, denigrated and relegated to institutions of lesser stature than medical science.

THE BIRTH OF SCIENCE

A nexus of ideas came together in the thirteenth century to determine the future of woman as healer, while the forefathers of experimental science wrestled with their theology and its relationship to women and healing. The outcome was a dubious recognition of the power of women, as well as the expression of man's primal fears.

The events of the seventeenth century formed a similar nexus. Smitten by the potential of Cartesian thought and the advances in science, learned men began to subscribe to scientific principles of discovery. It was most timely; change was due.

The tyranny of Galen had continued to hold forth. If anything, his dogma was reenergized in 1525, when the Aldine Press of Venice published the first copies of his work. It was neither medical science nor experiment that was being promulgated, but rather, pedantry.[2] If a human dissection did not conform to Galen's description, it was decided that the body was not constructed correctly, because Galen could not be wrong.

It was too much to expect that the likes of Paracelsus, Leonardo da Vinci, Andreas Vesalius, and William Harvey, to mention just a few of the early men of science, would believe information that was not consonant with their own empirical observations. Bravely, they contradicted the powerful mainstream of theology that ascribed to Galen's work the imprimitur of absolute truth. The union of their observations on the nature of life and Cartesian logic conceived a new medical heresy that became the orthodoxy that we now recognize as modern medicine.

Henry Oldenburg, a tutor to English noblemen and a skilled organizer, was dazzled by the provocative ideas of the loosely knit scientific community. Although not a scientist himself, he envisioned a parliament of these men. He agreed with the Italian proverb *Le parole sono femine, li fatti maschii* ("Words are feminine, facts masculine"). Thus, the factual, hence masculine, direction of science was institutionalized. The parliament, chartered in 1662, was called the Royal Society. This most learned body of men formed a "container" for scientific thought for the next few centuries. Its members communicated their ideas through letters, then books, and finally a journal.

As powerful as these men were in dictating the future of healing practices, that was not their intent. Frances Yates noted that the Royal Society was essentially for the advancement of natural science, aiming to find a niche within a preexisting society. "It did not envisage the advancement of science within a reformed society, within a universal reformation of the whole world. The Fellows of the Royal Society were not concerned with healing the sick, and that gratis, nor with schemes for the reform of education."[3]

The Fellows' imagery of nature, of woman, and of the role of the scientific community have become entrenched in modern thought. Evelyn Fox Keller, in her seminal work entitled *Reflections on Gender and Science,* observes a theme coincident with the "new science" and the economic, social, political, and intellectual upheavals of the period.[4] That theme is the "subtle but significant transformation in conceptions of and attitudes toward sexuality and gender roles. This transformation is reflected with particular clarity in the sexual language pervading much of the seventeenth-century discourse on what a 'new science' should look like."[5]

WOMAN AS NATURE

The writings of Francis Bacon provide a clear statement on woman and nature, a relationship obvious to earlier cultures that was reinterpreted to advance the aims of science. The belief prevailed that men were superior to women, and women were closer to the earth. Woman unfortunately was enslaved by the seventeenth-century metaphor linking her to nature, instead of enthroned by it, as she had been much earlier.

Nature could be known through its association with the feminine, and mastery and domination must occur if civilization was to progress. Bacon's vision was no less than the extension of the power of the human race itself over the universe; the "restituting and reinvesting of man to the sovereignty and power . . . which he had in his first state of creation."[6]

To meet these lofty aims, a chaste and lawful marriage between mind and nature must be established. It was nature, the bride, who was to be tamed and subdued by the mind of man. "I am come in very truth leading to you Nature with all her children to bind her to your service and make her your slave."[7] The tasks of the scientists were to "hound nature in her wan-derings," and subsequently the scientists would be able to "lead and drive her afterwards to the same place again."[8] Observation of nature's ways was thus advised, with a warning that gentle prodding alone might not uncover her mysteries. The scientist was advised to torture nature's secrets from her.

In Bacon's work "The Masculine Birth of Time," he proclaimed a race of "supermen" and "heroes" whose minds, because they were clear of false perceptions, could unlock the paths of sense, the greater light in nature. The work itself is representative of Bacon's belief "that older science represented only a female offspring, passive, weak, expectant, but now a son was born, active, virile, generative."[9] Much of Bacon's imagery was inspired by the witch trials: as attorney general for King James I, he had been present at the hearings and prosecutions.[10] Bacon's image of nature as a female whose secrets must be torn from her with mechanical devices was an obvious transposition of trial language into the "new science."

MATTER AND SPIRIT

One consequence of the Scientific Revolution especially important for our discussion is that not only were mind and matter disjoined but spirit was conceptually eliminated from matter. The separation of mind, body, and spirit tore at the very fabric of woman's healing power. Indeed, it invaded what I have described as the thread of consciousness connecting women healers.

When spirit no longer is seen to abide in matter, the reverence for what is physical departs. Hence medicine no longer regarded itself as working in the sacred spaces where fellow humans find themselves in pain and peril, and where transcendence is most highly desired.

The impact of the Scientific Revolution was dire for both woman as healer and for nature itself. Taking mind and spirit out of nature made way for an objective vision—one ostensibly separate from the invisible realm. The mind of man was cleared, as Bacon had prescribed, and the new vision led to unfathomable changes in understanding the physical plane. The goal of the Royal Society was accomplished. However, when clumps and lumps of matter are viewed as machines instead of living organisms, the consequences for the ecosystems of the earth are dire and far-reaching. "As long as the earth was considered to be alive and sensitive, it could be considered a breach of human ethical behavior to carry out destructive acts against it."[11] The crimes against women, their rape and destruction, were now permitted, by the rational overlay of the new science on the older theology, against the earth itself.

A new cosmology was created. The hierarchy of power had shifted only slightly. A male god who self-created the universe was still present, but his laws were now to be revealed to man, instead of held secret within the bosom of nature. This gave men, for the first time in group memory, the potential power to predict and control events of the world. The same power had previously been associated with women through the "nature as woman, woman as nature" metaphor, but, as we have seen, it had been waning for centuries. It had not been believed, for many hundreds of years, that women obtained their wisdom from God, but rather from powerful and evil resources. When spirit was taken out of matter, so was the devil likewise removed; the rational mind could no longer argue that women were wise because of their entrapment with the unseen.

HEALTH AND HEALING PRACTICES

Despite the energy of the Scientific Revolution and the revitalization of thought associated with the Renaissance in Europe, therapeutics did not change greatly until late in the nineteenth century. However, much information was gleaned and categorized. Developments and discoveries would eventually lead to a better understanding of the causes, the nature, and the cures for disease.

Although women have been omitted from the ranks of discovery and invention, it is not at all clear that this should be so. As we shall see, women were often the impetus for the very few therapeutic innovations that did come out of these years. Their involvement is increasingly trivialized in the writings of modern authorities on medical history, who are apt to pass off women's contributions as romantic fantasy.

The truth about who contributed what will never be agreed upon. Women frequently have been the developers and transmitters of health innovations;

men have been the popularizers. To say that one or the other is more important is a matter of opinion.

DISEASE PATTERNS

Until the eighteenth century most diseases remained unnamed, described in terms of only the grossly manifesting symptoms. So it is difficult to know just what our ancestors were afflicted with. Nutritional disorders, childhood infections, and complications of pregnancy and birth were constant, life-threatening problems. Diseases would change their nature and virulence as they moved through the population, stopped their attack, and moved through again.

The fifteenth century was noted for increases in sweating sickness, leprosy, and cholera, all of which had significantly decreased by the sixteenth century. Leprosy had become such a rarity that most of the leprosariums were closed down.

Then increases in typhus, diptheria, smallpox, and measles were reported. The seventeenth century saw the plague in virulent form, as well as more cases of measles, smallpox, scarlet fever, diphtheria, gonorrhea, and syphilis. Both scurvy and rickets were recognized and reported. By the eighteenth century, the old diseases of bubonic plague, typhus, malaria, and diphtheria returned, but in less lethal forms. Smallpox remained the great killer (inexcusably so, as we shall see below). The nineteenth century was faced with cholera, yellow fever, and typhoid, also of weaker strains.

THERAPEUTICS AND PROGRESS

What were the treatments prescribed for these cripplers and killers? From the fifteenth through the seventeenth centuries, they included incantations, complex botanic nostrums, urine diagnosis, and astrology. After that, medicine became far more heroic, with the regular physicians relying on purgings, cuppings, bleedings, and fumigations. Leeches, lancets, and highly toxic chemicals, such as mercury in its various forms, filled the physician's black bag. The emerging medical profession had little affinity for the gentler botanics.

The greatest progress during these centuries came as a result of the freedom from the ancient fathers of medicine—Pliny, Aristotle, Hippocrates, and Galen. As the new men of science looked at the world with vision unoccluded by the dogma from the ancient past, they made progress in the study of anatomy and botany.

Two brilliant, maverick physicians of the sixteenth century—Paracelsus and Agrippa von Nettesheim—expressed admiration for the empiric medicine of the wise women, viewing it as more advanced and effective than the practices of the fathers of medicine. Paracelsus ceremonially and with disdain burned the classic tomes, including those of Avicenna and Galen. Agrippa asked rhetorically, "Are not philosophers, mathematicians, and astrologers often inferior to country women in their divinations and predictions, and does not the old nurse very often beat the doctor?" Paracelsus is regarded as the father of modern chemistry; he is widely quoted as claiming to have learned his best prescriptions from women. A mysterious old Swedish woman may have been the inspiration and source of information for his unusually sensitive text *Diseases of Women.*

Paracelsus and Agrippa had a profound sense of the invisible aspects of disease and health, which have been linked to the feminine aspect of healing. In 1510, Agrippa stated:

> So great a power is there of the soul upon the body, that whichever way the soul imagines and dreams that it goes, thither doth it lead the body. . . . The passions of the soul which follow the phantasy, when they are most vehement . . . can thus take away or bring some disease of the mind or body.[12]

Paracelsus similarly declared that

> Man has a visible and an invisible workshop. The visible one is his body, the invisible one is imagination (mind). . . . The imagination is sun in the soul of man. . . . The spirit is the master, imagination the tool, and the body the plastic material. . . . The power of the imagination is a great factor in medicine. It may produce diseases in man and animals and it may cure them. . . . Ills of the body may be cured by physical remedies or by the power of the spirit acting through the soul.[13]

Interspersed between the highly magical, religious era of healing and the mechanistic modes of the new science, one finds statements such as these. They are harbingers of modern developments in psychophysiology and psychoneuroimmunology—fields that examine the role of mind in disease and health.[14] Despite the advances later attributed to Paracelsus and Agrippa, they were considered sorcerers by the mainstream scientists of the Royal Society. It was precisely their kinds of ideas, relating to spirit, imagination, and the invisible realm as factors in healing, that the new science had set about to expunge. These are also the ideas associated with the feminine myth throughout time.

William Harvey's work on the circulation of blood is usually mentioned as the major medical finding of the seventeenth century. He, and others, were probably unaware that his notations on the mechanical flow of blood did not differ greatly from the model proposed by Hildegard of Bingen in the twelfth century. This was not the only instance where a woman provided the infrastructure for medical advancement, as will be noted below.

A remedy for malaria was a major development in therapeutics in the seventeenth century.[15] The countess of Chinchon, wife of the Spanish viceroy to Peru, was cured of malaria by the bark of a tree. She imported a quantity of the bark back to Spain, where malaria was prevalent. The Peruvian bark came to be called "cinchona bark" in her honor. This story was chronicled in a thesis on the history of women in medicine written by Mélanie Lipinska, a respected colleague of Marie Curie, for a degree in medicine from the University of Paris. The thesis was awarded a special prize by the French Academy. Nevertheless, modern physicians and medical historians call this merely a "fanciful" story, attributing the introduction of cinchona into Europe to a man, Antonio de la Calancha.[16] Others give credit to Thomas Sydenham, an English physician, for the major advances in use of cinchona.[17]

There were two noteworthy events in the medicine of the eighteenth century: the discovery of digitalis and the development of an acceptable vaccination for smallpox. In both of these, women played a significant behind-the-scenes, role.

Digitalis, a chemical derived from foxglove, is a treatment for failing hearts, irregular heart rhythms, and fluid accumulation and swelling in legs and feet (or dropsy), which is also related to poor cardiac function. Credit for the discovery is given to Dr. William Withering, although he did little more than pass along an ancient remedy—a tea of foxglove leaves had been used by the wise women for centuries. It was only when Dr. Withering's fiancée persuaded him to visit an old woman herbalist that he became aware of the plant's medicinal properties. After some experimentation, he wrote a paper entitled "An Account of the Foxglove and Some of Its Medical Uses," establishing a reputation as one of the finest botanists of all time.

The second major boost to health in the eighteenth century was the announcement of Edward Jenner's method of vaccination for smallpox, using fluid from cowpox, a related disease found in cattle. In fact, vaccination has been called the single greatest outcome of the Enlightenment.

Jenner published his method in 1789, almost eighty years after Lady Mary Montagu related her observation of women's techniques of inoculation in Turkey. (It was then called variolation, from *variola*, the scientific name for smallpox.) Said Lady Mary,

> There is a set of old women who make it their business to perform the operation every autumn in the month of September when the great heat is abated. . . . They make parties for the purpose. . . . The old woman comes with a nut-shell full of the matter of the best sort of smallpox, asks what veins

you please to have opened. She immediately rips open that you offer her, with a large needle (which gives you no more pain than a common scratch) and puts into the vein, as much matter as can lie upon the head of her needle, and after that binds up the little wound with a hollow bit of shell; and in this manner opens four or five veins.[18]

In writing the above lines to her friend Sarah Chiswell, Lady Mary also expressed her concern that the medical profession would view variolation as a threat to their income as well as their knowledge. "I am patriot enough to take pains to bring this useful invention into fashion in England, and I should not fail to write to some of our doctors about it if I knew any one of 'em that I thought had virtue enough to destroy such a considerable branch of their revenue for the good of mankind."

Lady Mary was initially able to share the methods with royalty, and they were adopted by as many as could be convinced of their usefulness and safety. The accomplishments of this woman—one of the first great feminist writers—have recently been minimized. Genevieve Miller argues that it was really the king's physician and president of the Royal Society, Sir Hans Sloane, who should be credited with the adoption of the practice, and that partisan reports exaggerated Lady Mary's role.[19]

Even though Lady Mary was treated by Sloane for smallpox before she traveled to Turkey, she had no great respect for male physicians in general. In her essay *Woman Not Inferior to Man*, written under the pen name "Sophia," she states that women were more capable of practicing medicine

> to restore health to the sick, and preserve it to the well. . . . We can invent, and have invented, without the help of *Galen*, or *Hippocrates*, an infinity of reliefs for the sick, which [men] in their blind adherence could neither improve nor disapprove. *An old woman's receipt*, as it is termed, has often been known to remove an inveterate distemper which has baffled the researches of a college of graduates.[20]

Inoculation was unexpectedly successful in preventing death from smallpox. During the height of epidemics, one of every five victims died. In comparison, only one of every ninety-one persons inoculated in England died. Certainly, inoculation was not totally safe, because live virus was used and contagion was theoretically possible. Worse was the danger of blood poisoning from unsterilized needles. English physicians also insisted upon making deep incisions (unlike the Turkish methods of superficial scratches), contributing to the casualty rate. Too, they managed to make the practice very expensive by insisting upon medically supervised confinement and special diets weeks before and after the inoculation, rendering it unaffordable to the masses, who continued to die from smallpox.

Woman as Healer

Panic and "bad press" for the method resulted in it being forbidden at times in Europe and America. Religious issues also were raised concerning the evils of trying to defy Providence by preventing disease.

European wise women also had been performing similar injections, probably for centuries prior to the 1700s. The reluctance of the scientific and medical community to accept these practices indirectly resulted in millions of deaths.[21]

A comment by Dr. William Wagstaffe, a physician at St. Bartholomew's Hospital in London, fellow of the Royal College of Physicians and Surgeons, and the Royal Society, written in the early 1700s, is most telling:

> Posterity will scarcely be brought to believe that a method practiced only by a few *Ignorant Women* [italics his] amongst an illiterate and unthinking People should on a sudden, and upon a slender Experience, so far obtain in one of the most Learned and Polite Nations in the World as to be received into the Royal Palace.[22]

Dr. Wagstaffe's position won out. The women's skills were not introduced widely until William Jenner published his method of using cowpox instead of smallpox as a vaccination. Significantly, Jenner learned of the technique from a dairymaid he'd known as a boy. Dairy farmers were aware of the protection granted by cowpox, and deliberately exposed their children to the disease by making them touch the udders of infected cows. At any rate, medical science marched on. In less than two hundred years, smallpox appears to have left the face of the earth.

ANESTHESIA AND A POSSIBLE RELATION TO THE FEMININE

In the nineteenth century significant progress in treating disease was finally realized. The development of anesthetic agents allowed for major advancement in surgical procedures. Prior to this time, the qualities required of surgeons were that they be fast, strong, and determined. With the discovery of nitrous oxide (laughing gas), chloroform, and ether, more delicate surgery could be performed. Considering the association of anesthetic drugs with women's healing arts (they were the alleged witches' magical flying oil), the absence of anesthesia from medical practice from the fourteenth to the nineteenth century comes as no surprise.

The highly alkaloid or narcotic preparations may have been unreliable, but they had the benefit of having been compounded and tested for centuries. Also, natural pharmacological agents usually contain a combination of chemicals that is more likely to ameliorate the effects of overdose than the synthetic preparations. Given the option of dying from pain and shock associated with unanesthetized surgery, or from "never waking up," surely most patients would choose the latter. Surgeons had no qualms about giving their patients alcohol and opium; the dose required to cause unconsciousness was never very far from a lethal level. (Opium was not typically connected with women's medicine, although midwives were accused of giving their patients too much alcohol to ease their pains.)

Paracelsus had formulated a recipe for "sweet vitriol," comparable to ether. Still, since his work was in disrepute because of his association with women's medicine and his unconventional approach, the preparation was not employed as an anesthetic until it was rediscovered about a hundred years ago.

We must look beyond an explanation of "unreliability" to see why the wise women's herbs were not being used to mitigate the suffering of humankind. The association of the herbs with women was likely the reason they fell into disrepute, and then into disuse, and then into oblivion. They were also tainted by the suggestions of Albertus Magnus, Arnald of Villanova, and Roger Bacon that they were connected with the devil. That reason, coupled with the Christian dogma that women must suffer to atone for their (and Eve's) sins, assured that the herbs could not openly be administered for the pains associated with labor.

On Controlling Germs

By the end of the nineteenth century, the work of Lister, Pasteur, Koch, and the other "microbe hunters" led to the germ theory of disease, and to knowledge of sepsis and antisepsis. Hospital procedures and sanitation dramatically improved.

Even before the germ theory, another man—Ignaz Semmelweiss (1818–65)—was successful in learning to control the spread of puerperal (childbed) fever, caused by *Streptococcus pyogenes*. His is a long, sad story, representing the worst that can happen when one challenges the prevailing mode of thought.

Semmelweiss reasoned that dirty hands were the cause of puerperal fever. He noted that wards staffed by medical students had about a 10 percent mortality rate due to the fever, while those staffed by midwives seldom had even 3 percent. It didn't occur to him that midwives might just be better at their task; nevertheless, the observation was fortuitous. He also knew that medical students went straight from autopsy chambers to laboring mothers. They never washed their hands, but wiped them, instead, on aprons already coated with body fluids.

Semmelweiss ran several experiments requiring students to wash their hands with soap and water and rinse them in chlorinated lime solution before entering the wards. With each study, the death rate dropped to less than 1½ percent, only to return to the previous high levels when the procedures were curtailed.

Semmelweiss's work should have proven to be a boon to motherhood and life. Not so. His colleagues greeted his paper with jeers and scathing attacks on his character. They simply refused to believe that their own hands were the vehicle for disease. Instead they attributed it to a spontaneous phenomenon arising from the "combustible" nature of the parturient woman. Semmelweiss's academic rank was lowered, his hospital privileges restricted. Despondent, he was committed to an insane asylum, where he died of blood poisoning, a disease not unlike the puerperal fever he had almost conquered.

From the nineteenth century on, certain forces that had often had dramatic effects on people's health changed. For example, the inevitable cycle of famine and pestilence following a few bad farming years was mitigated. Agricultural and animal husbandry methods had improved and diversified sufficiently so that climatic shifts were no longer quite so devastating. In these and other instances, the need to control nature began to pay off.

Then, too, people began to learn that they could not live in filth and expect to survive. Major sanitary reforms began in the seventeenth century, although the concern had already been felt for some time. The stench of humanity had become so bad that even the hardy, perfumed Parisians could not stand the putrid odors emanating from each other's bodies and from stagnant sewage that was also their drinking water.[23] Slowly, human beings began to clean up their environment. The threat of disease borne by air, water, and the blood of other living organisms was reduced. Following the sanitary reforms, infectious disease began to recede like the tide, far in advance of the advent of the germ theory.[24]

None of the advances in health affected the abominably high infant and maternal mortality rates, however. The risks to life in giving birth and being born were exacerbated to epidemic proportions as increasing numbers of women gave birth in hospitals.

SUMMARY

This chapter scanned the developments that surrounded the major turning point in the history of medicine: its alliance with the new science. The Scientific Revolution itself, developed within the era of the witch-hunts, was vastly affected by the language and imagery associating women with nature. The emerging scientists conscripted what they believed to be feminine wisdom, and developed a methodology that lauded the masculine attributes of reason and objectivity.

Advances in science were only obliquely related to changes in clinical practice. Women's role in these developments was consistently downplayed. Women were neither uncreative nor shortsighted, but they tended to be the keepers of medical lore, rather than the popularizers. The presentation of medical and scientific discovery required membership in a special caste, which was disallowed women on the basis of their sex.

Women's role was redefined, progressively and significantly limited to domestic duties. The objections to women acting as independent healers changed radically after the Scientific Revolution. Whereas previously they had been forbidden on theological grounds, now the arguments against them related to their supposedly deficient reason and other weak mental capacities. As healers, women were legally allowed to practice midwifery only. The following pages detail the development and near-demise of this profession, as well as the more recent growth of other healing professions practiced by women.

Part Three

*Women and the Professionalization
of the Healing Arts*

12 *Gender and the Health Professions*

PROFESSIONALIZATION OF THE healing arts was the inevitable response to increases in knowledge about health, the demand for specialized treatment, and the development of large treatment institutions. Implicit in the formation of the professions was the need to establish standards for practice, training, and credentials. The healing professions were also established heavily along the lines of gender. The chapters in this section deal with the ontology of several women's healing professions: midwifery, the popular health movement, the unusual—and brief—era of nineteenth-century "doctoresses," nursing, and the healing ministry.

Far-reaching discovery and change took place in the years we are discussing in this section (about 1450 through 1900). Despite the wars and pestilences described previously, a sizable middle-class society was well in place, and with it, comfort and influence. The arts flourished. The sciences had established a theoretical framework and basis for inquiry which was challenging—and toppling—ancient fountainheads of knowledge. As early as the seventeenth century, outspoken women like Lady Mary Montagu were pressing for women's rights.

However, the practices of the healing arts changed little over these hundreds of years. Clinical care remained a travesty by current standards until the turn of the present century. Until then, therapeutics were inferior to those of Salerno in the eleventh century. The murders of the keepers of the healing wisdom and those with unusual healing abilities, and the suspicion of healing lore itself, had led to a dark and stagnant time.

Given the religious, scientific, and educational sanctions against women, it is remarkable that they attained *any* degree of professionalization. Indeed, they did so only about one hundred years ago. Before then, the occupational barriers created by religious superstitions had evolved into equally strong barriers erected by the superstitions of science. The shift from a theologically derived cosmology to one that had scientific underpinnings simply meant that women were forbidden to practice for different reasons. During the era of the woman-hunts, women were considered creatures teased by the devil.

As the hunts ended, women were considered merely weak and stupid. Women themselves do not appear to have had strength or interest in organizing or promoting their own advancement.

Women continued to be caught in the web of their own biology, with little governance over their reproductive functions. Repeated pregnancies left them sick and often in mourning for dead children. Complications of pregnancy and birth were often the causes of their own deaths. Small wonder then that women held their silence, failing to write of their aspirations, feelings, insights, and observations. Mere survival was a challenge—lofty achievement in a profession, a near impossibility.

For most of the period in question, the relationship between the elements and human wellness—the ecological dance that women so keenly experience—was not openly addressed. Not only had intellectual inertia set in, but apparently a spiritual amnesia as well. Women were caught in an abyss between the receding power of the supernatural and the eminence of the new scientism.

Until the nineteenth century, women had little energy, no tools, and scant permission to climb out of the abyss and build the bridge between the worlds of past and present, nature and science. Even midwives—probably the first health professionals in history—were increasingly constrained and legislated by the merging, scientifically focused profession of medicine. The spokesmen for medicine generally found women to be ignorant of progress, inept in their practices, and best replaced by men who had studied surgery.

The material in the next section shifts our discussion from the role of women in Europe to the role of women in America, consistent with the book's intent to examine the events influencing women and their healing practices in the United States today. Europe continued to influence modes of healing in America, but the influence was often of second-order importance compared to the realities of the frontier and the ideals of American individualism and opportunity.

In the American colonies, and later on the westward edge of the frontier, the healing professions overlapped due to the shortage of trained individuals. Anyone skilled in healing might be practicing dentistry, pharmacy, surgery, midwifery, and veterinary medicine, all at the same time. Women "doctoresses" who had received their training as apprentices, such as men in the colonies did, were well tolerated during significant doctor shortages. However, a professional physician (implying some university or college training), was, by definition, a man.[1] In seventeenth-century Boston, however, there were two women listed as physicians: Jane Hawkins and Margaret Jones. Both were later denounced as witches. Jane Hawkins was expelled from the city. Margaret Jones was executed. No other woman physician was allowed to practice in Boston until Harriot Hunt opened her office in 1835.[2]

Religious imagery also changed quite abruptly during the time covered by these chapters. Woman's persona had changed from Eve incarnate to woman as Angel in the House by the nineteenth century. With a few exceptions, Americans had little taste for the witch-hunts of their European forebears.

In the professions that emerged last century that were touched by woman's hand we can see the return to a reverence for nature's bounty of healing resources and an emphasis on healthy living as the primary means of preventing sickness. The tie that binds women healers—the focus on body, mind, and spirit as inseparable entities in the healing arts—came forth, but in separate professions.

Women's honorable entry into the professional world as independent caregivers occurred only during a small window in time. By the turn of the twentieth century, women had once again become handmaidens in the healing arts. The circumstances of this brief rise and fall will be examined.

I will often refer to the "warrior" quality of the clear-thinking, strong-minded women who established and sustained the professions, undaunted by the fact that what they sought was unprecedented in the written history of the healing arts. How they succeeded in enacting their vision, and why some of their visions ultimately failed, will serve as guide wires as we women healers of today begin to enact yet another vision that has no precedent.

13 Midwifery: The Mysterious Office

DURING MOST OF the years covered by this chapter (1450–1900) woman as healer was a midwife only, legally barred from the practice of every other healing art. Also, many of these years coincided with the accusations and murders of the witch-hunts, to which midwives were particularly vulnerable. Thus, for a time, women healers were legally restricted to a field in which they faced the probability of criminal charges and death. These issues should serve as a template for understanding the midwives and the medicine of the time. What they did, what they said, what was said about them—and what was omitted—remain dissonant bits of information unless their dilemma is considered.

MIDWIFERY: DEFINITION AND DESCRIPTION

The primary responsibility of midwives has always been to attend the mother through labor and delivery, and to give early care to the newborn. Because they have had access to the very private nature of reproduction, they have developed skills beyond management of the birth process itself. The early manuals written for midwives indicate they served as experts on most gynecological issues, including menstrual irregularities, uterine tumors, infections, and the various problems of pregnancy and parturition. Some midwives, not all, had a goodly font of botanical knowledge for ailments in general.

The qualifications for acting as midwife, until about the nineteenth century, related little to the skills needed for the profession. Rather, the women must have had children themselves, not be "young," and be Christians in good standing. Other factors of concern were their deportment, the size of their hands, and the state of their fingernails.

Our discussions in this chapter will focus primarily on midwifery as it evolved in England and then in the United States. The English system most influenced that of the colonies, despite gross differences in availability of resources and professional training.[1] However, we should note that the midwives of continental Europe were far more sophisticated in their practices than their counterparts in England, and support of their work was widespread. As early as 1452, the city of Regensburg, Germany, adopted a municipal plan for licensing midwives and soon after provided funds for midwives to serve the poor. Retirement benefits for aging midwives were also doled out of civic coffers. The Regensburg system soon spread to other areas of Europe—but not to England.

Midwifery in all countries drew overwhelmingly from women at the margins of society: old women, women disenfranchised from their families, women whose tolerance allowed them to be present at the "unclean" and torturous event of birth. The rank and file of midwifery was filled with women who had no other means of financial support, with the exception of a few women of means who attended births as a charitable function, and wives and daughters of physicians or surgeons who accompanied them as assistants. Percivall Willughby, seventeenth-century author of *Observations on Midwifery*, noted that many midwives, especially those in the country, were illiterate women of "the meanest sort who, not knowing how otherwise to live," had taken up midwifery "for the getting of a shilling, or two."[2] Yet Willughby's own daughter and other kinswomen were noted midwives of the genteel class. The midwife's status was therefore strongly contingent upon the standing of those she served.

Temperament, too, varied among the midwives: according to the widely circulated sixteenth-century text the *Byrthe of Mankynd*, many midwives were "ryght expert/diligent/wyse/circumspecte and tender." So too, many were "undyscreate/unreasonable/chorleshe."[3]

With the few rare exceptions, midwifery was a less-than-honorable profession. Birthing was regarded an objectionable, private, and nasty business. That the birth passage was placed between where feces and urine were eliminated was often cited as God's way of showing disgust for the birth of yet another sinner. The act of giving birth itself defiled the mother, who could be readmitted to the Church only after rites of purification, called "churching." These rites were based on older Judaic precepts, which regarded a woman as unclean for seven days after the birth of a son, fourteen days after the birth of a daughter.

Furthermore, the midwife was involved in a process that often resulted in the death of mother or child. Knowledge about even normal birthing, much less complicated births, had waned significantly since the time of Trotula. The skills of the midwife were limited to what could be gained from observation, common sense, apprenticeship, and the few manuals available, provided she could read. Birth was a traumatic event over which the midwife could exercise little control. Her scanty information, often superstitiously based and erroneous, was believed to contribute to the misery of mother and baby alike.

The midwives' story, like that of all women, is filtered through a distorted glass of words. What we know about them comes from the few midwife manuals that were handed down. What these books relate are ideal techniques, not what they actually did or their feelings about their work.[4] Additional sources of information include oaths and licensing requirements, references to midwifery in books written by male physicians, ecclesiastic concerns related to the association with witchcraft, and the observations of a few journalists. The writing is often a passionate and vicious diatribe against the midwife, her scurrilous character, her lack of training, and her incompetence. Less often, it is an emotion-laden defense of the midwives' practices.

Either way, the strengths and weaknesses of the profession can be assessed only in the broader context of women's healing history. Patently obvious from the writings is the disdain in which women were held, especially women attempting to serve other women during labor and delivery.

THE WRITTEN WORD

The presence of early manuscripts in Middle English attests to the fact that the profession of midwifery was being addressed with the intention of bettering it. Twelve such works have been identified. These may have been written by women, and most were certainly addressed to women. One of the earliest and most complete is referred to as Sloane 2463, and was probably written around 1450.[5] The work is a landmark in women's attempts to seek solace and assistance from other women, containing poignant and memorable passages on the necessity of freeing women from an embarrassing dependence upon male practitioners. It is a "moving lament against one form of discrimination . . . proving that English women of the late Middle Ages could express their female separateness and their own consciousness." One passage reads: "And so, to assist women, I intend to write of how to help their secret maladies so that one woman may aid another in her illness and not divulge her secrets to such discourteous men."[6]

The manuscript represents a compendium of knowledge that can be traced to the writings attributed to Soranus around the first century A.D. It is unusual in that, unlike most medieval medical works, it presents information on birth presentation, either natural or difficult. However, none of the beautifully drawn illustrations show informed knowledge of the embryo—the infants are in cherubic proportions, with mature genitalia. The work instructs the midwife to reinsert the abnormally presenting child into the vagina and try to rearrange it!

Several features of the book pique our curiosity about the nature of the woman of the time. For example, unlike most earlier works (such as those of Trotula or Hildegard), it contains no incantations, invocations, or other religious gestures. The prescriptions are almost exclusively botanic—rather than "magical" or religious—in nature. The omission indicates a responsiveness to the accusations of the Church of the connection between rituals and incantations associated with midwifery and, hence, with witchcraft. If midwives continued to use prayers and so forth, they chose not to write them down in this and other later manuscripts. Silence on spiritual or supernatural matters was probably necessary in order for midwifery to survive as a profession, even in an attentuated or modest state.

Also, there are references to abortion in the Sloane manuscript that are quite contrary to theological opinion: "Whan the woman is feble and the chyld may noght comy out, then it is better that the chylde be slayne than the moder of the child also dye."[7] One of the most potent prescriptions for abortions, and likely an effective one, is mentioned here: rue, savin, southernwood, iris, hyssop, dittany, quicksilver, bull's gall, and asafetida, among other things. (Other manuscripts mention mechanical abortions, as well as prescriptions to hasten "delayed menstruation.") Women may have aborted far more often than the Church's position would lead one to believe.

The Sloane manuscript (as well as others written over the next four hundred years) contains nothing that would be a major source of pain relief for a laboring woman. Botanics with significant anesthetic properties (henbane and nightshade) are mentioned only for external use, and then only for treating pestilence.

With the omission of pain-relieving botanics from the midwife manuals, we can surmise that: (1) they were protecting their knowledge, and themselves, from accusation; and (2) they had succumbed to the power of the Church authorities, who claimed that pain in childbirth was woman's just desert. Women's herbal lore was still vast, though, and it seems inconceivable that they selectively overlooked botanics that would offer them the most relief. Nevertheless, it was claimed that belladonna was not reintroduced into the care of the laboring mother until the last century.[8]

The midwives' manuals consist primarily of an amazing number of recipes, often listing twenty or more relatively benign ingredients, the majority of which were intended to be packed into the ailing woman's "privities." Oral ingestion, topical application, and fumigation were also prescribed.[9] The virtue of these prescriptions was in the cleansing and mildly soothing properties of some of the ingredients, in the great care that was shown to the patients by such complex preparations, and in the fact that they made women smell and feel better.

The first manuscript in English known to have been written by a woman was *The Midwives Book,* published in 1671 by Jane Sharp.[10] Mrs. Sharp, a midwife with over thirty years' experience, lamented the sorry state of much of midwifery, attempting to aid it with her good sense, vast experience, and personal remedies. The latter were neither more nor less bizarre than those of male midwives, whom she viewed as a serious competition. In her work, as in the earlier manuscripts, one is led to believe that woman was thought of as a living receptacle whose mechanical function depended upon being stuffed with one ingredient after another.

Jane Sharp presaged the future of midwifery by recognizing the difficulty women had in obtaining any type of higher education, and therefore the lack of prestige that would be associated with their work. Still, she also noted the irrelevancy of men's education to midwifery: "It is not hard words that perform the work, as if none understood the Art that cannot understand Greek."[11]

Since midwives were drawn primarily from illiterate classes, we can only guess how much the written information influenced their practice. And given the nature of the information, one wonders whether it mattered; or if, alternatively, the illiterate midwives had different (better or worse) ideas of their own, which were sustained through an oral tradition.

THE CODIFICATION OF HEALING

Prior to the 1500s, the Catholic church controlled the entrance into the profession of midwifery. Credentials were granted on ecclesiastic grounds alone. Even when civic legislation became common, the Church was still in charge of enforcing the law, and monitored the midwives in case they should try to mimic the activities of the other professions of healing.

The Church had several other reasons to continue to oversee the midwives' work. First, the authorities sensed a connection between witchcraft and midwifery, as discussed in the last section of this book. Second, the Church had to make sure that infants who died *in utero,* during, or shortly after birth, were baptized. (Midwives were required to perform this function if no other person was available.) Third, midwives were privy to sins and secrets, including the knowledge of how to perform abortions, paternity of illegitimate children, and the concealment of unwanted births. Finally, midwives had access to fetal tissue, which—while forbidden by the Church—was in great demand as a magical charm by healers and practitioners of the magical arts.

Despite the fact that the office of midwife was not an honorable position, it was clearly one of power, otherwise the Church would not have kept it under such close surveillance for so long a time.

In Tudor times, King Henry VIII began the systematic centralization of the healing professions, including the incorporation of the Royal College of Physicians in 1512. The first recorded attempt to license or register midwives in England was about 1550, with the bishop of the diocese and a "doctor of physicke" examining the aspiring midwives. Their primary concern was whether the women used witchcraft, charms, sorcery, or invocations, and whether they had ever exhibited behaviors offensive to the Church.

Midwives were required to swear to their diligence, faith, and readiness to serve the poor.[12] The latter clause was not included in the prerequisites for practicing any other health profession. In fact, as already discussed, the physicians' and surgeons' refusal to treat nonpaying patients had resulted in the "Quack's Charter." This allowed women and "quacks" to treat certain categories of disease, but only in the poor.

The midwives' oath contained fifteen items attesting to their integrity. Matters of training and expertise were not at issue in the sixteenth century. The midwives only promised to seek those more skilled than they if the labor proved difficult.

A midwife who failed to obtain a license could be imprisoned or excommunicated. Despite the serious tone of the oath and the threatened punishment for practicing without a license, enforcement was lax. It seems that most midwives, like all the other healers, ignored the regulations and went about their business as usual.

The legislation of midwifery followed a pattern that time has not altered. The codes have varied from era to era and place to place, but the progressive limitation of midwives' practice has been consistent. First, midwives were expected to register themselves following some kind of oath; then, concerns were voiced among the male professions about the midwives' expertise, at which time an examining committee, on which women were seldom represented, would be appointed. Even in France, where laws enabling women were more liberal and training was good, midwives were dropped from the examining committee by 1616.

Next, invariably, attempts would be made to limit midwives' participation to "normal" births, and then to be present only under doctors' orders. Finally, midwifery would become illegal or economically unfeasible. Interspersed through this course of events would be the establishment of educational requirements. It has not been unusual for the training required by law of midwives to be unavailable through any institution to which women had access.

"INNOVATIVE MEN" VERSUS "IGNORANT WOMEN"

When midwifery was first legally recognized, it was a profession of women exclusively. Stories (possibly apocryphal) are told of men who, curious about the birth process, masqueraded as women and observed the event, only to be caught, arrested, tried, and burned. Whether this happened or not, evidence suggests that the birth chamber was territory forbidden to male health practitioners. Within one hundred years after midwives were first licensed in England, men called man-midwives were attending "difficult" labors of those who could afford their fees. By 1700 they were attending normal deliveries as well. How did the profession of women give way so quickly, and why did the profession become more desirable to men?

Men's entrance into the profession of midwifery coincided with the end of the witch-hunts. The territory of the birthing chamber was apparently cleansed from whatever evils had been foisted upon it by the Christian doctrine. And, as the dark cloud lifted from the profession, male practitioners—soon to be further aided by the development of instruments to facilitate delivery—saw financial rewards from a wealthy and growing middle class. The reciprocal point must also be considered: perhaps because midwifery was viewed as a potentially lucrative profession, men in power were encouraged to erase the stigma associated with birthing and the women's practices.

Most opinion that has survived on these points is that of men, who generally viewed the masculinization of the profession of midwifery as progress in the interests of humankind. The esteemed physician William Hunter, for instance, noted that midwives "cram their patients with cordials, keeping them intoxicated during the time they are in labour, driving poor women up and down stairs, notwithstanding their shrieks, and shaking them so violently as often to bring on convulsive fits on pretence of hastening their labors, laugh at their cries, and breaking wretched jests upon the contortions of the women, whose torments would make a feeling man shudder at the sight."[13]

Willughby gives a seventeenth-century picture of women whose miserable knowledge of anatomy led them to believe that the baby could be stuck to the mother's back, an event that could be remedied only by stretching the labia, tying the mother-to-be to an obstetric chair, tossing her in a blanket, or pulling and jerking on whatever part the baby presented first.[14]

Midwives were accused of being unable to deal with the common instance of a difficult birth. It was claimed they used techniques that maimed the child—such as amputating parts of the infant's body—or killed the mother to save the child. Such reports are frequent enough—often by concerned midwives themselves—that the atrocities may not have been unusual. The man-midwives' promises of speedy, safe, and more comfortable deliveries must have been most welcome.

The major advances in understanding anatomy, labor, and birth were attributed to men acting in the spirit of the Renaissance. Whatever was "wrong" with midwifery as practiced by women was being rectified by men's science and medicine. Several of the ancient techniques, such as cesarean section and podalic version, were "rediscovered" by physicians. Credit for much advancement was given to William Harvey, Percivall Willughby, and Ambroise Paré, surgeon to the king of France. The accomplishments of these men were gradually attributed to men in general.

It is unlikely that women were as ignorant of birthing procedures as claimed by the man-midwives, but women's illiteracy, their failure to write when they could, and the plagiarism of their work when it existed were severe drawbacks in making their skills known. It now appears that motives of the men of science had more to do with greed than skills. According to the *Encyclopedia of Medical History*, "The criticism of midwives for having inferior training masked a conflict among disciplines seeking to provide health services and a bitter competition for the richest kinds of practice."[15]

Even modern writers refer to "ignorant midwives," at the same time reciting their unusual prowess. For instance, Herbert Spencer refers to Mary Donaly as the "ignorant midwife" who performed the first successful cesarean section in the British Isles in about 1738.[16] After making an incision with a common razor, she extracted the baby and sent for a surgeon to sew the wound. Until he arrived, she held the edges of the abdominal cut together with her fingers for two hours. Making incisions, suturing, and podalic version were considered surgical procedures forbidden to midwives. Having violated one procedure, she apparently decided she should go no further.

While the leading physicians of the seventeenth century—such as Willughby—were quick to criticize the midwives, the state of their own obstetric art was fraught with superstition and danger. For hemorrhage, Willughby prescribed a drink of hog's dung and ashes of toad, together with pessaries composed of the same substances, to be inserted into the womb.

Despite the promises of the new profession of obstetrics, the men were often viewed as doctors of death. When nothing more could be done to assist the birth, or if the fetus was dead, the man-midwife would do an embryotomy by plunging needles or scissors into the fetus's head. The cranium was then crushed, and the fetus was pulled forth, piecemeal, with the handles of the scissors, or with special crochets or hooks.[17]

Had man's claim to be able effectively to manage difficult births been vested only in their concoctions, podalic version, suturing, and embryotomy, it is doubtful they would have propelled themselves into the field of midwifery as easily as they did. Their hold on the profession was furthered by their vociferous testimony to their own superiority and to the midwives' inferiority in matters of birthing. Surgeon Benjamin Pugh wrote that some people mistakenly believed that "because Midwifery has been hitherto chiefly in the Hands of Women, it is a trifling Affair." Nothing could be further from the truth, he claimed: the "operation" of midwifery was one of the most difficult in all surgery.[18]

Other male practitioners were undaunted by Pugh's claims that midwifery was a surgical specialty. Anyone who saw the entrée into a woman's lying-in chamber as a lucrative venture tried out their untrained and inexperienced hands in the field. The unwarranted claims and clumsiness of some of these self-proclaimed experts were cause for concern by the serious and more scholarly physicians. In order to spare their own reputations, new techniques were required. In particular, the world awaited a gentler method of bringing along the baby's head.

INVENTION OF FORCEPS

The real milestone came, however, not with advancements in "knowledge," but in the development of the forceps. Why would such instruments be considered an advancement for a "normal" event, like delivery? Labor and delivery may indeed have been more perilous during this period in history because of frequent, repeated pregnancies and poor delivery practices. The result was often prolapsed uteri, vesicovaginal fistulas, and other health problems, including severe anemia. The bacterial infections associated with puerperal or childbed fever were debilitating at best, and more often deadly. Furthermore, poor nutrition contributed to richetic and deformed pelvic structures. There was no mercy for women of childbearing age, or for the fetus, whose life was at even higher risk. The forceps did indeed offer women hope for gentler deliveries.

Invented by Peter Chamberlen the Elder (1560–1631), the forceps remained a family secret until 1728. The lineage of Chamberlen man-midwives boldly advertised their expertise, claiming greater dispatch of the "operation," with fewer pains and less danger to mother and babe. Virtually every well-known man-midwife, including Pugh, William Smellie, and Edmund Chapman, attempted the design of satisfactory "extraction" tools. By 1750, several versions were in use. It is clear from the writings of these men that training in the use of the tools was to be given to men only—especially to physicians and surgeons, whose guilds had determined the use of instruments in health care was their exclusive right.

MIDWIVES, MAN-MIDWIVES, AND MORTALITY RATE

Juxtaposed with the vicious criticism of midwives is the contradictory report that country women attended by these midwives were more likely to survive their ordeal than those attended by man-midwives. William Harvey himself attributed the difference in survival to the fact that midwives allowed nature to take her unimpeded course.[19]

Later, the superiority of male midwives was very much open to question. Dr. Charles White, a man-midwife, wrote that the half-starved and diseased poor, serviced by midwives, had a lower mortality rate than those women in lying-in hospitals, or the more affluent women attended by men.[20]

Statistics are not available for the mortality rates for at-home deliveries. However, it is widely reported that the highest mortality rates were in the larger lying-in hospitals, where puerperal fever decimated the ranks of women. As more and more frequent digital examination became *de rigeur*, the less likely a woman was to escape the deadly bacteria on the men's probing fingers. Midwives, too, passed the disease around, but nothing equaled the spread by physicians and medical students in major hospitals. As recently as last century, maternal mortality rates were estimated as high as twenty eight per thousand for the major lying-in hospitals. Out-patient charity operations, where midwives provided direct patient care under the supervision of a physician, had rates as low as five maternal deaths per thousand deliveries.[21]

Even then, the statistics were questioned. If they were true, stated the eminent physician, Dr. James Matthews Duncan, one could draw the "absurd" conclusion that poor women, delivered in filth by imperfectly educated midwives or students, were at less risk than well-to-do patients attended by "educated *accoucheurs*." "Impossible," said he.[22]

The infant mortality rate in England in 1872 was an astounding 160 per 1,000 live births. The reponse by the British Obstetrical Society was to set up an examination board for all midwives, who had to have completed an approved program of study and been present at twenty-five deliveries. There was no set number of deliveries required of the medical students, and in hospitals that were not associated with lying-in facilities, they could graduate with no experience in delivery. Yet the midwives' license permitted them to participate only in normal births, whereas the physicians could legally attend the full range of complications.

MODESTY AND FASHION

It became the fashion, for those who could afford it, to be attended by a man. And, as prosperity increased, more and more women chose that option. Furthermore, apothecaries, dentists, and surgeons knew full well that the trust they gained from the family after a delivery increased the chances of their being consulted on other medical problems. The doctor's common boast was "that if he can attend one single case of midwifery in a family, he has ever after secured their patronage."[23]

Men were advised that while midwifery was a key to general practice, to engage in it full time would have an "unmistakably deteriorating effect on the medical practitioner, mentally, morally, physically and pecuniarily."[24] Once a man had established himself, he could turn over his nonpaying patients to midwives. The long-term care of patients who did pay could also be entrusted to midwives or nurses in the doctor's employ.

These developments came at a time of increasing modesty—from the late eighteenth century and into the Victorian era. The presence of a man in the lying-in chamber mortified "decent" women. Man-midwives likewise expressed their embarrassment and disgust at being present, and compensated by adopting a strict protocol: all examinations and even deliveries were done with the woman on her back, covered by a sheet under which the physician could feel but not look. The public had come to realize that childbirth was a risky business, and woman permitted "the knowledge of her danger to override this delicacy of her feelings and the modesty of her true nature."[25]

Physicians, too, were able to overcome their feelings. In the name of "distressing duty" they could "condescend" to conduct vaginal exams. Modesty and chastity, the foundations for love and respect of woman, the cornerstone of "civilization and order" must be preserved at all costs.[26] Other operations, such as the insertion of urinary catheters, were regarded as tasks too "odious" for a man to perform. "There is scarcely a more disagreeable operation to be performed than that of catheterism of the female; an operation which, I should think, every gentleman would be glad to commit to other hands than his own."[27]

Charles Meigs, an eminent, widely read, and widely quoted nineteenth-century physician, held forth on the moral and ethical dilemma faced by those who practiced obstetrics. In an age of such delicacy, men must thoroughly understand women in order to serve their needs. Woman, uniquely, he claimed, elevated and civilized mankind; all arts and sciences flourished under her spell, her smile made all achievements possible. Naturally religious, she martyred herself for country and family. Most charming of her traits was modesty, which bound her to home and family. Her head, he said, was "almost too small for intellect, but just big enough for love."[28] The works of Meigs and his colleagues helped complete the metamorphosis of carnal woman into "angel in the house"—an attitude toward woman that colors other nineteenth-century developments in science and medicine, discussed in the next chapter.

Opposition to man-midwifery was based primarily on the question posed by Meigs and others of his ilk. The presence of men in the birthing chamber compromised the dignity of women. Worse, men were known to give in to their most prurient lusts while undertaking their duties as midwives. Stories abounded of the wickedness of physicians, their antics, the threat they posed to the very fabric of society by attending birth. Charges ranged from the probably true (i.e., meddlesome and unnecessary procedures for profit) to the probably absurd ("a physician in Charleston, infuriated with the sight of the woman he had just delivered, leaped into her bed before she was restored to a state of nature").[29]

The anti–man-midwife movement never gained much force. Once men gained entry to the delivery room, they held their place, limiting the presence of women midwives. Male practitioners who taught midwifery were accused of charging higher fees of their female students, teaching them less, and in general, training them to be their servants rather than independent practitioners. Especially, they were discouraged from treating the rich.

The common argument was that men were better versed in anatomy, acquainted with more physical helps, and "commonly enbued with greater Presence of Mind," were "readier" and "discreeter, to devise something more new, and to give quicker Relief in Cases of difficult or preternatural BIRTHS, than common MIDWIFES undertand."[30]

It was a matter of survival, and out of fears of reprimand midwives restricted their position, becoming increasingly reluctant to perform any but the most routine procedures. Writing in 1795, Margaret Stephen carefully instructed women on anatomy and on use of the forceps, but advised them to send always for a man when forceps were necessary. Should the outcome be unfortunate, "people are more reconciled to the event, because there is no appeal from what a doctor does, being granted he did all that could be done."[31]

The men-midwives consolidated their position by overselling the dangers of childbirth, according to journalist Philip Thicknesse in *Midwifery Analysed*.[32] They frightened women into believing that extraordinary measures—that could be performed only by men—were more necessary than not. And men were quick to blame the midwives for anything that went wrong. Too, Thicknesse observed, the man-midwives made allies of the "monthly nurse."

The "monthly nurse" was a woman of lesser training than a midwife, hired by the family to care for the new mother and baby for a few weeks after the birth. These women could make more money if the midwife was left completely out. The "monthly" could be called in at the onset of labor. She would have no illusions about her ability to deliver the baby and would summon the physician at the appropriate time. He would perform the heroic and necessary operations and depart, leaving her a fine tip. By the mid-1800s more than three times as many monthly nurses were being trained in England as midwives. This is an example of the alliance between physicians and lesser trained technicians that is frequently the death knell for women's professions.

The story of English midwifery ends on a positive note. After a difficult struggle for survival, English midwives were aided by social reformers who argued for midwifery as an honorable professional outlet for the growing number of middle-class women who were seeking employment. The fate of poor women who could not afford obstetrical care was also a serious concern, and midwifery was seen as a partial solution to that ever-present problem.

Through the work of Louisa Hubbard, a Midwives' Institute was formed in 1881. In 1902, Parliament passed the Midwives Act, defining educational standards, and the relationship between midwifery and the medical profession. The jealous competition between the two continued until physicians' consultation fees were firmly established. Today, graduates of the Royal College of Midwives (formerly the Midwives' Institute) attend 80 percent of deliveries in that country.

MIDWIFERY IN AMERICA

Most of what has been written thus far applies to American midwives as well. Had American midwifery sprung from other sources, such as continental Europe, or even reflected the strong spirit of the pioneering American women, more midwives in this country might still be functioning legally and independently.

By the mid-1700s the "new obstetrics" with all its promises had become the vogue for the wealthy; by 1800 men were commonly attending normal births; and by 1850, they were a dominant force in the major cities. As in England, the practitioners of the new obstetrics had no intention of serving nonpaying patients. Primarily for this reason the practice of midwifery was allowed to continue. When state and federal funding became available for charity medical care, independent midwifery was significantly restricted.

The first two medical schools in America, the College of Philadelphia and King's College Medical School in New York, offered training in midwifery, which in and of itself ensured that delivering babies would become a specialty of doctors.

The first American manual of midwifery, *The Midwives Monitor and Mother's Mirror,* was written in 1800 by Valentine Seaman, a surgeon whose mission was to dispel the perennial problem of woman's ignorance.[33] While obstensibly intending to upgrade midwifery, he focused on instructing women in what they were *not* capable of doing, and affirming that they knew when to summon a physician for help. He, as well as others of his time, set an unfortunate precedent by describing pregnancy and birth as forms of disease.

Seaman wrote that the ideal midwife should bolster the patient's morale, be able to determine the extent of dilation, to support the perineum, to tie the umbilical cord, and to refrain from pulling on the cord to speed up the explusion of the placenta. He went so far as to describe how podalic version is done, but advised his women readers never to try it.

The most notable figure in American midwifery in the mid-nineteenth century was Samuel Gregory, an enterprising educator.[34] Having earned bachelor and master of arts degrees from Yale in 1840, he then developed an avid interest in anatomy and physiology—particularly that of the female. He wrote and lectured on such eclectic and sensitive subjects as *Licentiousness, its Cause and Effects,* and *Facts and Important Information for Young Men on the Self-Indulgence of the Sexual Appetite.* He even wrote a *Letter to Ladies in Favor of Female Physicians* and *Man-midwifery, Exposed and Corrected,* arguing for a corps of women who could attend to the needs of their own sex.

Gregory's lectures, at first ignored by the Boston medical community, caused an uproar when they began to look like they might engender serious competition for the medically trained men-midwives. Gregory's response was to establish the Boston Female Medical College. At first he offered courses in instruction of midwifery at three-month intervals, eventually offering certificates of proficiency. By 1853 the college had expanded its curriculum to include a degree in medicine. Although women were not included in the Female Medical Education Society, which Gregory created to raise money to meet his educational aims, they were heartily encouraged to donate money anyway. A large donation was *required* if women wished to serve on the Ladies Advisory Board of the school. (Donations were not required, however, from those who served on the all-male Board of Trustees.)

The reputation of the Boston Female Medical College was never stable, and the college's interest in the new wave of eclectic health practices such as mesmerism and homeopathy did not help to further secure it. Nevertheless, it survived. By 1856, the school had stopped awarding the midwifery certificate altogether, changed its name to the New England Female Medical College, and offered a complete course of study leading to a medical degree. Gregory was able to recruit decent faculty, including the very famous and competent woman physician Marie Zakrzewska. With her help, the school developed a clinical training program, which was unusual for any school at that time. In 1873, Gregory merged the school with Boston University Medical School.

And so, for all practical purposes, the energy surrounding the practice of midwifery dissolved and reshaped itself around a new breed of female physicans. Women were about to face some of the most exciting developments in their history as healers. A popular health movement was emerging, along with a surge of radical feminism, and the seeds of new pro-woman, pro-healing religions.

It is not quite correct to give a eulogy for midwifery, however. Even though it was overshadowed by the birth of American medicine, the midwives continued to practice for some time without the benefit of accredited training, regulation, or licensure. In 1910, as many as half of all births in the United States were attended by a midwife, and in the poverty-stricken areas of the cities, the figures were much higher. Immigrants clung to their cultural tradition of seeking a midwife to deliver their babies, and the poor had no other options.

Neither the unregulated practice of midwifery nor the obstetricians did the American mother any favors. At the turn of the century, the maternal mortality rate was the third highest among those countries that kept such records. The infant and maternal mortality figures have continued to be a source of shame, as the United States lags behind most industrialized nations, particularly those which employ a large cadre of trained midwives.

As the medical approach to birth came to resemble the management of a disease process, midwives were prohibited, restrained, or otherwise curtailed in their functions. The 1960s and 1970s saw a wave of renewed interest in home births and midwifery, associated with the strong feminist and popular health movements. History has repeated itself. As will be outlined in Chapter 16, legislation on midwifery is in a remarkable state of ferment right now. Some legislation is enabling, but most is prohibiting. Midwives are no longer being ignored. Once again, midwifery is posing a threat to the American medical establishment.

14 *Every Woman Her Own Doctor: The Popular Health Movement*

IN THE NINETEENTH CENTURY, events combined to create a popular health movement in the United States that was unlike any other until the 1970s. Creativity and freedom of expression in domestic health practices resulted in a safe, do-it-yourself type of medicine with great appeal for women who had long been restrained and scrutinized in their healing work. The women in this movement strove to return to the wisdom of nature as a healing resource, revitalizing the ancient connection between the feminine and the earth for the first time in many generations. Within three decades, women felt encouraged enough by their involvement to expand their talent beyond their own homes and the fringes of public health, into the professions.

Three major changes in thought precipitated and supported the popular health movement: the notion of a "cult of domesticity"; the corollary phenomenon, the "angel in the house" ideal of woman's morality; and a backlash against the more dangerous and ineffective practices of allopathic medicine. None of these changes was unique to the United States, although developments characteristic of the country's individualism flavored the movement, as described below, where each major change is discussed in turn.

THE CULT OF DOMESTICITY

A general change in attitude toward women during the first three decades of the nineteenth century meant that, curiously, women were able to gain professional freedom. At this time, any doubt about a woman's place in society had disappeared; her place was absolutely in the home. A man's place was in public, which meant everywhere except the home. So the lines were drawn, and yet from this "cult of domesticity" women gained the respect and courage to enter public life. Domesticity provided the springboard for major health reforms, and for women's eventual entry into fields such as medicine and the ministry.

The cult of domesticity was actually quite revolutionary, with impetus for its development coming from most of the industrialized Western world. For the first time in centuries, women's mysteries and power were no longer feared, *and* women were assigned an honorable role in society. This is a substantially different consciousness than that of the years of the witch-hunts, as well as the succeeding years when women were low in status and suffered from the prevailing attitude regarding their weakness and inferiority.

Industrialization and the growth of a working-class population meant that men were increasingly away from the family farm or estate. Only by women's taking a definitive role within the realm of the home could the integrity of family life continue. Assigning women a role with clear boundaries meant that their power was finally circumscribed to an area that need not be in competition with nor feared by men.

The "cult" was based on a paradoxical conception of woman.[1] Women's role within the home was respected, and their responsibility great. At the same time, women were politically and economically more subordinate than ever in the United States. Here, women's retreat into the home coincided with the uniquely American emphasis on "universal" (actually white male only) suffrage, and sensitivity to individual freedom. But freedom and the rights of full citizenry did not extend to women—a fact not lost on the bright, well-educated, and assertive reformists of the time. The social and economic situation that allowed for the development of the cult of domesticity also influenced the appearance of feminism. In fact, nineteenth-century feminism depended on the "cult" for both its moral and ideological power.[2]

The wedge that domesticity gave women was a result of their taking their assigned domestic tasks seriously. If they were to be the minions of the educational, physical, and spiritual well-being of America's sons, they would make a science of it. To some of these women, it became obvious that to guard and embellish the moral fiber of society would require that they be full citizens and professionals; but never did they lose sight of their fundamental connection with motherhood. Instead, they used it as the link to public life. Women chose not to compete, but rather to extend their special talents— as women and mothers—in fields that were the logical extensions of domesticity.

WOMAN AS THE "ANGEL IN THE HOUSE"

"The Angel in the House" is a Victorian ideal of womanhood. The term is adopted from a poem of the same name written by Coventry Patmore in honor of his first wife, Emily. She was beautiful, delicate, gentle, and self-sacrificing. Her face and demeanor inspired portraits by Millais and others, the ideas of Tennyson, Ruskin and Carlyle, and a work by Browning, entitled "The Face," which leaves a "clear impression on our minds of a sacred yet sensuous beauty, serious but inviting, always virginal, even though the honey should be sipped and the fruit plucked."[3]

She further conformed to the Victorian ideal by dying a lingering death from consumption, leaving behind her six young children and her wedding ring for the next Mrs. Patmore. "Angels" such as Emily Patmore were encouraged to write; indeed, she supported her husband for the years he worked on his poetry by writing children's stories and a guide for the homemaker.

The mystical eroticism in the tributes to Victorian womanhood and the image of woman as pure and morally superior are reminiscent of the medieval days of Mary-idolatry and the tales of courtly love. While we can scarcely believe that the idea ever pervaded all classes of society, it was nonetheless present, standing in stark contrast to the image of woman as embodiment of carnal lust. Not surprisingly, during both these times women healers found new outlets for the expression of their talents.

The elevation of women in the United States to a position of moral superiority has been associated with the "Great Awakenings"—religious revivals that swept across the country, first in 1740 and then in the early part of the last century. The evangelistic fundamentalism of the revivals posed a significantly brighter religious prospect for women than did Catholicism or its early Protestant offshoots. The new movement's leaders actually sought the support of women, reminding them that Christianity had raised them from the status of slaves to moral and intellectual human beings. The message was as persuasive as memories were short. Women soon constituted a strong majority of church membership.

The criterion for women's enhanced spiritual role was suppression of their sexuality, the element on which the witch-hunts had focused both directly and indirectly. "The clergy thus renewed and generalized the idea that women under God's grace were more pure than men, and they expected not merely the souls but the bodies of women to corroborate that claim."[4]

The "woman problem" was thereby effectively managed once again. Since the edge of the sword of condemnation was dulled, the churches could now attract sensible, modern women. Furthermore, the churches could honestly desire women to actively participate, since the worst of the pall had been removed from them. And finally, since women's new found spiritual image was not consonant with lust, there was less reason for men to fear them. In some sense, women lost their primal power. Within a remarkably short time, the stereotype of woman had changed to that of a passionless maiden.

Robbing women of their sensuality not only facilitated their welcome back into the Church, it also permitted a semblance of control over reproductive function. Birth control, limited primarily to abstention, was a giant step in the direction of progress and emancipation. The birth rate declined significantly. Men were advised to respect women's tender sensibilities by controlling their animal lusts in the marriage bed. Health reformers made quite specific recommendations about restricting intercourse for the well-being of both men and women. Most authorities claimed that intercourse once a month was plenty; others felt that the act should be performed only when a child was desired. Ideally, the timing of sexual intercourse was to be given over to women, whose primary desire is to please God.

Many women no doubt accepted the yoke of passionlessness more than willingly, as an acceptable way to limit the pain and grief of bearing children who might not live to celebrate their first birthdays. The prevailing belief that conception was unlikely if a woman did not reach orgasm surely also discouraged a sexual response.

This was an era of sexual mutilative surgery, too, designed to curb women's passions. Clitoridectomies were performed when a husband or physician decided that a woman was too sexually responsive, neurotic, uncontrollable, or might be pleasuring herself. Masturbation, "the solitary vice," was considered a terrible disease, to be cured by any means possible, including removal of the ovaries. It was also considered a disease in males, who were treated with reprimands and restraints rather than mutilative surgery.

The suppression of sensuality triggered a booming pornographic industry, provoking issues that extend far beyond the scope of this book. The prudery inherent in Victorian morality is important to our discussion here because it gave women an acceptable reason to enter the health field: to treat other women so that modesty and delicacy might be preserved.

THE ESTABLISHMENT OF ALLOPATHIC MEDICINE

In addition to the attitudinal changes associated with the "cult" and the "angel in the house," women's active engagement in health practices can be viewed as a reaction to the type of medical care offered by "regular" physicians. Medical practice, at least in the United States, took on a philosophy that disease was a malevolent entity that must be bludgeoned, bled, defecated, poisoned, and puked out. The strong preparations used to accomplish such aims were called "heroic" or "active" medications. The philosophy itself, called allopathy, remains the dominant type of medicine practiced in the United States today. While the methods have changed, the philosophical foundation of the practice of using medical tools to purge a body of disease has not.

The people of nineteenth-century America had a literal bellyful of the toxic materials that had become the standard for medical care. The women and men who spoke out for the grassroots movement faced irate medical men who defended their practices vigorously. The following excerpts from the *Boston Medical and Surgical Journal,* published in 1878, show the strong nature of the preparations that those in the popular health movement found so objectionable. They are from H. C. Wood, a well-known physician and professor, addressing the use of heroic medicine for idiopathic peritonitis:

> I remember my uncle, Dr. George B. Wood, saying that he never lost a case of peritonitis in an adult. . . . He always bled his patients from the arm until they fainted, and then put 100 leeches on the abdomen. I am proud to say that I am a thorough believer in the same plan of treatment, antiquated as it may appear. . . . What is to be done after venesection? I take my stand on the old theory that calomel [a preparation containing mercury] has power to modify inflammatory action. . . . In connection with the calomel, opium is undeniably of great value. . . . The ability to stand large doses of opium in peritonitis is wonderful. In one of my cases, seventy-five grains of solid opium were taken daily for five days, and the patient made an excellent recovery. . . . After the abdomen has been thoroughly poulticed for two or three days, blisters may be used, provided the temperature of the body has not remained high . . . do not put on a small blister. . . . I have ordered a blister eight by ten [inches].[5]

The following treatment was advocated for pulmonary consumption by Dr. Charles W. Wilder, speaking before the Massachusetts Medical Society: "Effective means are not wanting when the principle of action is once established. The lancet, the leech, the cupping-glass, the Spanish fly, croton oil, tartarized antimony, ipecacaunha, and mercury are instruments of power and great utility when skillfully used."[6]

The aim of the popular health movement was to disempower the dangerous techniques and drugs of the "regular" physicians. Its spokespersons advocated developing a healthy body and mind through nutrition, exercise, sunshine, fresh air and water, and clean living. In a person so strengthened, disease would not find a host. Pharmaceuticals, should they be needed, would best be botanics that engendered health in the body, not harsh chemicals that purged or punished it. Because of this emphasis, Oliver Wendell Holmes called the movement the "nature-trusting heresy."

WOMEN AND HEALTH REFORM

In addition to the antipathy toward the existing standard of medical treatment, other forces in the nineteenth century were operating to promote a new attitude toward health. The promise of good health and long life for the population of the Western world was at last imminent. Infectious disease was receding in the face of better nutrition and hygiene. Social reforms had already wrought more miracles than all the medical inventions put together. Small changes in lifestyle had made an enormous impact on the quality and quantity of survival. Sickness began to be viewed more as a violation of nature's laws than as God's retribution for sins. It was believed to be vital, therefore, to know what the laws of nature were and to follow them in order to maintain health.

Such progress encouraged middle-class Americans to believe that they could make a difference in the well-being of their nation, and that they could and should take responsibility for their own health. An air of optimism prevailed, enhanced by Jacksonian anti-elitism and the emphasis on the worthiness of the common person. The health reforms coincided with abolitionism and women's rights movements, all arising from an enlightened awareness of human value.

The antebellum period witnessed a flurry of reforms focused on physiological education, temperance, nutrition, hygiene, and new cures. Itinerate lecturers stumped the country preaching self-diagnosis and self-cures. Authors wrote expansively on health, and women were their primary constituency. "Because the changing structure of the nineteenth-century family increasingly required women to school their children in 'modern' values, they welcomed with relief the practical solutions to bewildering problems offered in health reform journals and tracts."[7]

Women played an important role as reformers in conjunction with the Ladies' Physiological Societies established throughout the northeastern United States. Dozens of women lecturers associated with these societies taught the laws of health to audiences that numbered in the thousands.

Issues of women's health—pregnancy, birth, diseases common to women, and birth control—were of major concern. Women, in short, were being taught the facts (as they were known) about their own bodies, so that they could better care for themselves and their families.

The popular health movement was primarily engaged in by women of the middle classes of society who viewed good health as a priority as well as a necessity for living the kind of active life required of them. Paradoxically, the women of the upper classes of the Victorian era viewed themselves as sicker than ever before. Some very famous women, including Elizabeth Barrett Browning and Florence Nightingale, stayed in bed most of their adult lives. Lifelong addiction to the doctor's draughts of opium played a major role in sustaining the delicate health of many women, including Browning. For this and other reasons of habit, the so-called "angel in the house" often did not have the stamina for organizing her domestic sphere. One reformer noted that in order for woman to find her place in the world, she must cease being "the puny, sickly, aching, weakly, dying creature that we find her to be; and woman must, to a very considerable extent, redeem herself—she must throw off the shackles that have hitherto bound both body and mind, and rise into the newness of life."[8]

Feminists and health reformers were rightfully concerned about the health of women of the lower classes who supported themselves by working twelve to fourteen hours daily at factory work, coal mining, and other grueling occupations. They were genuinely ill much of the time, and had few resources to sustain or regain health.

A WARRIOR REFORMER: MARY GOVE NICHOLS

Mary Gove Nichols was a particularly active reformer whose accomplishments illustrate the nature of the popular health movement. She was exceptional among women reformers in the breadth of her work, but representative in terms of her philosophy and purpose. Her life demonstrates the feisty warrior quality common to women whose work had a lasting influence.

Nichols was a lively writer and frequent contributor to the *Water Cure Journal,* a magazine addressing women's needs and their role in health reform, with a circulation of over 10,000. It was, in effect, a home-health-care guide—a substitute for the general medical practitioner, who was rapidly losing influence with America's women. Nichols stated her motives clearly. "I wish to teach mothers how to cure their own diseases, and those of their children; and to increase health, purity, and happiness in the family and the home."[9] Topics she wrote about included cooking, childhood problems, sexuality, bathing, teething, and domestic economy.

She and other reformers took on the huge and thankless task of trying to modify women's dress. Clothing was seen as a symbol of the women's rights movement as well as health reform. The "Gone with the Wind" styles, with their huge petticoats and whalebone corsets, were prisons which impeded breath and movement. "We can expect but small achievement from women so long as it is the labor of their lives to carry about their clothes."[10] Women were shown diagrams exaggerating the damage done to their internal organs by stays and tight lacings. Patterns of healthier styles such as bloomers and little dresses worn over trousers (in the East Indian fashion) were published. Such loose, healthy, sensible clothing did not overwhelm the world of fashion. Predictably, women who dared to adopt the new styles were ridiculed, and their femininity called into question.

An avid and energetic educator, Nichols argued that ignorance could no longer be an excuse for illness. She and other reformers thought medical information should be available to all and took issue with the jargon of medical journals. "If you cannot understand what an author is writing about, you may reasonably presume he does not know himself." Nichols supported the efforts of women to become physicians. "What will our Allopathic doctors say to this? We pause for a reply. In the meantime, our women are buckling on the armor for a struggle which must ultimately prove successful."[11]

Mary Gove Nichols was a protégé of Sylvester Graham (the developer of graham flour and crackers), whose followers ate a vegetarian diet, abstained from stimulants, wore sensible dress, and promoted the benefits of exercise, fresh air, and sexual purity. The latter usually meant infrequent or, preferably, no sex, and absolutely no masturbation under any circumstances. Whether Nichols agreed with "sexual purity," however, is doubtful. She clearly saw through the obfuscated idea of female passionlessness: "A healthy and loving woman is impelled to material union as surely, often as strongly, as man. . . . The apathy of [her] sexual instinct is caused by the enslaved and unhealthy condition in which she lives."[12]

From her experiences with Grahamism and other movements, Mary Gove Nichols developed her own sectarian enterprise—the water cure, which will be discussed in the next section.

SECTARIAN ANSWERS TO HEROICS

During the nineteenth-century challenge to medical care, schools of thought and techniques abounded. The patent medicine industry flourished. Lydia Pinkham's vegetable tonic for female problems, which was 18 percent alcohol, was a household staple. Pinkham's gentle face was everywhere. For some country publications, hers was the only female face in stock, so it was used when they published stories about other women, including Queen Victoria! Pinkham's influence went far beyond her face and potion. She also dispensed advice, promising the thousands of women who wrote to her of their female troubles that no man would ever lay eyes on her correspondence.[13]

Before the end of the century, gizmos and gadgets of all kinds were available to cure every manner of disease. Systems such as mesmerism, phrenology, and numerous "natural" botanics made their appearance. The three most influential systems were hydrotherapy (water cure), homeopathy, and the botanic remedies of Samuel Thomson.[14] The popularity of these systems largely relied on women's desire for more gentle, natural healing methods and for something they could use to help themselves and their children.

Hydrotherapy (Water Cure)

Nichols was one of three pioneers in the country who opened water cure establishments, general healing centers from which health care and domestic advice were dispensed. Here, water was used in every conceivable way. People were dipped, dunked, douched, and hosed, and given draughts of water to drink. The water cures could be administered by anyone after minimal study, in keeping with Nichols's goal of making physicians obsolete by teaching mothers to cure the diseases of their families and keep them in good health.

The most celebrated convert to the water cure was Ellen White, prophetess of the Seventh-Day Adventist church. White's two ailing sons completely recovered after being treated at a water-cure establishment. In one of her frequent visions, White was led to develop her own water-cure establishment. Her associate, John Harvey Kellogg (of Kellogg's cornflakes) became the most prolific writer on hydrotherapy. Through the strong influence of White, the healing mission of the Seventh-Day Adventists—with its emphasis on healthy living, combined with the best medical care—persists today.

Thomsonians

Samuel Thomson, a New Hampshire farmer, popularized a type of botanic medicine he had learned at the side of a female herbalist.[15] Unlike the water cures, Thomson's remedies were proposed as medical treatment for active disease. His battle cry, "Every man his own physician," argued that self-medication was better than being doctored to death.

The Thomsonian press was probably irresistible to all who harbored suspicions about the effectiveness of the heroic medicine of the "regular" doctors: "We . . . ardently long to lead our readers away from the rocky cliffs, the miney depths, and the scorching sands of the mineralogical practice, to the fruitful fields, green pastures, and flowery banks of sweetly-gliding streams and grassy fountain sides, to gather roots, and leaves, and blossoms, barks and fruits, for . . . healing."[16] Thomson and his agents sold a packaged and patented medical deal called "Family Rights." This enabled the family to enroll, receive his publications, and practice his brand of medicine. By 1840, an estimated three million persons were using his system. He emphasized the wife and mother as the physician, providing women with a medical practice of sorts—one that had no legal restrictions. A big sales feature was that women could be doctor to each other, avoiding the mortification of sharing their problems with the opposite sex.

As they opened botanic medical schools and expanded their vistas, the Thomsonians began to function more like regular doctors. Arguments and strife within the organization over the nature of medical education led to a significant waning in the influence of its methods during the 1840s.

Homeopathy

By 1840, however, homeopathy was on the rise. Homeopaths use infinitesimal doses of pharmacologic preparations, based upon the idea of similars or "like cures like." It is a medical philosophy that strengthened as time wore on, becoming a major competitor with allopathic medicine before the end of the century. Homeopathy is currently enjoying a rebirth of interest for many of the reasons it had allure over one hundred years ago.

Homeopathic preparations were not bad tasting and didn't have the side-effects of heroic medicine. Oliver Wendell Holmes quipped that homeopathy "gives the ignorant, who have such an inveterate itch for dabbling in physic, a book and a doll's medicine chest, and lets them play doctors and doctoresses without fear of having to call in the coroner."[17] Other regular physicians noted some distinct benefit from homeopathy, but tended to attribute it to the idea that homeopathic preparations were useless—but not harmful—with the patient's improvement due to benign neglect.

By 1860 there were an estimated 2,500 homeopathic physicians, with hundreds of thousands of followers, over two-thirds of them women.[18] "Domestic kits"—small mahogany boxes containing numbered vials of the remedies and a do-it-yourself cookbook for diagnosis—were the cornerstone of women's practices. "Many a woman, armed with her little stock of remedies, has converted an entire community," according to the American Institute of Homeopathy.

Homeopathy also interested Mary Baker Eddy, the founder of Christian Science. She was convinced that the effectiveness of homeopathy depended upon the power of the mind, since there was a relative absence of chemicals in the dosages. (Further elaboration of her ideas is presented in the next chapter.)

THE CONCLUSION OF THE POPULAR HEALTH REFORM MOVEMENT

The people associated with the health reform movement were remarkable women from an equally remarkable time. Had they lived in centuries past they would have been severely punished, murdered, or otherwise silenced. At last, after years barren of woman's influence, the profession of healing was being swayed by women's thought.

Women saw the light through the changing ideology of a culture, its health reforms, and through sectarian institutions. The latter welcomed their female constituents with open arms, seeing in them the portal to the families of America. The free-for-all antiprofessionalism of the Jacksonian era supported an eclectic approach to women's domestic medicine. Women capitalized on their long-awaited opportunity, crossing the bridge from the private to the public sphere, and into the healing professions. During their initial foray into the professions, they carried the traditionally female healing themes of prevention through healthy lifestyle, treatment with natural remedies, and compassion as a healing modality. The work of these women opened doors and laid the ground for others to practice in the three modern professions associated with healing: medicine, nursing, and the ministry.

15   The Warriors: Doctors, Nurses, and Ministers

THE IDEOLOGY OF the nineteenth century included a new concept of woman as morally and spiritually superior to males; she was no longer as greatly feared for her mysterious wisdom and primal power. With these changes in attitude as well as the emergence of the popular health movement, women began to enter the health professions. Many became physicians in independent practice. However, before the century closed, women were effectively pigeonholed into levels of service devoid of authority and independence. At the same time, the American medical system was taking on its unique character, moving toward becoming a monolithic organization that now dominates the present century. The strength of its medical dogma, subsumed under and supported by religious, educational, and business institutions in this country, can only be compared to the Church's long and powerful influence over the Western world. How did women healers allow themselves to be eclipsed by institutional domination once again? We will examine those issues in the context of the birth and development of women's healing professions.

THE WOMEN AND THEIR PROFESSIONS

The feminine healing perspective of the last half of the nineteenth century was manifested in three major ways: the training of a relatively large number of women physicians, the establishment of nursing as a profession, and the founding of churches which have an integral healing doctrine. This chapter will provide a picture of the women behind these movements, how they managed to move out of the shadows, and what can be learned from their experiences.

All three professional groups of women—nurses, physicians, and ministers—grew in different directions, but from the same Victorian roots. The women who made a difference in these fields had qualities that challenged the Victorian ideal—the qualities of warriorship: energy, strength, dignity, and a sense of purpose. Their visions projected far into the future, and they influenced their own time in remarkable ways.

Each had a single-minded vision beyond the ordinary. For example, Mary Putnam Jacobi, M.D., at age ten described a dream in a letter to her grandmother:

Vague longings beset me. I imagine great things and glorious deeds; but Ah! the vision passes like a fleeting dream and the muddy reality is left behind. I would be great. I would do deeds, so that after I had passed into that world, that region beyond the grave, I should be spoken of with affection so that I should live again in the hearts of those I have left behind me.[1]

The visions of Mary Baker Eddy and Ellen White were more concrete—guiding them to the establishment of their own healing ministries.

Furthermore, the women who made a difference were articulate. They wrote and they talked to whoever would listen. Many of them, particularly the women physicians, wrote volumes to each other, establishing a sisterhood that would sustain their bodies and souls through some of the most arduous work that women would ever be called upon to do.

They never took "no" for an answer. Instead, they learned the system well enough that if one way was blocked, they found another way to meet their goals. They had no illusions about the opposition to their presence and ideas. In order to get the hospital reforms she knew were needed, Florence Nightingale peppered the offices of government officials with her written demands, and when that didn't work, she pestered, cajoled, bribed, and blackmailed. She used friendships and family ties to meet her goals. The women physicians and their supporters also knew the power of the dollar—how to raise money and use it appropriately.

In the beginning, women's support networks were nonexistent, so it is of some note that most of the exceptional women also had an exceptional man in their lives: an indulgent father who saw to his daughter's superior education, or a nonconformist father, or a husband who provided emotional and financial support. A handful of brave and influential male physicians also believed that the profession would be exalted by the presence of women, and they actively supported their efforts.

Many of the women who made outstanding strides in health care were ornery and autocractic and didn't much care what anybody else thought of them. Florence Nightringale and Mary Baker Eddy had particularly sharp tongues. The women physicians, on the other hand, needed to exercise all their social graces for the sake of survival in the male medical community.

In discussing the three professional groups that women entered—medicine, nursing, and the ministry—the greater emphasis will be on medicine. It was that field to which many women aspired, causing heated debate and political furor. By no means does this focus imply that "woman as healer" was now exclusively synonymous with "woman as physician." Yet it is through the women physicians that the river of continuity flows with such breadth and brilliance during the nineteenth century.

LADY DOCTORS OR "DOCTORESSES"

Harriot Hunt, Elizabeth and Emily Blackwell, Ann Preston, Marie Zakrzewska, Mary Putnam Jacobi, and so many others—these are names well known within a limited circle of medical historians. Their pictures still grace dark hospital halls; their names are on plaques. Yet, women physicians today know so little of their predecessors, and those who have other healing vocations have not known to draw upon their strength and wisdom. Each of their lives reads like a good novel, full of action, courage, and great deeds. A few of their stories are briefly told below.

Harriot Hunt (1805–1875)

At age forty-two, Harriot Hunt decided she needed more medical education. She had practiced as a physician for twelve years, having served an apprenticeship with a husband and wife who were naturalist physicians. In those days, far less experience than Harriot had would have qualified a man for an honorary degree without further ado. Hunt sent her application to Oliver Wendell Holmes, dean of Harvard Medical School, stating that she hoped to get from Harvard a "scientific light." Holmes supported her application, convinced of her maturity and zeal. Her photograph perhaps also convinced him that this stout, matronly woman was unlikely to stir up any sexual longings among the students.

The administration dismissed her application without review as "inexpedient." Hunt thought the decision barbaric. Always a private person, and certainly not an activist, she joined the newly organized women's rights movement, seeing it as a ray of light penetrating the gloom.[2] When she learned that Elizabeth Blackwell had been accepted at a regular medical college, she resubmitted her application, reminding the review board that attitudes toward women were changing: it was no longer a question of women practicing, but of their receiving adequate training. This time, the administration softened and agreed to allow her and three black male applicants to attend lectures, with the warning that admission to classes should not be construed as the right to claim a degree.

Before Hunt could attend a single lecture, the senior class of students drew up a petition which protested the presence of Hunt as well as that of the "socially repulsive" blacks. The petition requested that they be asked leave to protect the dignity of the school. The protest against Hunt was worded in part: "We are not opposed to allowing woman her rights, but do protest against her appearing in places where her presence is calculated to destroy our respect for the modesty and delicacy of her sex."[3] They asserted that no woman of true delicacy would choose to be in the presence of men to listen to such discussions necessary for the medical student, and that women who would do so were predisposed to "unsex" themselves. In response, the trustees passed a resolution prohibiting the admission of women. Harvard enforced this policy until 1946.

Harriot Hunt led an active and productive life as a physician for over a quarter of a century, receiving an honarary degree from the Female Medical College of Pennsylvania in 1853. She worked with good cheer, and remained determined "to awaken public thought to the positive need of women entering the profession."[4] On the silver anniversary of her practice, 1,500 friends crowned her with a double wreath of flowers and gave her a gold ring to consecrate her marriage to the profession. The ceremony became a model for feminists who saw a need to honor the special lives of single women. When Hunt died in 1875, she was buried under a statue of Hygeia, the goddess of healing, a statue she had commissioned herself from Edmonia Lewis, a black woman sculptor.

Elizabeth Blackwell (1821–1910) and Emily Blackwell (1826–1910)

After her applications had been rejected by schools in Boston, New York, and Philadelphia, Elizabeth Blackwell was accepted by Geneva Medical College in upstate New York. Her acceptance was a fluke, an ironic circumstance of the first order: the students thought the application was a joke and voted unanimous approval. They were shocked when a young woman actually appeared on the first day of class. They survived the jolt, and tolerated her presence. An editorial in the *Boston Medical and Surgical Journal* described her as "a pretty little specimen of the feminine gender. . . . She comes to class with great composure, takes off her bonnet and puts it under the seat (exposing a fine phrenology), takes notes constantly. . . . Great decorum is preserved while she is present."[5]

In 1849, Dr. Elizabeth Blackwell graduated at the top of her class, the first American woman to obtain a medical degree. Soon after, Geneva Medical College closed its doors to women. Blackwell then encountered a difficulty that would plague women for the next century—the inability to obtain advanced study or quality residence training in the United States. She traveled to Europe where opportunities for clinical experience were more plentiful. Meanwhile, her sister Emily also decided to study medicine, despite Elizabeth's discouraging comment that "a blank wall of social and professional antagonism faces the woman physician that forms a situation of painful loneliness, leaving her without support, respect or professional counsel."[6]

After being rejected by eleven medical schools, Emily was accepted by Rush Medical College in Chicago. The state medical society objected to her presence, and pressured the college to rescind her application, which it did within the year. She then finished her training at Western Reserve Medical College in Cleveland, and, like her sister, went to Europe for the additional training that would make her an outstanding physician of her time.

Ann Preston (1813–1872)

Ann Preston began her studies with a Quaker physician in 1847, the same year Elizabeth Blackwell entered Geneva. After two years of apprenticeship, she submitted applications to four medical schools, and was rejected by all of them.

Preston was from a progressive Quaker family who had participated in feminist activities, and the temperance and abolition movements. Elizabeth Blackwell described her first impression of her:

> On a wild snowy winter morning, a delicate, refined Quaker lady, called at my consultation room, to tell me about the movement she was engaged in, for the establishment of a thoroughly organized Medical College for Women in Philadelphia. . . . The courage and hope of that fragile lady, who came to me out of the wild snow storm, was an omen of success. I felt sure that she would succeed.[7]

In 1850 Preston established the first regular woman's college in the world—the Woman's Medical College of Pennsylvania. She was assisted by a group of male Quaker physicians who were frustrated in their attempts to find college placement for their women apprentices.

Soon after her graduation, Preston became a professor of physiology. She managed to have her students admitted to lectures at Pennsylvania Hospital, where they were less-than-cordially received. One of her students, Elizabeth Keller (later to become chief of surgery at the New England Hospital for Women and Children), recalled, "We entered in a body, amidst jeerings, groaning, whistlings, and stamping of feet by the men students. . . . On leaving the hospital, we were actually stoned by those so-called gentlemen."[8]
Newspaper accounts corroborated the incident.

> Ranging themselves in line, these gallant gentlemen assailed the young ladies . . . with insolent and offensive language, and then followed them into the street, where the whole gang . . . joined in insulting them. . . . During the last hour missiles of paper, tinfoil, tobacco-quids, etc., were thrown upon the ladies, while some of these men defiled the dresses of the ladies near them with tobacco-juice.[9]

By 1879, about three hundred women had graduated from medical schools. The persistence of these women demanded that the opposition

---

formulate their views. And, in turn, the women were required to defend their vocational choice.

TAKING SIDES

The ensuing debate made the midwife controversy discussed in the last chapter look like a mere squabble. The case stated against women entering medicine centered on the traditional fear that their activities in the workplace would erode the fabric of the home, the family, and the nature of civilization. It was held that their pure and divine presence in the domestic arena was necessary to control the brute instincts of man and provide him succor during his weary hours. Women, it was asserted, were the moral guardians of society, whose role it was "to rear the offspring and ever fan the flame of piety, patriotism and love upon the sacred altar of her home."[10] Such rhetoric was common; overworked metaphors about women were rife.

Men also argued that woman's greatest charms—her modesty and delicacy—must be protected at all costs, for woman's sake as well as for the men who loved them. The rituals of the dissecting room, the blood and gore of surgery, and most of all, the unveiling of the mysteries of the human body would be more than a refined woman should bear.

On the other hand, physicians were encouraging women to become nurses, even though nurses, too, had to leave the home, work at backbreaking tasks, and be exposed to the "indecencies" of hospital life.

Another line of argument was that women must be protected from the dangers of education itself. Dr. E. H. Clarke's book *Sex in Education; or, A Fair Chance for the Girls,* evoked the most controversy. For years, Clarke had pretended to be a women's advocate, urging that the "experiment" be tried to see if women could master science and medicine. Then he homed in on the female physiology, addressing "the facts that physicians can best supply," claiming that "higher education for women produces monstrous brains and puny bodies, abnormally active cerebration and abnormally weak digestion, flowing thought and constipated bowels."[11] He cited case histories of women whose organs and functions were badly deformed by higher learning, and lists of symptoms a woman foolish enough to educate herself might expect. He spoke of his conclusions to alarmed women's groups, who, at that time, had no scientific retort.

Women's intellect and emotional stability were likewise assaulted. Limited by nature in their intellectual capacity, women were irrational, impulsive, unable to do mathematics, deficient in judgment and courage. Further, they were nervous, excitable, and subject to uncontrolled hysteria.[12] Dr. Horatio Storer, one of the most outspoken opponents of women, claimed that "although women make the best nurses, they do not inspire confidence as doctors since their judgment varies from month to month."[13]

Men also complained that women were badly trained. Some were, of course, but many were trained in state-of-the-art medicine. A comparative study of curricula and clinical offerings in several nineteenth-century medical schools suggests that women who attended the regular women's colleges had a vigorous, progressive, and demanding course of study.[14]

Menstruation—poorly understood and treated as a disease—was also used as a reason why women should stay out of the professions. A prescription of complete bedrest was not unusual. How could women be expected to practice medicine regularly under these conditions? Never mind that the majority of lower-class women had already entered the work force, returning home after fourteen-hour shifts to attend to domestic chores. There was little concern for their biological condition. Nor did the same objections apply to nurses whose labors often began before the light of day and ended long after the doctors had made their rounds—regardless of the time of the month. Nevertheless, biological justification replaced morality issues as arguments against professional women.

WOMAN'S POSITION/WOMAN'S DEFENSE

The position against women was so widespread—in the popular press, in medical journals, in public talks—that women were pressed into defining their goals as well as justifying their apparent violation of the Victorian ideology.

Women saw themselves as filling a niche unfilled by men's medicine. Their role was to address the special needs of women and children, as well as what they saw lacking in medicine in general. Women believed their natural abilities to nurture would provide a gentler and more caring side to medicine. Dr. Harriot Hunt suggested that men be given the curative department and women the preventative. Others agreed, including Prudence Saur, who in her graduation thesis in 1871 stated, "How much more God-like to prevent as well as cure."

Preventive medicine, despite its promise to move the nation's health forward, was and is a less-than-glamorous stepchild, consistently employing more women from many professional fields. It was the observation of the time that men shunned the time-consuming, often tedious task of educating others in self-help skills that would help people ward off many of their own health problems. Women, too, felt they had a natural talent for teaching; as it happened, they gravitated toward the lower-paying, less prestigious fields of public health and health education.

Women physicians and their supporters cleverly turned the morality arguments in their own favor, using them to justify women caring for other women. Elizabeth Blackwell claimed that it was both unnatural and monstrous that women had no resort to turn to other than men. Passively accepting this, she believed, "would indicate a terrible deficiency in some of the most important elements of womanly character." Decent, good women, then, must actively protest the medical opinion that holds that women have no place in medicine.[15] An active supporter of women, Dr. J. P. Chesney of Missouri, reminded his readers that if the traditionalists' own logic had been applied regarding feminine virtue and delicacy, "men would long ago have been banished from obstetrics." He went on to say, "It is an idea extremely paradoxical to suppose that woman, the fairest and best of God's handiwork, and practical medicine, a calling little less sacred than the holy ministry itself, should, when united, become a loathsome abomination . . . from which virtue must stand widely aloof."[16]

Women in medicine were not to replace men, but to serve in those areas dictated by modesty, and to enhance those fields in which male physicians were either uninterested or negligent. These are the integrative behaviors of a minority group: fill an uninhabited niche, take nothing away that belongs to the dominant class. Primarily, women viewed themselves as functioning in areas that were a natural extension of the domestic sphere. As the Blackwells stated, they were to be the connecting link between the science of the medical profession and the everyday life of women.

The creation of a noncompetitive arena within medicine was woman's only recourse at the time. Men would have never permitted women to make the grudging progress that they did if they had been competing on the same turf. Women's desire to specialize not only allowed them entry into medicine, it also reflected their deeply felt need to serve in a more feminized healing capacity. In the short run, it launched women's medicine; in the long run, though, women's medicine, taught by women to women and for women, was far too vulnerable to stand alone.

The question of woman's biological incapacity was, it seemed to women, one that must be thoroughly researched in order to counter medical opinion. Dr. E. H. Clarke's book had outraged the feminist community in Boston and elsewhere, triggering heated public debate. Harvard responded by announcing that the topic for the coveted Boylston Medical Prize competition was, "Do women require mental and bodily rest during menstruation and to what extent?"

Dr. Mary Putnam Jacobi submitted her research and won. After finding that their selection was written by a woman, the judges debated over breaking with convention in order to award her the prize, but decided in her favor.

Jacobi surveyed 1,000 women and ran tests on a smaller sample of women hospitalized in the New York Infirmary. Her results were at odds with Clarke's opinion. She showed that the majority of women suffered no incapacity during menstruation, but also that women could better tolerate any menstrual distress by continuing their normal work patterns. Harvard did not publish Jacobi's prizewinning monograph, but her wealthy publishing family—of the firm G. P. Putnam—saw her work into print.[17]

Study after study followed Mary Putnam Jacobi's work. In 1881, Drs. Emily Pope, Emma Call, and C. Augusta Pope, staff physicians at New England Hospital, published a study of 430 women who had graduated from medical school. Only 13 reported being in poor health during menstruation, and only 34 said they were periodically incapacitated.[18]

The impact of these studies is difficult to assess. At best, they tempered the arguments about women's biological inferiority, shifting them to other areas of concern. But the barriers to women's entering the profession did not self-destruct as a result of their publication.

By 1890, about 75 percent of female medical students were being trained in regular (as opposed to sectarian) colleges. However, few institutions offered clinical rotations, so medical education was primarily theoretical: one could graduate without having seen a single patient. The normal routes to postdoctoral clinical training were closed to the women of America, depending as they did upon acceptance by the "old boy" network. Women had two avenues available to them: to go to Europe, as the Blackwells had, or to establish their own clinical training facilities. The latter were exclusively for the care of women and children. Thus, despite the hurdles, many women managed to put together a program for themselves that compared favorably with those undertaken by their male colleagues.

Two of the most brilliant women, Marie Zakrzewska and Mary Putnam Jacobi, argued that women must outshine their male colleagues in order to survive within the profession. Taking up the tasks that men considered demeaning, boring, or otherwise of little consequence would only relegate women to the lower echelons of medical practice. Mediocre women doctors would doom their cause, as would those who had no grounding in general medical practice. The tactics that had sufficiently blunted male resentment would ultimately be their downfall. Both Zak (as she was called) and Jacobi were in the second wave of women, following in the wake of Hunt, the Blackwells, and others. Their struggle to enter the professions was cushioned by the work of the earlier women, and by a well-established feminist network. Therefore, their vision of the future was less occluded by the birth pangs of past years.

Marie Zakrzewska (1829–1902)

Marie Zakrzewska's story sets the stage for the beginning and the end of the gilded era in women's medicine. It also exemplifies the success of the woman-healer network, and the importance of the support of special men. At age ten, "Zak" had an eye infection, and was cared for by a physician who was struck by her intensity and interest in medicine; he took her on hospital rounds and loaned her medical books. At twenty, she was the youngest woman accepted to the government midwifery school. She trained under the mentorship of Dr. Joseph Schmidt, and later was appointed to the important post of chief midwife and professor at the Charité Hospital in Berlin. But fate intervened. Hours after her appointment, Schmidt, her chief supporter, died. Zak served in her appointed capacity for a while, but political infighting and jealousy caused her to resign and go to America. There, she was certain, science would have no sex. It is worth noting that during her tenure in Berlin, not one case of childbed fever was registered. She was applying higher standards of cleanliness long before they were widely accepted in the United States and elsewhere.

Zak had a dream of completing medical school and establishing her own hospital. Elizabeth Blackwell, recognizing her talent and ambition, found her to be the first student she thought worthy of a great investment of her time. Blackwell saw that she was admitted to Cleveland Medical College. Dr. Harriot Hunt provided a scholarship. Dr. Blackwell gave Zak her medical books. Caroline Severance, president of a ladies' physiological society and a suffragist, found funds to pay her board.

After Zak graduated in 1856, she encountered the obstacles of an un-friendly America. Her attempts to secure office space were met by landlords who thought she was a spiritualist in disguise, or who did not think a woman physician would meet the rents, or who asked prohibitively high rents. Finally, she opened an office in Elizabeth Blackwell's house.

Within a year, Zak's fundraising skills and the unflagging support of numerous men and women in the Northeast served to establish the New York Infirmary for Women and Children. It was the first hospital ever run entirely by women, guaranteeing that women would receive the clinical training necessary to attain knowledge and stature in their profession. Zak served as chief physician without pay; her only income came from private practice. Her work began each morning at 5:30 when she went to market to purchase groceries and to beg and buy hospital supplies. After a day of rounds, treatment, and consultation, she met regularly with her students at 9:00 p.m. They cut, basted, rolled, and folded towels and other hospital supplies as they recited their lessons; their work day ended shortly before midnight.

Zak established the post of "sanitary visitor," a person who visited the slums to offer treatment, as well as information on sanitation, nutrition, hygiene, and ventilation. Her work, and that of her colleagues, served as a bridge between domestic values and the professional world.

Her New York hospital flourishing, Zak then established the New England Hospital for Women and Children in 1861. She also sought membership in the Massachusetts Medical Society, with the encouragement of several male supporters in the organization. Acceptance within this society was extremely important to women, as it signified that they were no longer considered "pretenders" to the profession. An examination was involved, comparable to the licensure process that was instituted at a later date. Zak's application was refused repeatedly on the basis of her gender, but not without months of discussion. The opportunity to sit for the examinations was not offered to her until 1884, after she had practiced for twenty-six years. She declined. That same year, Emma Call was the first woman accepted into the society.

Zak's illustrious career was bolstered not only by powerful feminist support, but also by the goodwill of some established physicians. Accordingly, she advised women to stay away from irregular (in particular, homeopathic) practices. Her interests were clearly in the realm of body cure, not mind cure, and she had little respect or interest in the latter.

Zak heeded the conventions of regular medicine well, knowing that the life of her clinics depended upon referrals and support from her male colleagues. She strove to attain excellence within the system, in hopes of changing the system. This woman probably had more experience in obstetrics than any man in the country, yet she proudly told Dr. Lucy Sewall that her colleague, Dr. Samuel Cabot, did not feel it necessary that she call him for forceps deliveries. "You see, he rightly supposes we use the forceps *skillfully*."[19]

At the height of a childbed fever epidemic in Boston, only one patient in Zak's hospital died. Five hundred women died during the same time period at Boston Lying-in Hospital. Subsequent examinations of the records show that the female practitioners were more interested in antiseptic procedures and were more sympathetic to the women's conditions than those of their male colleagues. They were also more likely to let nature take its course during births, avoiding the frequent and unnecessary use of scalpel and forceps.

Mary Putnam Jacobi (1842–1906)

The next wave of advancement—integration into mainstream, coeducational training—came from women such as Mary Putnam Jacobi. She was a remarkable woman, even in comparison with the other physicians of her century. Had there been more like her, women and their medicine might have flourished through the twentieth century.

Mary Putnam received her medical degree in March 1864, and took her postdoctoral work at the École de Médicine in Paris. The first woman to graduate from this prestigious institution, she was also awarded high academic honors. She married a German revolutionary who was trained as a pediatrician; he became her colleague and father of their three children.

Mary Putnam Jacobi was a pathfinder. She sought to create a scientific spirit that she found lacking among American women. Too, she insisted that human compassion and pure science were equally essential to the practice of medicine.

Jacobi organized groups to support women in medicine, was a popular spokesperson, and published over one hundred papers. One of the first to warn women about their endangered careers, she was concerned that they not be educated exclusively in women's colleges. In 1882, she manifested her desire to see a masculine and feminine balance in medicine by accepting a teaching position at the male-run New York Post-Graduate Medical School, the first woman to be offered such a post. Always the professional, as she was dying she wrote an article on the malady with which she had been afflicted— "Early Symptoms of the Meningeal Tumor Compressing the Cerebellum."

At her memorial service, Dr. William Osler, one of the most eminent and humanitarian physicians of all time, said that the scientific character of her work gave a new distinction to women in this country. It was largely through her work, he further stated, that the strong animus that had kept women out of schools and medical societies had been allayed.

Mary Putnam Jacobi hoped to improve society at large by feminizing it. She saw women's entry into medicine as the vehicle for the greater good. Concerned that women receive due recognition as equal human beings in every respect, Jacobi believed that women themselves must change before this goal could be realized. "If you cannot learn to act without masters," she warned, "you evidently will never become the real equals of those who do."[20] She was dismayed at the turmoil among the ranks of women. "Unfortunately, it often happens with weaker parties that they intensify their own weakness by internal discords at the very moment that the closest union, the most frank and fraternal friendship, can alone save their cause and win the day."[21]

MONEY TALKS

Women did not unanimously agree with Jacobi that coeducation was vital, although some of the most powerful and vocal women were in firm accord. In 1865, women in Boston and New York raised $50,000 to endow women's scholarships at leading medical schools. Their money, summarily rejected by all to whom it was tendered, was eventually given to the Blackwells' hospital, but the spirit of the intent lived on.[22] In 1870, Cornell accepted women's gifts of a building and a $25,000 endowment for women medical students. In 1878, Marion Hovey of Boston offered Harvard $10,000 with the provision that women be admitted to the medical school. After much debate on the potential disasters that might strike if women were admitted, the administration decided to refuse the money, with the insinuation that next time the women showed up, it had better be with a bigger purse.

Through the fundraising efforts of M. Carey Thomas, Dean of Bryn Mawr College, as well as feminists and medical educators, $500,000 was gathered for the cause of medical coeducation. This time, Harvard was not even considered as a recipient—the endowment was given to Johns Hopkins University. For years, they had been trying to open a medical school but lacked the funds to complete their plans. With women's money, the most prestigious medical school in the country was established, on the condition that women were to be welcomed on the same terms as men. The admission of women was widely regarded as the most propitious event in feminist history.

When the medical school at Johns Hopkins finally opened for classes in 1893, about 75 percent of the other medical schools quickly adopted a coeducational policy. Women comprised 25–37 percent of the enrollment in the regular schools. Forty-two percent of the graduates of Tufts University Medical School in 1900 were women.

Despite the claims of women's intellectual inferiority, by 1897, women were capturing the greater percentage of academic honors in graduating medical classes. Furthermore, 90 percent of the women trained as physicians were working in the capacity in which they were educated, according to a survey taken in 1900.

THE END OF THE GILDED AGE

The gilded age for women in medicine ended quickly and silently. The reasons for its demise are ironic and complex. To understand their bearing on the present state of women in medicine, it is important to examine the problems and to identify causes when possible.

Around the turn of the century, after the wave of coeducation, all but one of the women's medical colleges had closed. Women saw little reason to keep them open. They had fulfilled their purpose of giving women a foothold in a medical world that was forbidden to them by the male institutions. With women so active and successful in regular coeducation schools, there was no need to provide separate educational facilities.

By 1898, physicians were singing the financial blues. An editorial in the

Journal of the American Medical Association complained, "The profession is overcrowded already to the starving point."[23] Their worst fears had been realized. The feminization of the profession had resulted in an inevitable decrease in salary and prestige. The American Medical Association declared that the standing and influence of the profession depended on "the material success and financial independence of its members,"[24] and both were seen as seriously challenged.

One by one the medical colleges stopped approving women's applications, or set up other, more subtle, barriers to their attendence, although the existence of quotas on women is typically denied.[25] The medical school at Johns Hopkins, which owed its existence to women's money, experienced a drop in women graduates from 33 percent of its total in 1896 to 3 percent in 1910. The worst offenders neglected to publish their enrollment figures during the times of the greatest cut in numbers of women, during which time the enrollments of Jews and blacks also dropped precipitously. Unfortunately, women's foothold was never strong enough to influence decisions at the administrative level.

Not being accepted into medical school was not the only problem women faced in establishing themselves as physicians. The "old boy" network was alive and well in the tracking systems that placed medical graduates in internship and residency training positions, so women had difficulty in fulfilling their postgraduate commitments. The tight referral network among physicians also worked against the women who elected to enter private practice.

Only a few short years before, women had been provided with ample clinical training and postgraduate experience in their own colleges and teaching hospitals. Many of these were consolidated or closed in the spirit of coeducational optimism. Women were left with nowhere to go, having trusted that they had reached a state of equality in medicine.

Did women contribute to their own problems? Jacobi and others believed so. In an age of increasing scientism and specialization, women's interests remained sequestered in an outmoded Victorian ideology. Furthermore, women could not come to an agreement on an effective stance. Should they bond together? Or should they act, think, talk, and try to associate with men so as to mask their differences? Should they try to add something new to medicine, fill undesirable roles, or excel on their male colleague's territory? They divided into factions, with no one position holding strength.

The women who would have recognized the danger signs were either very old or dead. The energy for activism was fading quickly, and there was no strong feminist movement to spearhead change and thwart the impending disaster. Women who had entered the profession without a struggle did not know how to fight, nor, in all likelihood, did they care to. They had already achieved their professional goals and were perhaps unaware that women's enrollment in the schools had declined so rapidly.

The argument favoring women treating women was no longer the issue it had been in the past. "Modern" woman no longer felt she needed to protect her virtue by seeking women physicians. A significant market therefore collapsed, and women physicians—because of their sex—were no longer in great demand. They had created a niche for themselves based on outmoded virtues. Those who were rejecting women as potential independent caregivers saw no need to drag out the old reasons having to do with female biology and psychology. Women had already proven themselves suitably robust for the task. It was much easier to just quietly close the door on women than to advance arguments or reasons. And so, supported by medical reform and an alliance of corporate power and money, medicine became masculine again.

After 1900, women who chose to be independent practitioners in the health professions were rare. Women were more likely to enter the blossoming field of nursing.

NURSING

There have always been nurses, just as there have always been midwives. Florence Nightingale herself often said, "Every woman is a nurse."[26] But the professional nurse is a modern development.

Information on the history and character of nursing and on legislation affecting it is readily available from many other sources. Our interest lies in addressing the issue facing a large number of nurses today: how might they function in the lineage of woman as healer, given the nature of the profession?

I believe the nurses who identify with the image of woman as healer will find kindred spirits in the Blackwells, Marie Zakrzewska, Mary Putnam Jacobi, and the other women physicians and reformers of the nineteenth century. Neither they, nor the nurse healers today, fit the conceptual mold of their professions. There is another territory here, one that both encompasses and transcends professional bounds. But because the professions, like the guilds, largely dictate practice, it benefits us to look at the ontology of nursing.

Nurses weren't much written about for centuries because they were servants. Nonetheless, we know something of the establishment of nursing orders, several of which have been mentioned in this book. The men and women who provided medical care to the Crusades and the monastic nursing orders made an exceptional contribution to healing. After the Reformation, the Catholic contribution to nursing diminished, and the Protestants lagged in fulfilling the demand for dedicated and free assistance to the sick.

Secular nursing was an abysmal substitute. Women of the lowest sort—prostitutes and drunkards—were the only ones willing to perform the duties of the nurse. Convincing them to sober up, clean up, and stop fighting were major problems faced by hospital administrators.

By the 1800s the elegant, towering medieval hospitals had been reduced to rat-infested, sewer-clogged nightmares. It was this world that Florence Nightingale entered as she began her lifelong campaign to establish nursing as a viable and honorable field.

Nightingale (1820–1910), an Englishwoman, was the privileged daughter of a doting father, who saw that she was tutored in history, mathematics, philosophy, Greek, Latin, and several other languages. The young girl showed interest in tending sick animals and a curiosity about the care of human beings. Later, she toured hospitals, spending some time in the more established facilities to learn about how they functioned. In 1853, she was hired as superintendent of the Institution for the Care of Sick Gentlewomen in Distressed Circumstances, installing progress with a heavy hand. For her work, Florence refused to take a salary. It was the least she could do for her family, who were always mortified by her nonconformity. The early years of her career were critical in determining the activities of her life.

When England declared war on Russia in 1854, Nightingale was chosen superintendent of the female nursing establishment in Turkey, the first official wartime assignment ever given an English woman. The conditions she faced were appalling. The hospital at Scutari had been built over an undrained cesspool. The wounded lay uncared for on stinking straw mattresses crawling with vermin, floors oozed slime, and there was no ventilation. The hospital was a breeding ground for diseases such as cholera, which claimed more soldiers than the war itself.

Florence Nightingale worked tirelessly during those years. Young men whom she nursed wrote home about her. Immortalized by Longfellow as "The lady with the lamp," she became highly romanticized. When her demands on the British government to establish a sanitary commission were realized, the death rate in the hospital dropped from 430 per thousand to 22 per thousand within a year.

While in Turkey, Florence Nightingale developed a plan for reorganizing all military hospitals. Upon her return to England in 1856, she led an arduous campaign that was ultimately successful in initiating changes there as well.

Through her work, she had gained a keen understanding of the architectural and staffing requirements of hospitals; within the decade, not a major hospital in the world was planned without her consultation. Despite her progress, she was obsessed with a sense of failure, and greatly fatigued by her political struggles in establishing reforms. By 1857, she had suffered a complete physical and nervous collapse from which she never fully recovered. Nightingale was a practicing nurse for only three years; for the remainder of her ninety-year-long life, she took to her bed as a semi-invalid, wielding her pen as a weapon.

Florence Nightingale was a world-class warrior, yet remains a paradoxical figure. She spoke eloquently about the suffering of humanity, but had little patience or affection for humankind. Her wartime experience fanned a permanent flame, and all else was relegated to the mission of reform of facilities and health care. Complaining that her demands weren't being met by the well-heeled aristocrats in England, she said:

> These people have fed their children on the fat of the land and dressed them in velvet and silk. . . . I have had to see my children dressed in a dirty blanket and an old pair of regimental trowsers, and to see them fed on raw salt meat; and nine thousand of my children are dying, from causes which might have been prevented, in their foreign graves! But I can never forget![27]

Florence Nightingale cared little for other women, and had an active distaste for the proliferative feminist writing of the time. The cause of suffrage would come to naught anyway, she believed, things being what they were. She by no means considered herself a "woman's missionary," remaining, by her own admission, brutally indifferent to the wrongs or rights of her sex. She wrote of women's problems as being self-created, but acknowledged that women were also victims of male oppression.

In June of 1860, the first group of fifteen students enrolled at the Nightingale Training School for Nurses at St. Thomas's Hospital, embarking on a year-long course of formal study that was a radical departure from the haphazard, on-the-job training previously given to nurses. The Nightingale graduates soon headed up schools of nursing the world over.

Florence Nightingale was a difficult taskmaster, demanding hard work and unquestioned obedience. She addressed her nurses:

> Nursing is said, most truly said, to be a high calling, an honourable calling. But what does the honour lie in? In working hard during your training to learn and to do all things perfectly. The honour does not lie in putting on Nursing like your uniform, your dress. . . . Honour lies in loving perfection, consistency, and in working hard for it: in being ready to work patiently: ready to say not "How clever I am!" but "I am not yet worthy; and I will live to deserve and work to deserve to be called a Trained Nurse."[28]

She reminded her students that if there was no cross, there was no crown; admonishing them to work, work, work.

At the onset, the financial autonomy of the Nightingale school protected the students from exploitation as mere hospital attendants, as did Nightingale's insistence that the superintendents of the hospital be women. In this sense, Nightingale's work was initially in line with feminist goals. Too, she elevated the calling far from the slovenly depths into which secular nursing had fallen. More women were seeking work out of necessity, and nursing provided honest labor.

NURSE AS WOMAN

From the beginning, 95–98 percent of nurses have been women. Women were viewed as natural for nursing, for all the reasons they were unsuited to doctoring. They were believed to be more humane and more sympathetic by nature. Nursing was seen as an inborn talent associated with being a wife and a mother. Nothing in the domestic sphere was seemingly violated by women becoming nurses. Nightingale saw nursing as so much a part of being a woman that when licensing examinations were proposed she reacted strongly, stating that one could no more examine a nurse than a mother. "Nursing should not be a profession," said Nightingale, "it should be a calling."[29]

Nursing was the scion of "an articulate and self-conscious elite," brainchild of upper-class, reform-minded women like Nightingale who in turn recruited other women (mostly lower-class, minimally educated) to do the work.[30] Were these women indeed exploiting other women? Were those in authority who bemoaned the lack of assertion and creativity at the same time suppressing it?

A further problem was posed, as Nightingale sought to define nursing. She acknowledged that nursing, as popularly conceived, was limited to little more than applying poultices and administering medications.

> It ought to signify the proper use of fresh air, light, warmth, cleanliness, quiet and proper selection and administration of diet—all at least expense of vital power to the patient. . . . The art of nursing [is to assist] the reparative process.[31]

In this, she echoed the words of the women reformers and physicians for whom she had so little regard.

The most pronounced conflict within the profession came later, when nurses themselves sought to increase their educational requirements, upgrade their skills, and bargain for more economic advantage. It was exactly what Nightingale feared they would do, once the calling became a profession.

In the United States, the larger women's and children's hospitals quickly established nurse training programs after 1860. Hospital administrators discovered that student nurses could be worked for a twelve-hour day with no pay save for room and board. Also, when student nurses were used, mortality rates dropped precipitously. (Hospitals were typically staffed by students; nurses, after graduation usually worked in home-care settings or assisted doctors.)

Funding for the support of nursing programs within standard educational institutions was difficult to obtain. Johns Hopkins had established a nursing school, however, in line with the modernization of medical curricula. Superintendent Isabel Hampton organized the first meeting of what would become the National League of Nursing Education. In 1896, a society was formed, open to all "graduate" nurses (meaning they had a diploma of some kind). This organization became the American Nurses' Association (ANA), which in 1900 established the *American Journal of Nursing*. In this same year, 432 hospital-based schools of nursing turned out 3,456 graduates. A survey revealed that by 1913 there were at least nine types of nursing personnel, representing various levels of training and specialty.

Nursing mirrored the development of American medicine in its organization and training structure. Philosophical conflicts that characterized the beginnings of the nursing profession did not go away. Physicians' attitudes toward nurses, even during the last century, were a mixture of gratitude and concern about their autonomy. An article in the Boston *Medical and Surgical Journal* sang praises to the nurses who went "into the slums of our city, through the dark alleys, among the ash barrels and swill, up the dark, dirty, rickety staircases of the tenements."[32] The physical limitations of being a woman had apparently disappeared. According to this same editorial, the ideal characteristics of a nurse were bodily strength, knowledge of symptoms, the ability to deal with emergencies, and mature judgment.

At the same time, physicians were sometimes patronizing toward nurses, advising them to keep their "proper station." It was apparent early on that some women were trespassing over the line. In 1901 the *Journal of the American Medical Association* charged that many doctors found that a nurse was "often conceited and too unconscious of the due subordination she owes to the medical profession, of which she is sort of a useful parasite."[33] The ability to be "useful parasites" with "mature judgment" was what was desired in nurses. It was also not expected that they would disrupt the medical system by disagreeing with it.

Nursing Sisters

The development of secular nursing has been emphasized here to show the foundations, values, and paradoxes encountered by large numbers of women in the health professions. However, the religious orders also deserve mention. After a rather quiet period following the Reformation, the Catholic commitment to caring for the sick was revitalized. Particularly outstanding were the Sisters of Charity in France, an order introduced into the U.S. by Elizabeth Ann Seton around 1800. Rose Hawthorne (Nathaniel's daughter) founded the Dominican Sisters of the Sick-Poor around 1850. Other orders also sprang up.

The Franciscan nuns associated with Drs. William J. and Charles H. Mayo opened the doors of St. Mary's Hospital in Rochester. "The nuns, by scrimping and saving, had raised all the money themselves and took the initial step leading to the development of one of the greatest medical complexes of all time."[34] The nuns also opened a nursing school and even enrolled in it themselves to refine their skills. The Mayo brothers had only praise for their work: "We had absolute confidence, then as now, in this group of women who have no thought outside their duty to the sick."[35]

American Catholics donated unprecedented sums of money for the brick and mortar of major hospital systems. Within less than a century, there were thousands of Catholic hospitals, serving millions of patients each year. Nearly all of these were the work of religious orders of women, who also established significant numbers of homes for the aged and nursing schools.

> But even thus professionalized, the sisters and their institutions of healing clearly gave priority to cure of soul over cure of body. They acted out of no mere humanitarian impulse, but out of the conviction that performing the corporal works of mercy was a primary means of securing salvation for those who performed them, as well as an occasion of supernatural grace to those for whom they were performed.[36]

Thus, the "good works" were sacramental, as well as ameliorative for those performing them.

The Conjoining of Religion and Health: Woman as Prophet

Healing and the sacred are yoked with the thickest of cords in the human psyche—a connection so stable that all advances in medicine, all the training to the contrary, cannot dislodge one from the other. From the earliest known shamanic cultures to the present day, most humans in most places believe that illness and health are controlled by an unseen deity or supernatural being. And, as in the case of the nursing sisters, caregiving is viewed as a means of securing one's own salvation.

Throughout this story of woman as healer, her fate has been intimately related to the gender of God. When God was a woman, the primary and independent healers were more likely to have been women. In spite of several thousand years of suppression in Western civilization, there were times when women practiced more openly and independently than at others. During the early days of Christianity, and in the eleventh and twelfth centuries, at the time of Trotula and Hildegard, for example, God took on a gentler, more bisexual character.

By the nineteenth century, the cosmology of Western civilization had shifted slightly. The changes did not come from any church, necessarily, but were reflections of the larger complex of issues associated with the Industrial Revolution. The same sociopolitical changes that allowed women to practice as physicians, also loosened the stronghold of religious dogma.

During this time, when women as healer flowered, religion was also becoming more feminized. The edge of women-hatred in the Christian Church was dulled and the fear of women ameliorated. Women were joining churches en masse, supporting them with actions and money, and generally participating in the evangelistic revival. They came forth as prophets, disciples, and the inspiration for many new religious groups.

With pomp and pandemonium, women evangelists were claiming the power to heal through their faith in God. Especially notable was Maria B. Woodworth-Etter (1844–1924), a Winebrennerian Churches of God member, who held mass healing rallies throughout the Midwest in the 1880s. Her healees fell prostrate at her touch, commonly known as "being slain in the spirit," or "resting in Jesus."[37] Her services were described by one journalist as sounding like the "female ward of an insane asylum."

> Dozens were lying around pale and unconscious, rigid and lifeless as though in death. Strong men shouting till they were hoarse, then falling down in a swoon. Women falling over benches and trampled under foot. . . . Aged women gesticulating and hysterically sobbing. . . . Men shouting with a devilish, unearthly laugh.[38]

The Pentecostals, among whom Woodworth-Etter could eventually be counted, waged a holy war, as one of her colleagues put it, against "doctors, drugs, and devils." Such a war against the establishment would not have been tolerated in previous centuries. Maria's great-great-grandmother, had she been associated with such unseemly behaviors, would have been seen not as a devil fighter, but rather a devil worshipper, and been burned, hanged, or boiled in oil.

The connection between women, religion, and healing was recognized on a number of fronts, not all as dramatic as Maria's. In the middle of that century, other religious stirrings could be seen. One movement was described by William James as the most significant religious force since the Reformation, a movement which he called the religion of healthy mindedness. It "gives to some of us serenity, moral poise, and happiness, and prevents certain forms of disease as well as science does, or even better."[39]

Never before had Western civilization witnessed a religious movement with more feminine emphasis than the one James described. Women were not only integral to the founding of the churches and sects, but were (and are) a majority of the membership. God, from the onset, was androgynous or bisexual.

Women viewed themselves as healers in another capacity—that of "mind cure." In process and philosophy, the mind-cure movement was significantly different from the type of faith healing described above. Furthermore, ideas of health reform were integrated into the body of church doctrine.

Despite the fact that they lived during the same years, and most within the same northeastern cities, mind-cure women and the women physicians who emphasized body-cure voiced disdain for each other's practices. They found no strength in the fact that time had finally released the bonds of women healers of all genres. Both groups offered new dimensions in healings which are only now being recognized and evaluated scientifically. The metaphysical thinking of writers and healers of the last century is an unsung precedent to many "new" directions in health today that involve the mind in matters of health and disease. The words *mind cure* are not used, of course, and *faith healing* is assiduously avoided. Instead, scientists and clinicians refer to the placebo effect, expectancy, the power of positive thought, mental imagery, hypnosis, and so on.

METAPHYSICAL HEALING

Most of the metaphysical healing sects have a Christian foundation, but others claim to be working with the laws of nature, which transcend religious dogma. The churches and sects, as they have evolved, present an eclectic combination of Eastern and Western religious thought, psychological orientation, the writings of Emerson and Whitman, and the work and teachings of Mesmer, Swedenborg, Hinduism and Buddhism, and the Jewish esoteric beliefs. The writings of several women are highly regarded, including the theosophists Annie Besant and Elena Petrovna Blavatsky.

The metaphysical ideas sprung from the common soil of an area extending only from Maine to New York, between the years of 1840 and 1875. Both the years and territory are coincident with the emphasis on popular health and sectarian medicine. The optimistic, do-it-yourself metaphysical movement was a reaction against the doom and gloom preachings of the evangelists. It was sometimes called the "Gospel of Relaxation" or the "Don't Worry Movement." Advocates would chant "Youth, health, vigor," while dressing for the day.[40]

Through the life and works of Mary Baker Eddy one can see the most extreme aspects of the mind-cure movement, but she certainly was not alone in deviating from the religious tide. Ellen White, prophetess of the Seventh-Day Adventists, was a contemporary, for example. Other women also helped to define the movement, including Myrtle Fillmore, who, together with her husband, Charles, wrote and established the early basis for the Unity church.

The institutions these women founded survived, in contrast with most of the hospitals and schools founded by women physicians. The women of religion differed personally in their blunt autocracy and absolute certainty that what they had to offer was divinely inspired. Their intuitive conviction was the truth, as far as they were concerned, and could no more be questioned than the visions of Hildegard or other mystics.

Furthermore, they were not trying to interpenetrate an existing institutional body. They were refugees from other religions that failed to tend to their spiritual needs. The new churches appealed to a large enough group to sustain themselves without needing to merge with mainstream religions. (Of course, organized religion in the United States is a diverse body whose heterogeniety is protected by the Constitution. Not so with medicine, which is a monolithic entity protected from diversity and competition by convention and law.)

The originality of Mary Baker Eddy's ideas remains a matter of dispute. She and partisan biographers naturally hold that the materials that became the doctrine of the Church of Christ Scientist (Christian Science) were a matter of her divine inspiration alone. The fact was, though, that she had ample exposure to the work of mesmerists, healers, philosophers, and sectarian medical practitioners whose ideas preceded hers and are reflected in her work.[41] She took those ideas and packaged and popularized them. As with the medical men who presented the ideas of women healers as their own, the question of who should be credited with discovery is a matter of opinion.

Nevertheless, the truth, as Eddy perceived it, is expressed only in her writings, principally *Science and Health, with the Key to the Scriptures,* first published in 1875. She specified that her inspiration superseded all others and must be read from her teachings in each church upon a given Sunday. Her arbitrary and autocratic leadership was questioned from the beginning, leading to a dispersion of her followers. After a major schism in 1888, Eddy disbanded her group and retreated, only to appear a year later with new vitality.

It was Mary Baker Eddy's personal bouts with poor health that guided her odyssey. As a child she was diagnosed with lung and liver ailments, gastric attacks, nervousness, depression, and a variety of acute and chronic disorders. When she was around eight years old, she heard voices that she interpreted as a signal of her prophetic ability.

Her experiences with medicines had convinced Eddy that "heroic" medications and treatments weakened the body. It was during a spontaneous recovery from a severe back injury that she discovered the principles regarding the power of the mind in healing that she set forth for her legions of followers.

According to Mary Baker Eddy, all is mind, and matter is an illusion. Healing disease is the most concrete demonstration of the power of the mind on the concept of the body. A mortal can obtain the harmony of health only when discord is forsaken, the supremacy of the divine mind is acknowledged, and material beliefs are abandoned. Disease is an image of thought externalized, and Eddy advised her followers to eradicate the image before it could take tangible shape in conscious thought, alias the body. She thought that by looking at the body one could view the images of the mind, just as the image that becomes visible to the senses can be seen on the retina.

The practitioners of Christian Science healing—and in the U.S. women outnumber men, eight to one—have been specially trained in Eddy's principles. They are called to sit with a patient during illness, diagnose, pray, and educate in the teachings of the church. The Christian Science church continues to hold its founder in esteem, honoring her wishes long after her death. Furthermore, modern science is beginning to vindicate her premises regarding the link between the mind and body. The principles of quantum physics, as they apply to health, are not so far afield from her metaphysics.[42]

The metaphysical churches and sects have continued to grow slowly over the years. Their tenets of positive thinking have found their way into some mainstream religions. And women continue to find in them a vehicle for extending the principles of health into spirituality, or vice versa. The metaphysical movement gave women an overdue taste of their own divinity.

SUMMARY

This chapter has surveyed the unusual women healers that lived during the last century. What I have hoped to convey is the complexity of the world they encountered, their survival tactics, elements that led to their downfall—when that occured—and their considerable accomplishments.

The mind, body, and spirit appeared to have been parceled out among professions. The most powerful essence of woman's healing art—connecting the triune—lay quiescent for another generation.

The words of Dr. Marie Zakrzewska provide a poignant closure to the nineteenth century. As she looked at the busts of famous men in the halls of Westminister Abby she wondered, Would there ever be a monument to the first woman physician

> because she had the energy, will and talent . . . because she is a landmark of the era marked by women's freeing themselves from the bondage of prejudice and from the belief that they are the lower being when compared with men? . . . We need such landmarks of civilization . . . because the now-living, as well as those who will live long afterward, need encouragement. . . . The person who is covered by a monument is of no consequence, but the fact that a "woman" can work and make an impression upon civilization needs to be known and to be remembered.[43]

The women healers of the last century, whether they were nurses, doctors, teachers, or ministers, were indeed landmarks of civilization.

Part Four

*Twentieth-Century Women and the State
of the Healing Arts and Sciences*

16 Woman as Health-Care Provider: Realities of the Marketplace

THE EVENTS OF the twentieth century have led to yet another pivotal era in healing, the outcome of which will intimately affect every man and woman in this country. In order for women to participate consciously in these changes, it is necessary for us to have an understanding of how the current situation evolved, and what we face from a vocational perspective.

At the turn of the century, American medicine was well on its way to becoming the most male-dominated system of health care in the industrialized world. Not a single health or allied health profession composed primarily of women was able to practice independently of the medical profession, of which 95–97 percent were men until the most recent years.

The vested interests of medicine were (and are) in a single, monolithic system associated with allopathic medical practices. All other healing systems are severely restricted or forbidden by law. This exclusivity is uniquely characteristic of the United States. Other countries with comparable standards of modernization show a significantly more benign attitude (if not outright acceptance) of medical alternatives to allopathy.

The above statements are not value judgments but simple facts. Whether the current system has worked in the best interests of the country—both from a consumer and provider standpoint—is a matter of ongoing debate.

The century itself has seen a vast number of changes in the practice of health care, grounded in increasing attention to basic science and technology and a meteoric rise in the industry of hospitalization. Major advances have taken place in the monitoring of body functions, acute care and diagnostic technology, the development of broad spectrum antibiotics, and the control of some of the major infectious diseases. The diseases that robbed families of all their young children—often in a single winter—are well controlled. Advances in pharmaceuticals have made life tolerable for those with chronic illnesses such as diabetes and epilepsy. Plastic surgery can correct hideous deformities and promises the appearance of eternal youth. Most would agree that sickness in general is more effectively managed in 1990 than in 1890, or, in fact, at any other time in history.

On the other hand, strong voices from both outside and within medicine claim that many of the so-called advances are an illusion created by propaganda and statistics.[1] They argue convincingly that major strides have been made in areas having relatively little impact on the well-being of a populace increasingly plagued by the chronic and catastrophic diseases associated with aging. Even the alleged progress in treatment of the two major killers—cancer and heart disease—has been made only in extending lives, not in curing disease.[2] New infectious epidemics, the most deadly being AIDS, are an unprecedented challenge to the bureaucratic machinery, the already deep pocket of health-care expenses, and the methods of health-care delivery. Among "first world" countries, the United States lags woefully behind in health matters, particularly with its high infant mortality rates.

Whether one chooses to believe that American medicine is the best possible system, or a highly overrated one, there can be no question that health care in this country is in a state of crisis. The problems ostensibly center around the escalating costs of an industry that has mushroomed beyond affordability. Such a system must either change or collapse.

Serious criticism of the "heroic" aspects of medicine, the significant number of iatrogenic (medically induced) illnesses, and the stark omission of caring and compassion in the healing arts are reminiscent of conditions of the last century. Like the popular health movement, a grassroots reaction has steadily gained force, with components almost identical to those of a hundred years ago. Lifestyle changes regarding nutrition, exercise, etc., and healing systems such as homeopathy that promise a kinder impact on the human body than allopathy's onslaught are all included in what is sometimes referred to as the holistic health movement. (Other names for this movement include "alternative," "adjunctive," or "complimentary" medicine, which imply a peripheral role; or "unorthodox" medicine, which suggests a somewhat unsavory practice.) In academic circles, the field of behavioral medicine encompasses a range of ideas from lifestyle changes to mental techniques such as biofeedback or guided imagery for altering body functions.

Additionally, far outside the boundaries of allopathic medicine (and outside the law in most states) one finds a growing number of treatments for various diseases such as cancer. The public demonstrates its frustration with the unfulfilled promises of allopathic medicine by seeking out these alternatives in increasing numbers.

There are some differences between the health movements of the nineteenth and twentieth centuries. In the middle of the last century, the country was in the throes of an anti-elitism and anti-professionalism. Licensing was

        Woman as Healer

considered restrictive of fair trade, and most existing statutes regarding the health fields were removed. Organized medicine or organized anything was viewed with distrust. The American public did not buy the American Medical Association's (AMA) party line that its members represented science and were better than the sectarians who represented something else—presumably non-science. From the consumer point of view, the sectarian brand of medicine was about as good as any. Now, whatever changes occur in American health care must contend with well-established laws, customs, and statutes which support the autocratic interests of the AMA.

However, the alternatives are supported by a growing body of research, not available last century, that demonstrates that some of the procedures are quite effective. As usual, what Oliver Wendell Holmes called the "nature trusting heresy" has a larger number of women supporters, and tends to represent the feminine consciousness in healing.

The role of women in the healing arts for most of this century has been one of quiet service, interspersed with flares of feminist activity and, in the 1960s and early 1970s, progress in achieving equal opportunities with men. In discussing the tasks assigned to women, it is difficult to use the phrase *woman as healer* to describe their function. *Woman as health-care provider* describes far better the multiple roles that women play in the treatment system. *Healing,* which suggests some independent effort to help others "become whole," also implies that sometimes people are also cured in the process. If, indeed, the healing professions are to broadly encompass both caring and curing, it must be said that women have been almost exclusively involved in the former. Curing has been the province of the physician only.

Women have professionalized the art of caring, however, in numerous fields unheard of last century, including subspecialities of nursing, the allied health sciences, social work, and the behavioral sciences. The growth of very specific areas of expertise has also led to guilded societies of practitioners, incumbent with legal definitions of who might seek membership, educational criteria, and delimitations of the scope of practice. We have moved not so far from the Middle Ages, for the guilds are still formed around issues of gender.

This chapter will examine these issues in more detail, beginning with developments at the turn of the century that predicated the male-dominated health-care system. Transitions currently being faced by women and their professions, and facts and figures of the present reality will be briefly discussed.

REFORM AND THE FLEXNER REPORT

Abraham Flexner, like René Descartes, is often viewed as having propelled medicine into a new dimension, and accelerating the demise of irrational, natural, and holistic healing practices. Descartes's writing provided the philosophical basis for separating mind from body in the seventeenth century; Flexner, in 1910, wrote a report that altered the course of American medicine.[3] Both men have been overcredited (or overaccused, depending upon one's point of view), but have remained figureheads for the new ideologies of their time.

As the reform of the American system began in the last part of the nineteenth century, it channeled women away from medicine into nursing and other professions. The reform included the need for university-associated medical training, a decrease in the number of medical schools, control of the clinical experiences of medical students, and the establishment of scientific laboratories in conjunction with medical training. The schools in Europe, especially Germany, provided a coveted model.

Other needs expressed before the turn of the century included the recruitment of teachers and heads of departments who would be exempt from the demands of private practice, as well as willing to forego its lucrative reimbursement. Teaching and clinical care would be secondary to research. In 1902, Lewells Barker, who later succeeded Sir William Osler as dean of Johns Hopkins University, claimed that a teacher who was not also an investigator had no place in a medical school, and might actually be harmful to the students.

Based on these reforms, the hospital–university–medical-school complex was considered the only type of entity that clearly served to advance American medicine. The funds necessary to operate such institutions far exceeded student fees, requiring major investments on the part of government and industry.

The AMA established a Council on Medical Education to advise schools on the development of a sound medical curriculum. By 1905, recommendations included prerequisites for admission, and expanded medical training to minimally a five-year program, including two years of basic sciences, two of laboratory experience, and two in supervised patient care. The Council also established a rating system for medical colleges, based upon the scores their graduates obtained on state board examinations.

At this time, major sums of money were becoming available through trusts formed by the new billionaires. The Carnegie Foundation, in particular, sought to upgrade higher education with its philanthropic efforts. The AMA asked the foundation to investigate the state of medical training, and to strengthen the advisory role of the Council on Medical Education. The foundation agreed, hiring Abraham Flexner, an arrogant and power-hungry schoolmaster who had no experience in medicine at any level, to do the job. Flexner's dogmatism and zeal were reflected in the way he conducted the investigation and, later, in the Machiavellian way in which he handled millions of dollars from the foundation's coffers.

Flexner visited 155 medical colleges. He announced that after one-half hour of examining student credentials he could tell whether standards were being upheld. In a matter of hours, he could determine whether or not the school was worthy of money. Johns Hopkins, which owed its beginnings to monetary gifts from women, was the only school given unconditional approval.

The Flexner Report accelerated the ongoing reforms. But more important, it directed which way the money would flow. The union of corporate trust and medicine was complete. The scientific direction of American medicine demanded large sums of money; colleges that did not receive it would wither and die. Schools that could not hope to mimic the Johns Hopkins model would not be financed, nor would any sectarian, nonallopathic college. In 1907 there were 160 medical schools in this country; by 1914, there were only 100. All but one of the women's colleges was closed; all sectarian schools rapidly disappeared. Hence, the death of all competitive systems of healing. The percentage of women in medical school dropped to about three percent within the first decade of the century, and did not increase for about sixty years.

PROFESSIONAL HELPERS

Nurses

Coincident with medical reform and the Flexner Report was the professionalization of health-care workers. The majority were always women, with the field of nursing the largest specialty. The AMA recognized that the new breed of physician needed helpers. In 1908, the organization formally recognized the nurse as a member of a learned profession (which was to formalize the distinction between them and members of labor unions.) By 1914, forty states had adopted nurse practice acts, with licensing boards or qualification statements in place. The status of the profession was enhanced during wartime, but even so, after World War I, there was a shortage of nurses (the "White Cap Famine") that would never be resolved.

The reasons for the supply and demand problem in nursing speak to the problems endemic to the field.[4] When there was a threat of physician shortages, major efforts, including large government grants, were made to subsidize medical education. During the nursing shortage no such efforts were made. In fact, nursing schools were closing in the midst of the most severe shortages. Why?

As early as the 1930s the National League for Nursing and the American

Nurses' Association (ANA) were following the lead of physicians. Recommendations for upgrading education and specialty training were endorsed. The diploma schools associated with hospitals were closing in deference to college-based programs that would provide the desired academic foundation. Physicians complained from the beginning that nurses were overeducating themselves; in times when nurses were in short supply they have even advocated reducing the educational requirements.

Recruitment efforts have never been particularly successful except during wartime, when the image of nurses has been glamorized. A low-salary structure combined with increasing responsibilities has been largely responsible. After 1940, in the face of the doctor shortage, nurses have been expected to do jobs like administering inoculations and I.V.'s—previously the province of the physician. Hospitals have been slow to reimburse for the expanded service requirements, and nurses are less and less convinced that they should be working for love, not money.

The word *nurse* itself has grown more ambiguous over time, encompassing a wide range of training and expertise. The term is applied to graduates of the fading number of diploma (hospital) schools and four-year programs leading to a bachelor's degree as well as to those with associate degrees from junior colleges or with master's or doctorate degrees. Furthermore, there are proliferating areas that demand advanced training, including nurse practitioners, and clinical nurse specialists.

The profession continues to be as paradoxical as it was in the last century. It is characterized by continued pressures from within medicine to upgrade, at the same time to quickly produce large numbers of nurses who will be able to meet the overwhelming demands of the hospital industry. Furthermore, the emphasis on professionalism has resulted in the desire for expanded, and even independent practice, which places the interests of some nurses at odds with the medical profession. Nurses themselves have voiced concern about all these issues, including the attrition of the "caring" aspects of nursing as increasing emphasis is placed on technological skill.

Currently, there are about 1,900,000 nurses in this country. Ninety-seven percent of them are women. They function under two layers of male authority: hospital and physician. A third layer of authority—that of the insurance carrier—is gathering momentum. The companies tend to be physician-driven, representing the doctors' interests. However, their profit orientation may temper or override their partisanship to any single profession.

The nurses' struggle to attain legal recognition in their own right has been ongoing, and is characterized by the landmark Laverne-Pisani Bill, passed in 1972 in New York.[5] The Nurse Practice Act proposed by the bill, as well as every other proposed legislation to advance nursing as a profession, was blocked by the Medical Society of New York and the Hospital Association of New York State. The bill was passed in a modified form, but only after significant lobbying, including a march by approximately 4,000 nurses on the capital at Albany.

The definition of nursing contained therein became a model for adoption in other states. It essentially defined the registered professional nurse as "diagnosing and treating human responses to actual or potential health problems through such services as case finding, health teaching, health counseling and provision of care supportive to or restorative of life and well-being, and executing medical regimens prescribed by a licensed or otherwise legally authorized physician or dentist."

Thus, the nurses' autonomy as a *profession* was declared, but certainly not their *independence* as practitioners. The practical issues of nurses' functioning subordinate to multiple layers of authority have not even begun to be resolved. Even the limited independent practice granted to nurse practitioners in some states is an uneasy situation. The nurse practitioners originally claimed for themselves a new niche, almost identical to the one claimed by the women physicians of last century. Their duties may include long-term monitoring of patients with chronic disease, administration of medications under blanket physician orders, and routine physical examinations. In 1988, nurse practitioners claimed that "certain groups of the population—especially children, the elderly, and women, all of whom need regular exams—are the nurse's natural constitutency."[6]

Nurse practitioners functioning without the direct authority of a physician are always at risk for charges of practicing medicine without a license should they be targeted as a threat to vested interests. At the onset of their drive for independent practice, nurses offered needed health services because of a shortage of primary-care physicians in the early 1970s. They were particularly welcomed in rural areas of the country where physicians were always in short supply. However, it is estimated that there is now an excess of 70,000 physicians in this country (according to the Graduate Medical Education National Advisory Committee, created by the Secretary of Health and Human Services). What this surplus means is that every aspect of nursing activity viewed as overlapping the responsibilities of physicians will be under scrutiny.

The barriers to nurses' autonomy as practitioners are also attitudinal. Bonnie Bullough, a professor at the University of California School of Nursing, wrote at the beginning of the nurse practitioner movement that "the weight of past tradition, the subordination of nurses, the sex segregation, and the apprenticeship model in nursing education have left a mark on the attitudes of present-day nurses. . . ."[7] A few nurses who are still practicing will remember being taught to stand up when a doctor entered the room, and to open the door for him. A very, very few will remember when learning to pour tea was part of the curriculum.

Nurse practitioners are currently facing two significant challenges. State agencies are re-examining the nurse practitioner legislation. New York, for example, revoked and then returned certain privileges for independent practice within a year. Also, a block of major insurance companies have either refused to insure them, or raised premiums to prohibitive levels. On the other hand, nurse clinical specialists in psychiatry in one state have received tentative approval to administer psychotropic drugs; in another, to practice counseling under a licensing law totally independent from medical practice acts. The best that can be said of these discrepant moves is that the field is in a state of transition. From history, we know that active legislation in women's health fields should be carefully monitored.

The chief issues for those nurses who envision themselves as "nurse healers" are: how to straddle the worlds of art and science, of caring and curing, and how to develop and implement new techniques that better fit their own notion of the role they serve. Currently important tools and strategies are therapeutic touch, mental imagery, biofeedback and other self-regulation techniques, modes of relaxation and meditation, and certainly, health education in its most comprehensive form. These nurses see sound nursing education and clinical experience not as incompatible with the new techniques but as the foundation upon which the expanded functions can build. Several organizations have emerged to serve their interests, including the Holistic Nurses' Association, and the Nurse Healers Cooperative.

The most significant challenge to the field of nursing is yet to come. In the summer of 1988, the AMA voted to proceed with a pilot program to train what it calls "registered care technologists" in a two-year training program with a physician-designed curriculum. The decision came after a long period of critical shortages and unsatisfactory solutions, including the hiring of poorly trained "technicians" to fill nursing vacancies. The aim was to fill significant unmet manpower needs in hospitals. The AMA accused nursing officials of discouraging potential students by their support of four-year academic programs for all nurses.

As of this writing, the ANA still holds that the shortages would be best ameliorated by improved working conditions and higher salaries, and not by undermining their educational foundation. The organization continues to present a unified front in opposing the AMA's decision.[8]

Other Women's Health Professions

Nurses are not the only ones currently wrestling with the dilemma posed by the masculinization of American medicine. Patient care over the twentieth century has been parceled out to a number of professions largely composed of women.

The proliferation of health professions is occasioned by increasing demands of technology, the specialization of medicine, and a health industry that profits from additional services. Also, the post–World War II emphasis on services for the handicapped engendered the growth of professions associated with rehabilitation.

The allied health professions, from the onset, emphasized submissiveness and conformity to the male-dominated medical profession. For example, in 1922, graduating occupational therapists pledged, "I will walk in upright faithfulness and obedience to those under whose guidance I am to work."[9]

Women continue to outnumber men in the allied health professions by a ratio of three to one. In a survey of those areas accredited by the AMA Committee on Allied Health Education and Accreditation, male students outnumbered female in only two fields—emergency medical technology (paramedic) and perfusion.[10] Major health specilizations, such as speech therapy, physical therapy, and social work, are not accredited by this body. Including them would increase the female-to-male ratio even more.

People practicing in these fields face problems similar to those faced by nurses at the advanced levels: they are more-or-less autonomous, have their own research base, and have refined clinical techniques, and yet they must work under the orders of physicians who have less knowledge of their field than they do. Some—physical therapists, speech therapists, and social workers in particular—have made some headway in working independently, but all have proceeded with caution. Clinical psychologists, legally independent practitioners in their own right, must acknowledge deference to medicine (especially psychiatry) in order to pass licensing examinations. Psychologists may well have more training and experience in therapeutic processes, psychodiagnostics, and even in psychopharmacology than psychiatrists; they are still seen as impinging on the territory of the physician, nonetheless. Psychologists in many states have active proposals before their legislatures requesting hospital admission privileges, and some are pressing for permission to prescribe certain medications. In other areas, psychiatrists are actively lobbying to restrict the practice of psychology.

The other side of the picture is that non-physician professions tend to be viewed as owing their livelihood to the paternalistic good graces of both the physician and the hospital system. Opposition is viewed as mutinous insubordination—in effect, biting the hand that has fed them so well for so long. Physicians have assumed the full burden of responsibility for the consumers of the health system and, in doing so, feel justified in wanting to control how and through whom that system delivers.

The allied health specialists are less likely to be accused of practicing medicine without a license, than are nurses or even clinical psychologists. The tedious activities of care giving and laboratory work have never been coveted by medicine and would likely not be viewed as competitive except in the worst of financial times. The spectrum of work of these specialists might profitably be expanded. A broader, more effective use of health-care personnel would benefit the industry as a whole, not to mention reduce its costs. Harold M. Schoolman, M.D., put it thus: "There is a need in fulfilling the requirements of medicine to use professionals other than physicians. The concept that the doctor, the physician, is the only professional who can exist in the execution of the functions and requirements is idiocy."[11] It is estimated that 75–80 percent of primary adult care and 90 percent of pediatric primary care could be safely turned over to non-physician professionals, including nurses.

The thornier problem for the vested interests of American medicine is posed by practitioners who are distinctly at odds with allopathic medicine. Interest has proliferated in older healing systems such as Eastern forms of medicine, native tribal medicine, naturopathy, and homeopathy, as well as techniques associated with "New Age" or holistic health. This problem is a woman's issue because women are more likely than men to gravitate to these "alternatives" both as consumers and practitioners. Furthermore, many represent women's traditional interest in lifestyle, prevention, and botanics as viable healing tools.

In the twentieth century, just as before, some women who regard themselves as healers have made the choice not to enter the mainstream of health care with its educational and practice requirements. These women trust their natural healing abilities, often using unusual methods. Indeed, it seems that a select few do have talents that are most apt to flourish in a situation unfettered by the usual professional dictates; for others, the dubious and solitary road of the periphery may be marked by self-doubt and even self-delusion.

In addition to the nonguilded healers just described, there are quasi–health guilds springing up on all fronts, formed by like-trained individuals who sense that what they offer has a positive impact on a broad definition of health. Among these are expressive therapists in music, art, and dance, who occasionally find a role in the medical mainstream.

In order to understand what might be in store for these sundry groups, we will examine the experience of twentieth-century midwives. While nurses and allied health professionals were created and sanctioned to meet the needs of doctors, midwifery has consistently been outside the mainstream of American medicine.

Midwives

Over the past eighty years, midwives have been banned, prosecuted, ignored, or regulated, depending upon the mood of the state medical societies. As mentioned in the last chapter, despite the fact that medicine saw midwifery as a dangerous and archaic profession, at the turn of the century over half of the births in this country were attended by midwives. It is now estimated that midwives attend approximately one percent of births, which attests to a small but persistent choice for their services.

Unfortunately, neither midwife nor obstetrician knew much about the birthing process in the early decade of this century. According to a survey conducted by Johns Hopkins Professor of Obstetrics J. Whitridge Williams, in 1912, the medical student in the best programs witnessed an average of four births; in the substandard programs they were lucky to witness one.[12] Each child delivered by a midwife was seen as an opportunity lost to study by medical science. Midwives, unless they were European trained, were found to be dirty and incompetent. So, with this bleak situation on both sides of the issue, the saga of the American midwife continued.

Massachusetts, always the stronghold of mainstream masculine American medicine, banned midwifery in 1907. The state supreme court stated that the practice was indistinguishable from obstetrics, and therefore violated the commonwealth's Medical Practice Act.[13] The outcome of the ban was that maternal and infant mortality rates immediately increased. In 1916, the maternal mortality rate was 6.5 per thousand in Boston (where midwives were banned), as compared to 1.7 in Newark, where a program of education combined with midwife home delivery was instituted. In Washington, infant mortality *increased* as the number of births reported by midwives *decreased.*

In New York, despite a dwindling number of midwives, their success in controlling puerperal fever and prevention of stillborns was superior to that of the doctors, a finding that has not changed in seventy years.[14] Whenever the results of midwife home births are compared with those overseen by an obstetrician in a hospital, all things considered, the midwives fare equally as well or slightly better.[15] Midwives, of course, are allowed to attend only normal vaginal deliveries, and the comparisons are made on these.

When prohibitions existed on midwifery, the practicing midwife had several options: to give up her practice (as many did), to practice surreptitiously, to become an obstetrical nurse and work with a physician, or to join with other midwives and battle the medical associations. The last option was not chosen. The midwives never developed sufficient political awareness, nor were they organized enough to respond successfully to their male competitors.[16] Until recently, any networking among midwives was only cordial, at best.

The medical profession fought the ongoing presence of midwifery by medicalizing childbirth, and convincing the population that they were the only safe caretakers of pregnant women. Pregnancy and childbirth became diseases, and "active management" of labor more and more common. The trend has replicated like a virus. Today, the figures of active intervention are astronomical—approximately 20–25 percent of all babies are delivered by cesarean section, and in some hospitals the rate is over 50 percent.

In any event, the medical campaign was initially successful. Most women chose to have their babies in hospitals, and the midwives served primarily the rural poor. Midwives continued to serve the large immigrant population who could neither afford nor abide a doctor in the birthing chamber. In the 1960s a number of women began to protest hospital routine as an indignity and not in the best interests of mother or baby. They sought, instead, more natural birthing alternatives to "active management," and home births increased.

As a medical alternative, midwifery is in a very interesting position right now. Like nursing, the field is in transition, with the outcome uncertain. Over the past five years, there has been a flurry of state legislation that makes any review quickly obsolete. Furthermore, laws are not always clearly written, and there is also a discrepancy between the law and what is really taking place. The underground of American midwifery is alive and well, supported by numbers of people who tend to be well-educated, health-conscious, and ecologically aware. How widespread the movement is, and how much medical support it has, cannot be known. Privacy is essential to its existence, as will be made clear by the following brief discussion of state laws.

Midwives fall into several categories: certified nurse midwives (registered nurses with advanced training), lay midwives who are recognized (licensed, certified, or registered) by the state, and lay midwives who are practicing without legal recognition.

The certified nurse midwives (CNMs) are allowed to practice in virtually all states, but under a jumble of laws, boards, and councils that may or may not represent their interests. The American Council of Nurse Midwives proposes licensing standards that are followed by most states. The CNMs must work under the supervision of a physician, who typically bills "over" them, and takes a chunk of the fees. Their practice may become a moot issue—all major insurance companies now refuse to insure them with malpractice coverage. The decision was unwarranted: to date only 6 percent of nurse midwives have been sued, whereas 66.9 percent of obstetricians have been sued at least once, according to the American College of Obstetricians and Gynecologists. Hospitals will not hire anyone who is uninsured. As a stop gap measure, nurse midwives have formed their own mutual insurance company, but the exceedingly high costs (around $5,000 per year in premiums) may be impossible to meet for most nurse midwives, whose average salary is only $27,000 per year.

The lay midwives are also in a precarious situation. While the American College of Obstetricians and Gynecologists officially opposes their activities, their actual legal status varies from state to state. Most lay midwives, given the choice, would prefer to be included as recognized health professionals within the mainstream system of medical care, much as they are in Europe. They cite the poor showing of the United States in infant and maternal mortality rates, as compared to Europe, where midwives are often employed. For instance, in Holland, where over one-third of the births are attended by midwives, the mortality rates are among the lowest in the world. (The actual mortality rates in the United States have improved slightly over the decade; however, the relative position among industrialized countries is still close to the last, behind the European countries, Canada, and Hong Kong.)

Training for midwives in most parts of Europe has been exceptional for several hundred years. But in the United States, it is the training of midwives that forms the "Catch 22." It is old business for women, the reader will recall from previous chapters, that they may not formally practice the healing arts without being trained. Yet no official or accredited training in midwifery is offered in this country, and the twelve "unofficial" schools that exist at the time of this writing will remain unstable without official sanction. American midwives take their training either through these programs, or in Europe, or through an apprenticeship with other midwives. A few junior colleges also offer courses on birthing which are relatively technical, and useful to the aspiring midwife. Some lay midwives have nurse's training; many do not. Others are licensed under "grandmother" clauses which recognize previous experience.

The most recent update on state law and lay midwifery is based on a survey published in mid-1987.[17] According to these figures, most laws are in a state of transition. Positions held by the states range from prohibiting the practice, to regulating it, to ignoring it altogether.

Of the ten states that have established regulatory bodies for midwifery, all but one have enacted their laws since 1980. These states include Arizona, Arkansas, Florida, Louisiana, Washington, Alaska, New Mexico, Texas, South Carolina, and New Hampshire. Legislation varies in terms of whether licensure, certification, or merely registration is required. The first two imply that an examination—usually oral and written—is in force.[18] The survey concludes that opportunities for lay midwives are *better* in those states (twenty-one at present) that have *no* legislation on midwifery.

The establishment of licensing, certification, or registration of a professional group is meant to protect the consumer. Therefore, the law may prove to be more restrictive than enabling for the profession.

A landmark study of lay midwifery in Arizona exemplifies the difficulties midwives have experienced as licensed practitioners.[19] Educational requirements formed an initial obstacle. Since 1978, applicants have been required to have completed a formal course of instruction and clinical training, with curriculum specified by law. Only an unaccredited "study group" existed in the state, and that closed in 1981. The qualifying examination was viewed as another obstacle, a common complaint of midwives in all states where they are required. In most, the questions and decisions are made by a board on which lay midwives have little or no representation.

The biggest obstacle to practice in all states where legislation exists is the requirement for medical cooperation, since midwives' activities are usually met with hostility by the rest of the medical community. However, midwives are required to obtain formal medical backup, and they are therefore legally dependent upon the physician and hospital system. The backup includes the availability of medical services in case of emergency, and usually pre- and postnatal physician care. The scope of the midwives' practice is also clearly specified. They may attend only normal vaginal deliveries. However, in case of unforeseen emergency, the law jeopardizes the mother's life and well-being because the midwife is forbidden to use any operative procedure (including suturing) and in most states may not legally administer a single dose of antihemorrhagic drugs or herbs.

Finding even one physician to back up their services remains an obstacle to practicing midwives. The physicians who are so inclined are pressured by their peers not to assist the midwives. They may also lose their hospital privileges, and their own malpractice insurance coverage if their carrier finds out they are providing backup services to even one midwife. Hospital personnel are not always accommodating to mothers who require emergency services as a result of postpartum complications after having been served by a midwife. In the Arizona survey, midwives reported that their patients were lectured severely and even physically abused in some of the situations. For example, one patient was sutured without anesthesia in an apparent attempt to teach her a lesson about not having come to the hospital in the first place. Other hospital staff proved to be quite sympathetic and accommodating.

In summary, the midwives bear watching. Never before in history have they been so organized, or so much in tune with the nuances of the law. This profession of women serving other women has the support of a small, but potentially influential, community. They are no longer the "last resort" of the poor and immigrant population, but the conscious choice of educated men and women. The midwives have survived the AMA, the bureaucracy of the hospital industry, the insurance companies, the lack of official training facilities, and the fickle mood of the American health consumer. It is something to be said for women as healers.

A FEW MORE FACTS AND FIGURES

What has happened to women physicians since 1910? There are more of them than at any time since the heyday of the last century. Between the years 1970 and 1986, the number of women physicians in the United States increased by 241.2 percent.[20] By 1986, 86,670 women physicians were practicing. Women in residency programs in 1987 constituted 27.4 percent of the student body, indicating a continued increase in the number of women in medical practice in the future. Their specialty areas have changed from pediatrics and general practice (the areas most frequently chosen by women in 1967) to internal medicine and pediatrics, followed by general practice (the areas most frequently chosen in 1986).

Of the women practicing medicine, less than 10 percent are involved in professional activities such as medical teaching, administration, and research. Women are more than twice as likely as men to be employees. In 1986, only 23.5 percent of men were employed by another person or corporation, whereas 45.4 percent of women were.[21]

The exceptional increase in the number of women in medicine is felt by many to reflect the doors that were opened in the wake of feminist activism of the 1960s. Women who entered medicine at that time were also "warriors."

On the other hand, today's increasing numbers of women in medicine may not reflect any inroads on the part of women. Rather, it may well be that women are filling the vacuum caused by the white male flight away from an increasingly unattractive profession. From all perspectives, medicine is undergoing what is called the "feminization" of a profession—lowered prestige and remuneration—that is invariably associated with entry of large numbers of women in any field.

Further, because more women are practicing medicine does not automatically guarantee that the practice of medicine itself will benefit from the feminine point of view by becoming more nurturing or compassionate. It is only when women exercise conscious responsibility that such changes might be expected in the institutions and professions they serve, as will be discussed in the final chapter of this book.

Another fact should be kept in mind as women rise into conscious responsibility: in all health fields where numbers of women predominate, the men in those professions receive higher average salaries. Hospital jobs held mainly by women pay less than those held primarily by men. For example,

74 percent of the membership in the National Association for Social Workers are women. The average annual salary for women is $22,500; for men it is $32,250.[22] Further, the more women enter a particular occupational field, the more likely remuneration is to decrease.

Sophisticated data analysis of forty health-care occupations in fifty-two hospitals revealed that wage differences continue to exist, with hospital jobs held by males paying about five percent more than those held by women.[23] Wage inequities take two forms: women are paid less than men for the *same* work, or they are paid less for *comparable* work. The former violates the Equal Pay Act of 1963, and is relatively easy to prove in a court of law. The latter requires complex analyses and formulas to determine the comparable worth of various jobs.

As an example of the latter form of wage inequity among the predominantly male occupations, chief pharmacists commanded the highest minimum starting wage in the hospitals studied ($8.74 per hour); among the predominantly female occupations, nurse supervisors received the highest minimum starting wage—$6.75 per hour.[24] But the evaluation of these positions found the nurse supervisor's job to be substantially more demanding.

We need not belabor the point. No matter how we look at the statistics, if wages are taken as an indicator, we must conclude that women's work in the health professions is undervalued.

SUMMARY

The thrust of the material presented in this chapter is that women and their health-care occupations are in a state of transition that includes both advances and retreats within any given field. Legislation of the female-dominated professions is at an all-time high. More and more women are studying to become physicians, but with no guarantee that they will be practicing in the prestigious and high-paying profession that medicine is currently perceived to be.

The current time is an era of crisis, characterized by financial exigencies and demands for a different type of health care than is being delivered in this country. Women healers find themselves at a double threshold of danger and opportunity, the twins born of crisis. Never before have women been faced with such challenges, nor has there been so much hope that they might creatively participate in the design of the future.

17 *Life in the Balance*

OVER THE PAST few years, a new healing consciousness has been gathering momentum. Both men and women are beginning to recognize and integrate the feminine perspective into their professions and into their lives. The new direction was born out of crisis and frustration with living in a rather constant state of dis-ease, out of fears that we as a species had passed a point of no return. It was also born out of scientific findings that validate the mutual domain of mind, body, and spirit, and support the necessity for addressing the triune nature of humankind in any healing system. The healing consciousness that embodies the feminine also recognizes that we are all part of a living, breathing, global entity. The focus on the health of human tissue alone—without similar due concern for feelings, spirituality, relationships, and the environment upon which all health, all life is dependent—is dangerously myopic, according to this emergent point of view.

An unusual and growing body of women healers who express the feminine as well as the traditional virtues and values associated with various professional practices provided the incentive for researching and writing this book. As their historical lineage reveals, their lives and the expression of their talents reflect the social, religious, and political events of their times. The implications of the material in this book extend far beyond the vocational functions of women who practice the healing arts, as has been duly noted. The institutions that are related to healing—including religion and government—stand only to gain from the influence of women's voices.

The situation should not be idealized beyond its current reality, however. To do so fails to reckon with the fact that women's position in the world of health is at least as tenuous as ever, based upon shifting legislation, wage and status inequities, and other old business. The economic crisis of health care itself breeds uncertainty. The desire of some to interject spirituality back into healing has already created its own backlash among fundamentalists in religion and in health. The usual pack of opportunists who confuse power and healing, "shamanship" and showmanship, are ever present. How to transform the crisis into challenge becomes the issue.

I have used Elizabeth Blackwell's words *conscious responsibility* in conjunction with woman's potential for exorcising the demons of the old order. For the next few pages, I will explore what that might entail.

WRITING A NEW COSMOLOGY

In England, there are numerous sites that have been used for religious ritual from the beginning of human settlement. Among these are the great megalithic henges. When the cosmology of most of the world began to shift about three to five thousand years ago, the stones of the henges were realigned with the new belief that the sky, not the earth, was the dwelling place of the divine. Were these sites still in use, a few men and women would no doubt be seen beginning the monumental effort of moving the stones once again. The cosmic story that dominates the world of tomorrow must honor the divinity in both earth and sky, man and woman, so that life itself might be affirmed.[1]

The cosmology of the culture has determined the position, role, and status of women healers from the beginning of time. That relationship has been reviewed for each era covered in this book. To reiterate briefly, healers are primarily those who are created in divine image. This is still true even though religion has ostensibly been long separate from the everyday aspects of healing. The gender of the primary, independently practicing healers depends upon the gender of the god(s).

The cosmology upon which the foundations of the Western world rest evolved thousands of years ago. The Great Mother was unseated from her reign in favor of one male god residing outside of, or above, the earth. Women are still deeply connected at every intrapsychic level—in all prevailing cultural ideologies—with the earth. The fate of the earth, the fate of women, and the extant cosmology are inseparable.

Throughout time, the life course of women healers has been influenced by changes in the ecosystem, famine, and pestilence. Now, the ecosystem is changing once again. This time, the devastation is being wrought by human greed, thoughtlessness, outmoded ideas of power and boundaries, ignorance, and denial. The most relevant danger to the earth is adherence to a cosmology in which humanity is seen as alien from the concerns of the planet.

When the gods lived in the earth, the whole planet was worshipped as the manifestation of the divine. The rivers, the rocks, and especially humans were the inhabitants of a sacred place. All—what we call living and non-living alike—was alive and related. All humans breathed the breath of the spirit and drank the waters of the spirit. In most tribal and early cultures, this was the prevalent system of belief. In the monotheistic religions of today, the earth,

Woman as Healer

and indeed all that is physical, is either ignored, dominated, or transcended. Honoring the earth is part of the old religions that must be reinterpreted to strengthen the new.

As we have noted, the Earth Mother, represented by the physical world, was believed to have betrayed humankind at several intervals. Seas rose, the summers cooled, and the rains seldom came. Crops withered and children died. The people looked to another savior, one who was not of earth, to help them. They sought dominion and control over the forces of nature so that life might go on. As a consequence, information about the physical world unfolded at an unprecedented rate. Even within one lifetime, understanding of physical forces and the development of technology to harness the elements has proceeded at a lightning pace. These are not problems in and of themselves, but rather signs of progress. The problem is that wisdom has receded in the shadow of advancing knowledge and technology.

Fading wisdom left a dying earth. Women cannot bear the brunt of this ecological crisis as they have in the past. In order to spare humanity, they must be seen not as the problem but as part of the solution.

Consequently, we must develop a new cosmology, a radically new story about the reason and purpose for human life, and how we stand in relationship to each other and to all things in the material world. We must describe anew who we are and what we will become in the unseen places of dreams and death.

The story must be one that saves us from the destruction of our own doing. Thus, it shall honor what is most real, most human, and whatever it is that sustains those values. It must honor the earth and man and woman and child with equanimity. It must acknowledge that true healing will take place only when men and women come to full consciousness, allowing the expression of those dimensions of being which have been held silent. The new cosmology must recognize that spirit is immanent in all life, as well as transcending the living, or life will not continue.

The conscious knowledge that we have the opportunity to devise a spirituality that will sustain life is as big a step in human evolution as has been known to our species, at least equal to when men and women began to reflect upon themselves as thinking beings and to ponder their mortality. This evolution of the self-conscious mind has allowed humans to interpret a cosmic story—indeed, any cosmic story—and map the landscape of immortality.

Now, though, we are pressed into writing a story that will preserve the best in us, and prevent poisoned air and poisoned relationships. All other cosmologies were devised with far more limited, less moral, and certainly less lofty goals. Cosmologies of the past and the present were usually counter-

---

feited by an elite group to gain power, and the personalities of saviors were embellished so that religions and governments might triumph. Our goal can no longer be so secular. We must think beyond all present institutions into the depths of what is richest and most enduring, and what moves beyond boundaries and race and the meanness of attitude. Together we can, and must, become the creators of a new story of meaning, origin, and presence; in doing so, we enter the next and finest stage of our existence.

But institutions are slow to move in a direction that facilitates envisioning such a story. Their self-proclaimed infallibility and vested interest in the status quo, built on layer upon layer of rigid belief and denial, must be eroded, and normally only time alters the faces of monoliths. Moving into another paradigm does not happen quickly, except when the world is perceived to be at an end. Then, panic and loss of nerve become the foundation of a new order. Conscious creators need not wait until such a point of desperation.

This new paradigm will be based upon eternal need to add meaning to existence, bring order out of chaos, and preserve humanity. It need not exclude the principles of religious faith, nor can it ignore the findings of modern science. What will be required, however, is a reordering of priorities, and a balance to be effected by including the feminine perspective. In order for life-honoring balance to be achieved, women must be active in its development, assuring that the cosmic story has both a male and female voice. Women's history has taught us the high cost of complacency, and of failing to make our perspective known. We have labored under the false assumption that if we would just express enough unconditional love, if we would pray and stand fast by morality and principles of right living, then life would flow justly, and peace and high-level wellness would automatically enfold us according to some divine plan. The assumption has proven false; the dangers of the passive stance for the health of society are clear.

THE FEMININE PERSPECTIVE AND MERGER OF THE CULTURAL MYTH

What is the feminine voice, and if fully expressed, how might it affect society, in particular the institutions related to health? The concept of the feminine—and masculine—voice, myth, perspective, or principle (terms used interchangeably) is derived from several sources: Eastern philosophy, personality theories (especially Carl Jung's), research on cognitive styles of males and females, and long-held and widespread cultural mythologies. The typical traits associated with masculine and feminine are relatively—but by no means completely—consistent across time and culture.

The masculine and feminine are regarded as polarities that, together, comprise the whole of the process of being. Neither aspect of the polarity is complete in and of itself; each depends upon the manifestation of its opposite for full expression. Men, of course, have a feminine aspect, and women, a masculine aspect. The myths no doubt have some basis in genetic differences but also are formed through environmental forces. Some of the traits usually associated with the masculine and feminine myths are listed in the accompanying table.[2]

The Myth of the Masculine and Feminine

Masculine	Feminine
Intellect	Intuition
Rational	Irrational
Light/sun	Dark/moon
Linear	Nonlinear
Right	Left
Knowledge	Wisdom
Power	Compassion
Analysis	Synthesis
Mastery	Mystery
Active	Passive
Expansive	Contained
Proactive	Reactive
Giving	Receiving
External/public	Internal/private
Technical	Natural
Unique	Unity
Form	Process
Competition	Collaboration
Sky	Earth
Focus	Perspective
How	Why
Objectivity	Subjectivity
Doing to	Being with
Curing	Caring
Fixing	Nurturing
Reason	Feelings
Physical world	Invisible realm
Decisive	Flexible

From earlier days of science, men such as Bacon and Newton set forth to design methods and practices that were exclusively masculine in nature. The traits believed to be related to the feminine were carefully deleted from the pursuit of science and relegated to a low status in the practice of the healing arts. We have been acculturated to believe that the traits of the feminine are darker, weaker, substandard, or of a menial nature. They have been regarded as appropriate for the domestic sphere, and unsuitable for the public world of professionalism.

The feminine voice is raspy from disuse, but many men and women now wish to express their long-suppressed female consciousness. The feminine perspective is an appealing alternative especially in times when technology has caused pain, and male-dominated institutions have not rid human beings of their miseries. But a healing system based upon the feminine perspective alone is not progress. To take the next step, the myths of the masculine and feminine perspective must merge and actualize in the practices of healing.[3]

Women are most able, I believe, to lead the way toward integration. We have nothing to lose and less to fear than men by heralding a new direction. Research on feminine cognition reveals the ability to move more gracefully from intellect to intuition, and from linear to nonlinear thought, than men. The more extensive connection between the two hemispheres of women's brains validates that they are better able to move from "right brain" to "left brain," as the popular conception goes. To women, the events of life are less likely to look black or white, and more likely to appear as a continuum; women are, more than men, apt to sense all sides of a controversy.[4]

Based upon the premise that any claim to absolute truth ultimately will prove limited, erroneous, or just plain ignorant, flexibility of thought might herald more advances in healing than delusions regarding what is and what is not the absolute truth. Adding women's voices, then, is not simply adding new and lost dimensions to health care. It also brings balance and flexibility because those are precisely the qualities of the feminine mode of processing information.

Historically, whenever women have been welcomed back into the healing fold, it has been to supply the "caring" to the "curing," the latter always having been associated with men and power. The caring dimension of healing has had little status, and few financial rewards. Traditionally it is a realm dominated by and exploited by men. Major changes are on the horizon to alter this course.

First of all, caring and curing are now meshing as healing forces. It is becoming less and less possible to believe that one is more important than another, or that, in fact, caring and curing are different. The aspects of healing associated with caring—hope, love, joy, expectation—are being documented as ingredients in the remission of disease. Second, negative forces such as loss of hope or love and the failure to adequately cope with stress have been identified as factors in both the onset and exacerbation of the symptoms of major illness. Even a decade ago, research was sketchy on these points. Now it extends through all fields of science and behavior. In short, the lack of caring or nurturing may be a primary causative factor in disease, and the "carers" are involved in directly facilitating cure.[5]

The change in the health-care needs of the industrialized world also implies the importance of integrating the feminine myth into the masculine medical model. The majority of people being treated are chronically ill or disabled, or suffering from diseases for which there is no cure. Therefore, a system, the model of which is to actively "fix" or otherwise return a person to a normal state of health with advanced technology, is no longer appropriate for most of whom it serves. A steadily aging population will require more than ever in the way of long-term care. Thus, the change from services primarily for the acutely ill to those for the chronically disabled mandates the expression of the feminine myth in order to render high-quality care.

THE HEALER AND THE HEALING SYSTEM

In a balanced viewpoint that includes both the masculine and feminine perspective, healing is seen not as technique, but as process. The healing system moves beyond its intense and limited concentration on molecular biology to the integrity of community, environment, and concerns for the spirit. The healer takes on new dimensions, with wisdom gained from superb professional training as well as from the depths of personal experience.

Healing: A Redefinition

Healing is a concept that requires a redefinition in the Western mode of health care. The term currently tends to be associated with quacks, evangelists, or others who do not use the standard allopathic modes of treatment. Self-healing is paid little heed by the scientific community, even when the results are dramatic. The internal mechanisms of mind and body (such as the immune system) that are equipped to heal and repair virtually every type of trauma or disease have only recently received a measure of scrutiny by the scientific community, which has been intently focused on external healing forces—primarily chemicals and surgery. Health, or healing, is far less understood than the pathophysiology of disease.

On the other hand, the idea of curing has sustained prestige in the allopathic system, which that emphasizes technology, power, analysis, and fixing broken parts. Curing implies that the one who offers the cure is active, the one receiving the cure, passive—again, a dichotomy of the masculine and feminine myth.

In a balanced system, neither healing nor curing is something that one person *does* to another. Instead, both terms refer to internal processes, reflecting a more basic definition of health which implies harmony and wholeness. As such, physical health—or the molecular biology—may or may not be changed or relevant to wholeness. The end-points of being "healed" or "whole" are more a matter of personal opinion than the results of a urinalysis, or a psychological test, or anyone else's criterion of what constitutes "well." Furthermore, through the healing process, a person may be more whole, more harmonious, or more "well" than before, having gained strength and insight. Disease or suffering, in fact, may be regarded as critical events in the path toward personal transformation.

I believe that a balanced view of healing would also include the following concepts:

1. Healing is a lifelong journey toward wholeness.
2. Healing is remembering what has been forgotten about connection, and unity and interdependence among all things living and nonliving.
3. Healing is embracing what is most feared.
4. Healing is opening what has been closed, softening what has hardened into obstruction.
5. Healing is entering into the transcendent, timeless moment when one experiences the divine.
6. Healing is creativity and passion and love.
7. Healing is seeking and expressing self in its fullness, its light and shadow, its male and female.
8. Healing is learning to trust life.

The Healing System

A system that allows for the fuller expression of health is multifaceted: it is a web of individuals, their relationships, and the sustaining environment (see accompanying diagram). It should be visualized as a web, however, and not a unidimensional hierarchy. Each level touches every other level, and the connections are complex and infinite. Healing, or disease, or disruption any place in the system reverberates to all levels. The web is replete with feminine imagery, in contrast to the more common systems models of linear, hierarchical relationships—a masculine order of thought.

The bonds among and within levels are invisible and nonmaterial. They include conscious and unconscious thought, motivation, love, and will. In fact, as life begins to show its most intimate nature, it appears that the basis for all that is physical is the invisible bond. These findings from the world of quantum physics are a jolt to a materially, physically minded people. Again,

---

Woman as Healer

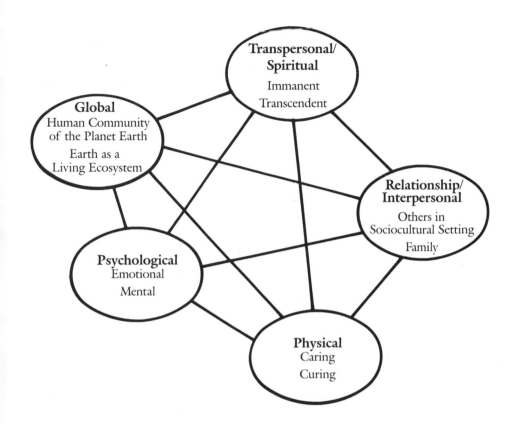

The Healing System

An Interconnected Web

one is reminded of the necessity for including the characteristics of the feminine myth into any pursuit of knowledge. The polarities of visible and invisible, physical and nonphysical, are required for the understanding and pursuit of global health.

Each level in the healing system demands a technology and a data base. What manifests at the physical level demands attention and treatment on the physical level. What manifests psychologically demands knowledge of psychopathology and normal psychological functioning. The lessons, message, and meaning of disease may relate to understanding and accepting the genetic structures inherited from one's parents, to lifestyle issues, or to more esoteric concerns. All are equally valid, equally sacred, and deserve equal recognition in a balanced approach to health.

In a multifaceted, balanced healing system, it cannot be assumed that any single view is the primary cause of suffering or disease, nor that treatment should emanate from a single body of practitioners. It is tempting, if one is a psychologist, to assume that emotional imbalance or dysfunctional relationships are the "real" cause of disease. Medical scientists are prone to describe cause in genetic or other physical terms. Other practitioners regard energy imbalances, spinal misalignments, stress, past-life transgressions, or failed spiritual disciplines as primary causes and loci for treatment.

Issues of cause and cure in this healing system cannot be resolved with simple answers, platitudes, minimal or narrowly applied skills, or egocentric approaches. The challenge is to integrate feminine values with masculine standards: to couple flexibility with decisiveness, perspective with focus, synthesis with analysis.

The Healers

For those who seek a healing vocation in a balanced system of healing, the demand for diversification and breadth of knowledge is greater than ever before. Surely, not everyone should go to medical school. But change in a system as omnipotent as American medicine demands familiarity with its history, language, and legislation, and an objective sense of what it does and does not do effectively.

The experiences of past and present advise that women, particularly, must invest in many levels of expertise in the healing professions. The desire to heal and the awareness of an ability to heal (whatever that might mean in the broad context of health) is only just that: a motivation and an awakening. The work of healing may be a "calling," as Florence Nightingale maintained, but it is also inescapably a profession. Having hands filled with healing light and a heart full of love may be necessary, but not sufficient, for the women who will truly redirect the course of human life. The healing path is long and costly, as we have seen from the lives of Trotula, Hildegard, and Mary Putnam Jacobi, among others. In traditional cultures, the propensity to become a healer is made known during the vision quest that usually takes place in adolescence. The healer-to-be is then an apprentice to a master for most of his or her adult life. The true work of healing is not performed independently until the trainee's hair shows streaks of silver.

The current "New Age" belief that healers can know of their healing tools just by plugging into their intuition and bypassing the world of amassed information poses a danger to a balanced healing system. These would-be healers may offer a quickly learned technique, perhaps coupled with compassion, unconditional love (a difficult concept at best), and a nurturing attitude, but their training with real people is often minimal and their understanding of suffering and disease, poor. Promoting the feminine aspects alone, to the exclusion of what is admirable and effective from other bodies of thought, is not exercising conscious responsibility.

The current popular concept of the "wounded healer" is also relevant to the development of a balanced healing system. It implies that personal transformation, inner work, or crisis is encountered, directing one toward a healing mission. The experience then allows one to be present more effectively for others who are suffering, and to assist them in their quest for relief or healing.[6]

Transformative events in the lives of health professionals do often lead to a vocation. Experiencing severe disability, catastrophic disease, addiction, and even having a child with a handicap have been wounding or initiatory events for many in the health-care field. The wounding may also be from psychic pain or the texture of a complicated life. Becoming "wounded" in these ways does not occur merely by going to school and learning a trade. Rather, the tools and techniques taught in health-care professions serve as a shield to protect one from the wounding—from the arrow of understanding. The stress on objectivity in all professions keeps the practitioner removed, aloof, and untouched by his or her work. The "wounded healer" is an apt metaphor for the empathy, understanding, and a certain richness of character that are lacking in the current system of health.

The mission of the wounded healer, in any era, any culture, is difficult and treacherous. Intense involvement in healing is a challenge to one's own life. The initiatory journey of the wounded healer that involves personal growth and transformation distinctly parallels the healing journey toward wholeness, embracing what is feared, learning to trust life, and so forth. Because of this, the healer and the healed are able to join each other on the path of self-awareness and self-development; each is able to be deeply affected by the presence and experience of the other.

The feminine principles of healing—subjectivity, relatedness, understanding—*are* the qualities of the wounded healer. The decision to adopt those principles should be undertaken seriously, and with great reservation. To follow in the tradition of the wounded healer is to work in sacred space, in places where the meaning of existence is constantly being confronted, where life and death in their awesome and terrible dimensions are being faced. Those who chose, or are chosen, to work in such space feel honored and humbled to be part of the transcendent process, knowing full well that the demands are far reaching, sometimes overwhelming. Entering that space requires passion and courage and knowledge that not a single moment is banal. It requires not only an appreciation for the body-mind bridge, but also an awareness of the presence of spirit. The wounded healer consciously shares another's life, moving with that person into the realms of the spirit and recapturing, together, the knowing that was lost, the memories of the infinite.

The work of the shaman, which I have previously described, is the work of the wounded healer. Shamans are capable of

> pearl diving in the collective unconscious and discerning the information writ in their own entrails and bones, the knack of humming the bloodsong on the heartstring. . . . The shaman, like Plato's philosopher, has found the Sun Door and gone outside the cave, has burrowed into the depths of the cave and found that door, too. His (her) job is to bring back images for healing of the soul.[7]

The role has been long abdicated by priests, by physicians, by therapists, and even by artists who have forgotten the healing function of their media.

The rewards of this work are many. For, if it is true that work is love made visible, in no other place or function is there more opportunity to make love visible. Such work is a way of learning who we are—the charge given to human beings by most religious disciplines of the world. As Theodore Roszak said about the wisdom of the Buddha,

> Responsible work is an embodiment of love, and love is the only discipline that will serve in shaping the personality, the only discipline that makes the mind whole and constant for a lifetime of effort. There hovers about a true vocation that paradox of all significant self-knowledge—our capacity to find ourselves by losing ourselves. We lose ourselves in our love of the task before us and, in that moment, we learn an identity that lives both within and beyond us.[8]

GIVING VOICE/ADDING BALANCE

The collective voices of women healers from generations past have much to offer on how to best facilitate a balance in the healing arts and sciences. The following points are derived from their experiences in order that we might actively and consciously determine our own.

Honoring Life

Honoring life is the essence of the healing arts, the heart of medical oath throughout time. All other points are trivial in comparison. The phrase should not be taken to mean that one uses all possible means to avoid death, as the creeds are usually understood. Honoring life is also honoring death. To honor life is also to appreciate the richness of existence, to know that many paths lead toward wholeness. This is of concern to woman as healer in developing her skills in a vocation.

Women must ensure that life is honored by preserving our rights and responsibilities for the biological aspects of our nature. The lessons of the

---

past speak clearly to this point. When women lose their knowledge of or individual responsibility in reproductive control, everyone suffers. This is precisely what happened when the church and state began to speak authoritatively on these matters—there ensued a downward spiral that included: loss of respect for woman's unique biological role in reproduction; depreciation of birthing, conception, and lovemaking as shameful activities; the increasingly demeaned status of women who serve other women as midwives; and the physical and mental devastation of women who are forced to bear, or not to bear, children.

The call for women healers to honor life is not a statement on the current abortion issue, but rather a warning of the devastation that occurs when women's individual responsibility is lost. When governments and other social institutions determine reproductive control, then abortions, birth control, or the killing or "exposure" of live infants are as likely to be mandated as the prohibition on abortions. When, for any reason, societies decide that life must be declared surplus, it is usually the girl babies that are quietly smothered at birth.

I believe that, given the chance, women will reinstate the ability to bring forth new life to its true rank of miracle among miracles. The rituals of birth will then bear little resemblance to the activities of the obstetric chamber. We have seen the beginnings of this movement in the past two decades with the resurgence of natural birthing practices, of home births attended by family and friends, and of the use of midwives among an educated, health-conscious people.

The greatest mischief in medicine has occurred because life was not honored. Women have been robbed of the glory of their own bodies with, in recent times, removal and mutilation of reproductive organs and breasts, and the treatment of natural passages of life—birthing, menstruation, menopause—as disease.

Paying Our Dues

Today's woman healers must have skills sufficient to include the masculine-feminine polarities of the cultural myth. Women, over time, have not moved with the currents of intellect, power, or technology—for reasons that are various and complicated, as we have seen. Their interest was not welcomed, but also, women often were uncomfortable with the aggressive power-based healing systems that have dominated the Western tradition.

During the nineteenth century, the pioneering women physicians warned that women would be left out of the healing professions if they ignored the scientific turning of the tide. The problem is not that new technologies were developed, but that they developed without the feminine voice, and therefore were liable to abuse. In hands devoid of compassion, advanced technologies have become weapons—from the invention of the forceps and advanced surgical techniques to the harnessing of the energies of the planet.

As the woman health reformers of the nineteenth century discovered, if they wanted to change society, they had to form a bridge between their world and the public sphere. They had to enter the institutions in order to be change makers. The same applies to women now. *Paying dues* means that we can no longer shirk what many of us consider the dreaded tasks of administration and leadership. As we saw from the role of women healers throughout time, their absence in the governance of institutions, on faculties, on boards, and on committees was a major contributor to their vulnerability as professionals. It enabled medical schools to close their doors to women almost overnight, has kept salaries and prestige low, and allowed licensing committees to exclude women from examining their own professions.

Women throughout the ages have chosen to do the actual work of healing. Thus, the machinery of the health professions, which includes writing, discovery, research, and administration, has been left to men. History shows that this division of labor has done women no favors. Not all women will decide to abdicate the clinical work—nor should they—but support and encouragement should be tendered to those who do.

Women today, especially those in their middle years, are admirably equipped for these tasks of bridging worlds and leadership. The last two decades have provided an unusual environment for "consciousness raising" and for self-reflection. As a consequence, women have sought ways to empower themselves, as mothers, wives, professionals, and members of a spiritual community. They now have a sense of where they've been, who they are, and what they can become to fill their lives with adventure and meaning. Men have rarely been afforded such luxury. It is time, though, for the self-empowerment to lead to the next step, which is to inject balanced action into the public sphere.

It is especially important that women make a written record of our ideas, our accomplishments, and the way the world appears to us. From the very earliest roots of Western medicine, in ancient Sumer, the scribes structured reality. By selectively omitting women from their writings, they left us with an obtuse lineage and little vision of the future. In modern works, again, we witness the selective omission of women and the minimization of their contribution. Women's names and their ideas have been quickly buried under the avalanche of words that have flowed from the pens of men. Yet the lasting contributions of a few great women live still in their writings.

Written works are the legacy we offer our daughters—and their daughters—who seek the path of healing. They will ensure the continuity of women's thought. Women have always written valuable personal missives; these sustained the network of women in the past century. Women have founded publishing houses to effect the movement of their thoughts into print, and typed newsletters, and established journals. When women healers and scientists write from their hearts, the works are often rejected as too mushy, nonlinear, nonrational, convoluted, emotional, and illogical. The world is not accustomed to reading an impassioned and unabashed feminine voice. This creates some problems in publishing through normal channels, ones that need to be circumvented in any way possible in order to keep our thoughts in print.

Women who have made a difference in the world with their writing usually are able to write only after a long day's work, and while everyone else sleeps. Writing under such circumstances requires enormous energy and support. The unity of woman's effort is also critical in a broader sense, as will be discussed next.

The Sisterhood

Women have always found solace and joy in each other's kitchens, and arms, and words. Sisterhood has been the bond that has held women healers together in the dimmest days of Western civilization. The support groups of women were so powerful, and so greatly feared, that they became a target of witchcraft accusations for several hundred years. Women healers taught each other the healing arts when training was forbidden and the guilds closed to them. The oral tradition of woman's domestic medicine carried through the centuries the best of the healing lore available. The energy that has sustained midwifery, albeit at a much diminished level currently, has been through a sisterhood of women helping other women.

It is in times of women's most openly coming together that their healing arts are most likely to flourish. During the latter half of the last century, and again in the 1960s when feminist movements flowered, the greatest advances in the women's healing professions have taken place. Today, when groups largely composed of women act together for a single goal, they can be extraordinarily successful. The problems we face in networking with each other are difficult, but not insurmountable. Women do not have much experience at being team players. We don't take well to the jockeying and sparring that characterize a group's setting and achieving goals. In the past, women have been unclear about their strategies. Would strength come from standing apart from men? Or would it come from integrating so completely that we looked, talked, and thought like them? Weaknesses arose from indecisiveness and factionalism within the ranks of women themselves.

We must recognize strength in numbers. Granted, sheer numbers of women won't alter the way of healing, unless we contribute something different to the system. The new genre of woman healer fully intends to do that. The women's guilds have already made headway. Nurses have made significant gains in lobbying for their needs. Social work, a profession largely of women, has likewise been successful in many states at obtaining independent licensure. Women medical students and faculties in some schools have been instrumental in revising the curriculum to include the teaching of holistic and humane practices. The groups of women healers that draw from many professions are powerful in bringing together and presenting the feminine point of view. The impact of women on institutions has inestimable potential.

What is presently being written by women healers shows that gaining equality in the Western health-care system is no longer the main issue. Women healers now find the system itself unsatisfactory; rather than equality, they seek massive change and vitalization of the institutions.

Another lesson from the sisterhood of women healers is that we must support each other in tangible ways. The women physicians of the nineteenth century were exemplary in this. They, and women's support groups, financed the opening of Johns Hopkins Medical School, insisting that women be accepted on the same basis as men. The event was regarded as the biggest victory for feminism of the century. They made it happen with money. Women's money also opened the hospitals that gave women an opportunity to practice and provided the best medical care available to women and children. Florence Nightingale's financial means and the contributions to her name enabled her to found her school of nursing. Furthermore, her private funding provided some protection to women against the roughest edges of exploitation.

A significant amount of the financial resources in this country is in women's names, yet control is usually abdicated to men—stockbrokers, investment counselors, accountants, and husbands. We need to take a hard look at why we let this happen, and regain our influence. Whenever women control their own resources, just as when they control their own bodies, life gets more humane.

We can donate private funds, using them wisely to help one another. We must place contingencies on our gifts, insisting that women be hired and promoted, or that women being treated within the system receive humane care. We should appoint ourselves to the boards of those agencies dependent upon our money to ensure that our desires are not forgotten. We can determine that funds be diverted away from medical schools and other graduate and undergraduate training institutions that uphold models of education that exploit women as professionals or as patients. As women rise in conscious responsibility we will serve in decision-making roles in government and industry. In such positions, women can insist that no grant or contract be awarded nor wage be paid to organizations or individuals who violate human rights. We can do that now and in the future, but only if we speak collectively.

CONFRONTING THE SHADOW

In my search for the historical precedent of woman as healer, my great hope was to uncover a sanctioned lineage that ran strongly through time. Women healers do, of course, have a rich and honorable history, and the messages from the past are profound. However, a most overpowering specter has also come forth which must be confronted in light of incontrovertible evidence. Women healers have borne, and still bear, the brunt of man's failures and his uncertainties in the healing professions. Women have, willingly or not, taken on the shadow side of humanity's healing function. This is summarized by the following points:

1. Women's accomplishments in the healing arts and sciences have been minimized, trivialized, or forgotten.
2. Innovations by women, their writings, and their tradition of domestic medicine have been stolen or plagiarized by men who have failed to give credit to the originators.
3. Women have been irrationally blamed for men's failures to cure, becoming the scapegoats for problems as diverse as ecological stresses, poor medical practices, and the evil believed to be inherent in humanity.
4. Women's healing arts, or professions where women form a majority of members, have been banned without rational cause, legislated against, made the focus for persecution, and placed under the direct authority of male professionals.
5. Women in the health-care professions have been exploited.

None of the above is ancient history. Everything listed happens on the scientific and medical scene today. The subjugation comes overtly in wage inequities and in legal restraints, and more covertly in terms of attitudes.

Sadly, we women are so socialized into the hierarchal, power-based model of healing that we also blame, scapegoat, minimize, exploit, and mistrust the contributions of other women. We are very hard on each other. We are burned out, oppressed, unhappy, demeaned, and victimized, and have been for centuries. None of that makes us easy to live with.

Despite the strong sense of sisterhood, when stresses mount, we attack each other. Like all victims, we know only two primary models of behavior:

our own cowering demeanor and the victimizer's aggressive stance. The latter is the putated model of strength, and what we turn to in defense. The bonds of sisterhood, although ancient, are also fragile, readily overwhelmed by greed and power, and the need to do whatever is necessary to survive in a system.

Those of us who have managed to practice autonomously and independently, to lead in male-dominated fields, or to spearhead scientific discoveries, have paid a price. Our role models were men. We learned to speak, think, dress, and act like men. In doing so, we failed to cultivate our precious femininity and, more often than not, were unaware that we had lost half of ourselves. Now, as so many of us, men and women alike, chart a more balanced course, we are required to strike out into untamed territory without a map, naming the places and obstacles, the paths and turning points, as we move along.

BALANCING OUT THE ART AND SCIENCE OF HEALTH

Women must take a proactive, rather than reactive, stance to ensure that history does not repeat itself. Deciding who we will be as the twenty-first century opens is the first step. For professions in transition, such as nursing, this is most critical. As goals are redefined, the healing process will begin.

The growth and change in health care will obviously depend upon the breadth of our energies and the richness of our creative process. Changes most likely to result from women exercising their conscious responsibility include:

1. Differences in the nature of medical education and in the practice of medicine itself.
2. A shift from the hierarchy of a power-based health system to one of more egalitarian proportions.
3. The elevation of women's professions to higher levels of competency, respect, and responsibility.
4. More attention to larger systems of health, including the ecology of the earth.
5. The inclusion of therapeutics that treat the mental and spiritual aspects of health within the mainstream of health care.
6. A more human-centered healing system, which will be assured if the feminine nurturing voice is included.

All of this portends significant changes in the art and science of healing. When the balance is finally achieved, and the feminine voice is heard, much of what is now practiced in the name of health care will be deemed clearly unethical.

We must be fearlessly willing to manifest in our lives and healing arts what women have always known—the unity of being and the reality of the invisible spaces. We can neither exclude nor can we accept unconditionally and exclusively the products of the intuition or the products of intellect; instead we can unite these and all other polarities that characterize the myth that has divided us. The fully expressed feminine voice can only occur when the masculine is recognized as part of our own totality. Women healers can know power and compassion; they can, like the women healers of the past, be gentle warriors. There is no incompatibility here, but only wholeness and completion.

When women healers emerge fully, the tradition of gender bias in American healing guilds will end. The thread of sisterhood that reaches back into the epochs of prehistory will take on a fuller life. Naturally, the women who honor the balance of the masculine-feminine myth in healing are aligned with men of similar sentiments. There are fewer men openly embracing this position, perhaps because they fear it and dare not, or because support in the professions for balanced men who acknowledge their feminine self is so very limited. Often, they are disenfranchised souls who have fled the inhumanities of medicine. All are wounded healers who have come to the position of balance from their own personal experiences.

Together, we will begin to learn how to speak to one another across the chasm of different worlds; to work together in ways that are creative and not destructive. We will learn to love each other, and in doing so, fulfill the prime mission of the healer by honoring life.

Notes

Introduction

1. Quoted in R. M. Morantz, C. S. Pomerleau, and C. H. Fenichel, eds., *In Her Own Words* (New Haven: Yale University Press, 1982), preface.

Chapter 1: The Primeval Turning Points

1. For resources on the goddess figures see: F. Hančar, "Zum Problem der Venusstatuetten im eurasiatischen Jungpaläolithikim," *Praehistorische Zeitschrift*, XXX–XXXI Band, 1/2 Heft, 1939–1940; M. Gimbutas, *The Goddesses and Gods of Old Europe* (Berkeley: University of California Press, 1982); and B. Johnson, *Lady of the Beasts: Ancient Images of the Goddess and Her Sacred Animals* (San Francisco: Harper & Row, 1981).
2. W. Schmidt, *Der Ursprung der Gottesidee,* 12 vols. (Munster in Westfalia; Aschendorff, 1912–1955); and W. Schmidt, "The Position of Women with Regard to Property in Primitive Society," *American Anthropologist,* Vol. 37 (1935): 244–56. Reported in J. Campbell, *Primitive Mythology: The Masks of God* (New York: Penguin, 1987). The latter is an informed source on both Paleolithic and Neolithic myth.
3. J. E. Harrison, *Themis,* 2nd rev. ed. (Cambridge: University Press, 1927), p. 459.
4. J. Campbell, *Occidental Mythology: The Masks of God* (New York: Penguin, 1964), p. 86.
5. G. Lerner, *The Creation of Patriarchy* (New York: Oxford University Press, 1987), p. 223.
6. Campbell, *Occidental Mythology,* pp. 26–27.
7. Ibid., p. 70.

Chapter 2: Sumer

1. Campbell, *Primitive Mythology,* pp. 143–150.
2. D. Wolkstein & S. Kramer, *Inanna: Queen of Heaven and Earth* (New York: Harper & Row, 1983).
3. Ibid., p. 4.

4. J. Ochshorn, "Ishtar and Her Cult," in C. Olson, ed., *The Book of the Goddess* (New York: Crossroad Publishing, 1983).
5. H. Zimmern, "Babylonische Hyumnen und Gebete in Auswahl," *Der Alte Orient,* 7 Jahrgang, Heft 3 (Leipzig, 1905).
6. B. Landsberger and M. Reiner, eds., "Old Babylonian Proto-Lu List," *Materials for the Sumerian Lexicon,* vol. 12 (Rome, 1969) quoted in G. Lerner, *Creation of Patriarchy.*
7. R. C. Thompson, "Assyrian Medical Texts," *Proceedings of the Royal Society of Medicine* 17 (1924): pp. 1–34.
8. See, for example, G. Majno, *The Healing Hand: Man and Wound in the Ancient World* (Cambridge: Harvard University Press, 1975).
9. S. N. Kramer, "Poets and Religious and Anthropological Aspects of the Legacy of Sumer," in D. Schmandt-Besserat, ed., *The Legacy of Sumer: Invited Lectures on the Middle East* (presented at the University of Texas at Austin, 1976).
10. A. S. Lyons and R. J. Petrucelli, *Medicine: An Illustrated History* (New York: Harry N. Abrams, Inc., 1978).
11. K. C. Hurd-Mead, *A History of Women in Medicine* (Haddam, Conn.: Haddam Press, 1938). This book, now out of print, is the most thoroughly documented compendium in English on women healers who lived prior to the nineteenth century.
12. Majno, *The Healing Hand,* pp. 29–68.
13. Ibid., p. 54.

Chapter 3: Denmark

1. These same geological conditions have yielded recent finds in England, Northern Germany, and the Netherlands. See D. Brothwell, *The Bogman and the Archaeology of People* (London: British Museum Publications, 1986). In this book, I have restricted discussion to the territory and culture of Denmark.
2. P. V. Glob, *The Mound People* (London: Paladin, 1983), p. 70.
3. P. V. Glob, *Denmark* (Ithaca, N.Y., and London: Cornell University Press, 1967), and E. Roesdahl, *Viking Age Denmark* (London: British Museum Publications, 1982). Both publications provide excellent descriptions of life in ancient Denmark, from which these and the following notions on healing were derived.
4. Glob, *The Mound People,* p. 116.
5. S. Odman, "An Attempt to Explain the Berserk-Raging of Ancient Nordic Warriors through Natural History," *Nya Handlingar,* Vol. 5 (Kungliga Vetenskaps Akademien: Stockholm, 1784): 240–247. Gordon Wasson, however, disagrees that the mushrooms would produce the frenzy noted in battle. See R. G. Wasson, *Soma: Divine Mushroom of Immortality* (New York: Harcourt Brace Jovanovich, 1968).
6. H. R. E. Davidson, *Gods and Myths of Northern Europe* (New York: Penguin, 1964).

7. P. V. Glob, *The Bog People* (London: Faber and Faber, 1969).
8. Brothwell, *The Bog Man,* pp. 56–76.
9. Glob, *The Mound People,* pp. 162–164.
10. Glob, *The Bog People,* p. 159.
11. Tacitus, *Germania,* trans. H. Mattingly, rev. S. A. Handford (Harmondsworth and Boston: Penguin Classics, 1948).
12. Glob, *The Bog People.*
13. Brothwell, *The Bog Man.*
14. Glob, *The Bog People,* p. 162.
15. M. Eliade, *Shamanism* (New York: Pantheon, 1964), and M. Harner, *The Way of the Shaman* (San Francisco: Harper & Row, 1980).
16. Glob, *The Bog People,* p. 157.
17. S. Sturluson, *Prose Edda,* trans. L. M. Hollander (Austin: University of Texas Press, 1962). Quote is from Davidson, *Gods and Myths,* p. 114.
18. Davidson, ibid., states that the harmful aspects of *seiðr* were minimally emphasized; H. P. Duerr, *Dreamtime* (New York: Basil Blackwell, 1986) believes the practitioners were often prosecuted or executed, and therefore that the practices should not be overly romanticized. While most of the stories support the shamanic aspect of the Vanir, M. Eliade (*Shamanism*) believes that since they did not go to the "underworld" in their shamanic journeys, they were not practicing classic shamanism. I would like to propose the thesis that European women shamans typically go to the "upperworld" in trance, unlike men, in part supported by the witch accusations discussed in Chapter 10 of this text.
19. Davidson, ibid.
20. Tacitus, *Germania,* p. 108.
21. Strabo, *Geography,* cited in Glob, *The Bog People,* p. 176.
22. W. Alexander, *The History of Women: From the Earliest Antiquity to the Present Time Giving Some Account of Almost Every Interesting Particular Concerning That Sex, Among All Nations, Ancient and Modern* (London: printed for W. Strahan & T. Cadell in the Strand, 1779).
23. Ibid., p. 58. "Thorbioga" may have been Thorgerda, a legendary Danish woman linked with the Vanir in the Norse sagas.
24. Glob, *Denmark,* p. 167.

Chapter 4: The Healing Legacy from Greece

1. This material from Homer's *Odyssey* (about 700 B.C.) has been quoted from C. Palmer and H. Horowitz, *Shaman Woman, Mainline Lady* (New York: Quill, 1982). This book presents an intriguing picture of women's use of drugs in the healing arts.
2. J. H. Baas, *History of Medicine,* 2 vols., translated by H. E. Anderson (Huntington, N.Y.: R. E. Krieger Co., 1971).
3. K. C. Hurd-Mead, *History of Women in Medicine,* provides the most extensive categorization of ancient women healers in myth, as well as citations of the

contributions of women to the healing art. She sought her information on tombstones and epitaphs and in osbcure works. Classic mythologies, such as T. Bulfinch, *Myths of Greece and Rome* (New York: Penguin, 1979), recite the Olympian pantheon only, an era when the goddesses had taken on roles of war and the hunt, and when the healing aspects were minimized. The works which focus on the earlier, pre-Hellenic mythology, such as J. E. Harrison, *Myths of Greece and Rome* (London: Earnest Benn, 1927), address the feminine healing pantheon. A readable current resource is C. Spretnak, *Lost Goddesses of Early Greece* (Boston: Beacon Press, 1981).

4. H. Kursh, *Cobras in the Garden* (Wisconsin: Harvey Press, 1965), summarized in M. Stone, *When God Was a Woman* (New York: Harcourt Brace Jovanovich, 1976).

5. M. Stone, *When God Was a Woman,* p. 203.

6. Menstrual blood has been the subject of primal fear and worship since the beginning of time. It was used as a panacea, a primary ingredient in casting spells, and even as a pesticide—menstruating women ran through the fields with their skirts raised to kill the bugs. Pliny, writing around the first century A.D., thought that menstrual blood drove men and dogs mad.

7. For an expanded list see Hurd-Mead, *History of Women in Medicine.*

Chapter 5: Women of Rome

1. See Hurd-Mead, *History of Women in Medicine,* for expanded recitation of Roman goddesses of healing, pp. 48–50.

2. M. R. Salzman, "Magna Mater: Great Mother of the Roman Empire," in Olson, ed., *The Book of the Goddess,* pp. 60–67.

3. Quoted by Hurd-Mead, *History of Women in Medicine,* p. 41.

4. Soranus, *Gynecology,* translated, with introduction, by O. Temkin (Baltimore: Johns Hopkins University Press, 1956).

5. Celsus, *De Medicina,* translated by W. G. Spencer (Cambridge: Harvard University Press, 1938).

6. Scribonius Largus, "De compositione medicamentorum liber," cited by Hurd-Mead, *History of Women in Medicine,* pp. 59–60.

7. Ibid., pp. 62–64.

8. Ibid., pp. 64–65.

9. Ibid., p. 69.

Chapter 6: Brilliant Early Christian Flowering

1. M. Fox, *The Coming of the Cosmic Christ* (San Francisco: Harper & Row, 1988).

2. E. S. Fiorenza, "Women in the Early Christian Movement," in C. P. Christ and J. Plaskow, eds., *Womanspirit Rising* (San Francisco: Harper & Row, 1979).

3. E. Pagels, "What Became of God the Mother?" in Christ & Plaskow, eds., *Womanspirit Rising.*

4. The summary is derived from Pagels, ibid.
5. St. Jerome is quoted in F. Heer, *The Medieval World* (New York: New American Library, 1961), p. 322.

Chapter 7: Medieval Christian Cosmology

1. Heer, *The Medieval World;* J. Huizinga, *The Waning of the Middle Ages* (Harmondsworth: Penguin, 1985). Both of these authors eloquently describe life in the Middle Ages. While not feminist historians, by any means, they write with unusual sensitivity about woman's role and the interplay between religion and the feminine as the Church crystallized into form and dogma. Both are regarded as premier scholars of these times.
2. D. R. Hopkins, *Princes and Peasants: Smallpox in History* (Chicago: University of Chicago Press, 1983).
3. M. Bishop, *The Middle Ages* (New York: American Heritage, 1985).
4. B. S. Anderson and J. P. Zinsser, *A History of Their Own: Women in Europe* (New York: Harper & Row, 1988). This recent volume is thorough, novel, and exceptional in its presentation of woman's history.
5. A major source of information on prescriptions from the Middle Ages is L. Thorndike, *Magic and Experimental Science During the First 13 Centuries of Our Era,* 2 vols. (New York, 1923).
6. F. Gies and J. Gies, *Life in a Medieval City* (New York: Harper & Row, 1969).
7. F. Gies and J. Gies, *Women in the Middle Ages* (New York: Barnes & Noble, 1978).
8. Gies and Gies, *Life in a Medieval City,* p. 53.
9. Bishop, *The Middle Ages.* This provides a concise summary of the disease-ridden medieval population.
10. S. de Renzi, ed., *Collectio salernitana,* 5 vols. (Naples, 1852–59).
11. History suggests we should not be too hasty in classifying what is superstitious medicine and what is "real." The power of the imagination, or the placebo effect, has been well documented in modern research. Furthermore, research on many of the ingredients in botanical preparations, and on the psychophysiological effects of ancient rituals, suggests that they may have significant healing properties. See, for extensive documentation: J. Achterberg, *Imagery in Healing: Shamanism and Modern Medicine* (Boston: Shambhala, 1985).
12. de Renzi, *Collectio salernitana,* Vol. IV, p. 23.
13. M. A. Nutting and L. L. Dock, *History of Nursing,* Vol. 1 (New York: Putnam & Sons, 1907), pp. 260–265.
14. Bishop, *The Middle Ages,* pp. 146–148. An additional resource on relics is: E. Maple, *Magic, Medicine and Quackery* (New York: A. S. Barnes, 1968).
15. S. de Beauvoir, *The Second Sex,* translated by H. M. Parshley (New York: Alfred A. Knopf, 1953), p. 171.
16. Fox, *Coming of the Cosmic Christ.*

17. C. Singer, "The Scientific Views and Visions of Saint Hildegard (1098–1180)," in C. Singer, ed., *Studies in the History and Method of Science* (Oxford: Clarendon Press, 1917).

18. Hildegard has several biographers, including C. Singer, ibid.; L. Thorndike, *Magic and Experimental Science*, Vol. 2, includes a summary of her medical works; Gies and Gies, *Women in the Middle Ages,* offer a chapter overview. S. Flanagan, *Hildegard of Bingen, 1098–1179* (London and New York: Routledge, 1989), gives an interesting account of her life. Other resources include: G. Uhlein, *Meditation with Hildegard of Bingen* (Santa Fe: Bear & Co., 1982). M. Fox, *Illuminations of Hildegard of Bingen* (Santa Fe: Bear & Co., 1985).

19. L. Thorndike, *Magic and Experimental Science,* Vol. 2, pp. 154.

20. Heer, *The Medieval World,* pp. 118.

21. Ibid., pp. 317, 323.

Chapter 8: The Tapestry

1. S. Griffin, *Woman and Nature* (New York: Harper & Row, 1978). This book contains a wealth of information on woman's connection to nature; history, poetry, science, and culture are interwoven in Griffin's thesis.

Chapter 9: Women Healers as Heretics

1. Campbell, *Occidental Mythology,* pp. 13–14.

2. J. Michelet, *Satanism and Witchcraft,* translated by W. R. Allinson, 1860 (Secaucas, N.J.: Citadel, 1939).

3. Thomas Aquinas, *Summa theologica.*

4. J. B. Russell, *History of Witchcraft* (London: Thames & Hudson, 1980). Russell, a professor of history at the University of California, Santa Barbara, presents a concise discussion of the monism/dualism issue that fueled the heretic hunts, and continues to be a source of debate in modern religions.

5. Ibid., p. 33.

6. R. H. Robbins, *Encyclopedia of Witchcraft and Demonology,* 1959 (New York: Bonanza Books, 1981), p. 271.

7. Dr. Lynn Thorndike's work, *History of Magic and Experimental Science*, two volumes, was the first and most thorough exposition of the early bridges between magic and science and is a premier source of information on these earliest scientists. While the inquiry of *Woman as Healer* is slightly different from Dr. Thorndike's, a significant debt of scholarship is due nevertheless.

8. Arnald of Villanova, *Antidotarium,* cap. 3 (from edition of his complete works, published in Lyons, France, 1532).

9. Arnald of Villanova, *De epilepsia,* cap. 25; *Brevarium,* III, 4, and *Brevarium,* II, 45.

10. Michael Scot, *Physionomia (De secretis natural* [alternate title]) caps. 46–50. (Amsterdam, 1740).

11. Michael Scot, *Liber introductorius*, Bodleian 266 manuscript, fifteenth century.
12. Albertus Magnus, *Sleep and Waking*, translated by Petrus de Prussia, 1621, cap. 12.
13. Thorndike, *History of Magic and Experimental Science*, Vol. 2, summarizes Magnus' work.
14. R. Bacon, *Opus tertium*, edited by A. G. Little (Aberdeen, 1912).
15. T. Aquinas, *Quodibet*, translated by E. Frettle and P. Mare, *Opera omnia* (Paris, 1871–1880), cap. 11.
16. T. Aquinas, *Contra gentiles*, III, 103, *Opera omnia*.
17. Arnald of Villanova and Roger Bacon were themselves repeatedly challenged by the Inquisition for having ventured opinions on controversial issues of healing and theology.

Chapter 10: Fate of the Wise Women

1. Huizinga, *The Waning of the Middle Ages*, provides a description of the schizophrenic and abrupt temper of the times, where, he notes, one smelled both blood and roses.
2. F. Braudel, *The Structures of Everyday Life: The Limits of the Possible*, trans. (New York: Harper & Row, 1981).
3. Bishop, *The Middle Ages*, p. 306.
4. Russell, *History of Witchcraft*.
5. Bishop, *The Middle Ages*, p. 313.
6. E. Power, "Some Women Practitioners of Medicine in the Middle Ages," *Proceedings of the Royal Society of Medicine*, 1922, History of Medicine Section, pp. 6, 21.
7. Ibid., p. 22.
8. Ibid., p. 22.
9. K. Bücher, *Die Frauenfrage im Mittelalter* (Tübingen, 1910).
10. Maple, *Magic, Medicine and Quackery*, p. 64.
11. Ibid.
12. Ibid., p. 66.
13. E. Boulding, *The Underside of History* (Boulder, Westview Press, 1976).
14. Michelet, *Satanism and Witchcraft*, xix.
15. Robbins, *Encyclopedia of Witchcraft*, p. 3.
16. C. Larner, *Enemies of God* (Baltimore: Johns Hopkins University Press, 1981), p. 100.
17. Ibid.; B. Walker, *The Crone* (New York: Harper & Row, 1985); B. Walker, *The Women's Encyclopedia of Myths and Secrets* (San Francisco: Harper & Row, 1983); B. Ehrenreich and D. English, *Witches, Midwives, and Nurses: A History of Women Healers* (Old Westbury, N.Y.: Feminist Press, 1973); M. Daly, *Gynecology: The Metaethics of Radical Feminism* (Boston: Beacon Press, 1970); M. Daly, *The Church and the Second Sex* (Boston: Beacon Press, 1985).

18. W. Pressel, *Hexen und Hexenmeister* (Stuttgart, 1860), reprinted in Robbins, *Encyclopedia of Witchcraft*, p. 510.
19. M. Gage, *Women, Church and State*, 1893 (Watertown, Mass.: Persephone Press, 1980).
20. These stories by children of being forced to engage in satanic adventures are not unlike those of children who recently have accused adults of identical crimes in the United States.
21. Russell, in *History of Witchcraft*, notes that most of the accusations were originally associated with the heretic trials, and hence, were not new ideas during the witch craze.
22. Figures are derived from primary sources by Robbins, *Encyclopedia of Witchcraft*, unless otherwise noted. N. Cohn, *Europe's Inner Demons* (London: Paladin, 1975), identifies exaggerated numbers in a few secondary sources and suggests that in some regions the trials did not claim as many lives as is typically stated. To adjust the figure downward, as Cohn has done, does not ameliorate the atrocity.
23. Robbins, *Encyclopedia of Witchcraft*, p. 551.
24. Gage, *Women, Church and State*.
25. J. Springer and H. Kramer, *Malleus maleficarum*, trans. by Montague Summers (London: Pushkin Press, 1948).
26. E. Clark and H. Richardson, *Women and Religion* (New York: Harper & Row, 1977), p. 120.
27. Springer and Kramer, *Malleus maleficarum*, Part I, Question 6.
28. Ibid.
29. Springer and Kramer, *Malleus maleficarum*, Part 2, Question 1; Chaps. 6 & 7.
30. Ibid.
31. Ibid., p. xviii.
32. From Aquinas, *Quodibet*. The Inquisitions often cited the Church Fathers in this regard, believing that women (or witches) had control over the "generative" forces.
33. The studies are reviewed in D. O'Keefe, *Stolen Lightning* (New York: Vintage, 1983). The sociological analyses of the witch phenomenon have yielded more precise—if circumscribed—data than most approaches.
34. V. Bullough, *The Subordinate Sex* (Chicago: University of Chicago Press, 1973).
35. William Perkins, *A Discourse of the Damned Art of Witchcraft* (Cambridge, 1608, 1610). Note: the use of the male pronoun was common to refer to either sex—much as it is today.
36. G. Gifford, *A Dialogue Concerning Witches and Witchcraft*, 1593, 1603, 1842, ed. Beatrice White (Oxford: Oxford University Press, 1931).
37. C. L. Ewen, *Witchcraft and Demonism* (London: Heath Cranton, 1933).
38. Springer and Kramer, *Malleus maleficarum*.
39. R. Scot, *The Discovery of Witchcraft*, 1584, 6, 1.

40. Quoted in Gage, *Women, Church and State*, 281.
41. Duerr, *Dreamtime*.
42. Discussed in Robbins, *Encyclopedia of Witchcraft*.
43. F. Bacon, *Works*, (London, 1876), Vol. 2, p. 664.
44. J. F. Rubel, cited in Duerr, *Dreamtime*.
45. J. Harttliepp, quoted by Duerr, p. 4.
46. M. Harner, *Hallucinogens and Shamanism* (New York: Oxford University Press, 1973).
47. Larner, *Enemies of God*, p. 129.
48. M. Harris, *Cows, Pigs, Wars and Witches: The Riddles of Culture* (New York: Vintage, 1978).
49. M. Murray, *The God of the Witches* (Oxford: Oxford University Press, 1970). J. G. Frazier, *The Golden Bough* (New York: Avenel, 1981).
50. Meyer's work and thesis are discussed in Russell, *History of Witchcraft*.
51. J. Michelet, *Satanism and Witchcraft*, pp. 88, 89.
52. G. Zilboorg, *The Medical Man and the Witch During the Renaissance*, 1935 (New York: Cooper Square, 1969).
53. Ibid., p. 58.
54. Ibid., p. 73.
55. Ibid., p. 63.
56. Larner, *Enemies of God*, p. 195.
57. H. Leventhal, *In the Shadow of the Enlightenment* (New York: New York University Press, 1976). Quotes Samuel Johnson: "No sir, witchcraft had ceased; and therefore an act of parliament was passed to prevent persecution for what was not witchcraft. Why it ceased, we cannot tell, as we cannot tell the manner of many other things."

Chapter 11: Absent at the Birth of Modern Medicine

1. M. Hooker, ed., *Descartes* (Baltimore: Johns Hopkins University Press, 1978).
2. D. J. Boorstin, *The Discoverers* (New York: Random House, 1983), p. 347.
3. F. Yates, *The Rosicrucian Enlightenment* (Boston: Shambhala, 1978), p. 190.
4. E. F. Keller, *Reflections on Gender and Science* (New Haven: Yale University Press, 1985).
5. Ibid., p. 47.
6. J. H. Robertson, "Valerius Terminus on the Interpretation of Nature," in *The Philosophical Works of Francis Bacon* (London: Routledge & Sons, 1905), p. 188.
7. B. Farrington, *The Philosophy of Francis Bacon* (Chicago: Phoenix, 1964), p. 197.
8. Quotes from Keller, *Reflections*, p. 36.
9. Farrington, *The Philosophy of Francis Bacon*, p. 194.
10. C. Merchant, *The Death of Nature* (New York: Harper & Row, 1980).
11. Ibid., p. 3.

12. H. C. Agrippa, *Three Books of Occult Philosophy or Magic* (Chicago: Hahn & Whitehead, 1898).

13. F. Hartman, *Paracelsus: Life and Prophecies* (Blauvelt, N.Y.: Rudolf Steiner, 1973), pp. 111–112.

14. Achterberg, *Imagery in Healing*.

15. M. Lipinska, *Histoire des femmes médicine*, 1900, p. 58.

16. Lyons & Petrucelli, *Medicine, Illustrated History*, p. 454.

17. F. B. Rogers, *A Syllabus of Medical History* (Boston: Little, Brown, 1962).

18. M. Wortley Montagu, "Letters of the Right Honourable Lady Mary Wortley Montagu: Written during Her Travels in Europe, Asia and Africa to Persons of Distinction, Men of Letters, etc. in Different Parts of Europe," 3 vols. (London: printed for T. Beckett, 1717).

19. G. Miller, "Putting Lady Mary in Her Place: A Discussion of Historical Causation," *Bulletin of the History of Medicine*, 1981, 55: pp. 2–16.

20. "Sophia, a Person of Quality," 1739, *Woman Not Inferior to Man*, facsimile reprint (London: Bentham Press, 1975).

21. Hopkins, *Princes and Peasants*.

22. R. P. Stearns, "Remarks upon the Introduction of Inoculation for Smallpox in England," *Bulletin of the History of Medicine* 24 (1950): pp. 103–22, 115.

23. A. Corbin, *The Foul and the Fragrant* (Cambridge: Harvard University Press, 1986). Corbin presents a well-documented book describing the role of odor in the advent of sanitation and public health.

24. R. Dubos, *The Mirage of Health: Utopias, Progress, and Biological Change* (New York: Harper & Row, 1959).

Chapter 12: Gender and the Health Professions

1. R. M. Morantz, Introduction, in Morantz, Pomerleau, and Fenichel, *In Her Own Words*.

2. M. R. Walsh, *Doctors Wanted, No Women Need Apply* (New Haven: Yale University Press, 1977).

Chapter 13: Midwifery

1. J. Donnison, *Midwives and Medical Men* (New York: 1977). An excellent summary of English midwifery.

2. P. Willughby, *Observations on Midwifery. As Also the Countrey Midwifes Opusculum or Vade Mecum*, H. Blenkinsop, ed. (Warwick, England, 1863).

3. E. Röesslin, *The Byrthe of Mankynd, Otherwyse Named the Woman's Boke*, trans. from Latin, Thomas Raynalde, 1545, London. Quotes are from the preface.

4. J. B. Donegan, *Women and Men Midwives: Medicine, Morality, and Misogyny in Early America* (Westport, Conn.: Greenwood Press, 1978).

5. B. Rowland, *Medieval Woman's Guide to Health: The First English Gynecological Handbook* (Kent, Ohio: Kent State University Press, 1981).

6. Ibid., p. xiii.

7. Ibid., p. 14.
8. Michelet, *Satanism and Witchcraft*.
9. Fumigation required that the woman sit straddling a pot of burning or steaming plants, preferably those which had a pleasant odor. Some recipes also required that she smell foul odors (such as burning dog hair) at the same time, the purpose being to expel the vapors of disease.
10. J. Sharp, *The Midwives Book or the Whole Art of Midwifery*, 1671, quoted in H. Smith, "Gynecology and Ideology in Seventeenth Century England," in B. A. Carroll, ed., *Liberating Women's History: Theoretical and Critical Essays* (Urbana, Chicago and London: University of Illinois Press, 1976).
11. Ibid., p. 112.
12. The oath is discussed in many texts, including Donnison, *Midwives and Medical Men*. The original source appears to have been an anonymous book of oaths published in sixteenth-century London.
13. J. H. Aveling, *English Midwives: Their History and Their Prospects* (London: Churchill, 1872), pp. 125–126.
14. Willughby, *Observations in Midwifery*.
15. E. McGrew and M. P. McGrew, *Encyclopedia of Medical History* (New York: McGraw-Hill, 1985), p. 205.
16. H. Spencer, *The History of British Midwifery from 1650 to 1800*, cited in Hurd-Mead, *History of Women in Medicine*, p. 463.
17. W. Smellie, *A Treatise on the Theory and Practice of Midwifery*, 3rd ed. (London: D. Wilson & T. Durham, 1756).
18. B. A. Pugh, *Treatise of Midwifery, Chiefly with Regard to the Operation, with Several Improvements in That Art* (London: J. Buckland, 1754), pp. 64–65.
19. W. Harvey, *Anatomical Exercitations, Concerning the Generation of Living Creatures* (London, 1653), p. 488.
20. C. White, *Treatise on the Management of Pregnant and Lying-in Women* (London, 1773).
21. Figures produced by Dr. Farr of the Registrar-General's Office in England, 1876, reported in J. Donnison, *Midwives and Medical Men*.
22. J. M. Duncan, *Mortality of Childbed* (London, 1870).
23. Report of the College of Physicians, November 15, 1835, in W. R. Penman, *The Public Practice of Midwifery in Philadelphia*, transactions of the College of Physicians of Philadelphia, 37 (October 1869): p. 129.
24. Donnison, *Midwives and Medical Men*, p. 92.
25. J. van Pelt Quackenbush, An address delivered before the students of the Albany Medical College, Introductory to the Course on Obstetrics, November 5, 1855 (Albany: B. Taylor, 1855), p. 7.
26. H. Graham, *Eternal Eve* (London: W. Heinemann, 1950). The quoted material is from a discussion of C. Meigs' philosophy of women.
27. C. Meigs, *Females and Their Diseases* (Philadelphia: Lea & Blanchard, 1848), pp. 19–21.
28. C. Meigs, Lecture on some of the distinctive characteristics of the female,

delivered before the class of the Jefferson Medical College, January 5, 1847 (Philadelphia: Collins, 1847), pp. 6–17.

29. T. Ewell, *Letters to Ladies, Detailing Important Information Concerning Themselves and Infants* (Philadelphia: W. Brown, 1817).
30. J. Maubry, *The Female Physician* (London: James Holland, 1724), quoted in *A Short History of Midwifery* by J. S. Cutter and H. R. Viets (Philadelphia: W. B. Sanders, 1964), p. 12.
31. M. Stephens, *Domestic Midwife: or the Best Means of Preventing Danger in Childbirth considered* (London, 1795).
32. P. Thicknesse, *Man-Midwifery Analysed, and the Tendency of that Practice Detected and Exposed* (London: R. Davis, 1764).
33. V. Seaman, *The Midwives Monitor and Mother's Mirror* (New York: Isaac Collins, 1800).
34. A. Johnson, ed., *Dictionary of American Biography*, vol. 2 (New York, 1951).

Chapter 14: Every Woman Her Own Doctor

1. N. Cott, *The Bonds of Womanhood* (New Haven: Yale University Press, 1977).
2. R. M. Morantz, Introduction, in Morantz, Pomerleau, and Fenichel, *In Her Own Words*, p. 8.
3. K. Moore, *Victorian Wives* (London and New York: Allison & Busby, 1974), p. 4.
4. N. Cott, "Passionlessness: An Interpretation of Victorian Sexual Ideology, 1790–1850," *Signs: A Journal of Women in Culture and Society*, vol. 4, 21 (1978): pp. 219–236.
5. H. C. Wood, "The Heroic Treatment of Idiopathic Peritonitis," *Boston Medical and Surgical Journal*, 98 (1878): pp. 555–560.
6. C. Wilder, "Pulmonary Consumption, its Causes, Symptoms and Treatment," *Medical Communications of the Massachusetts Medical Society* 7, 2nd series, Vol. 3 (Boston, 1848).
7. R. Morantz, "Making Women Modern: Middle Class Women and Health Reform in Nineteenth Century America," *Journal of Social History*, 10 (Summer 1977): pp. 490–507.
8. S. E. Selby, "A Bloomer to her Sisters," *Water Cure Journal* 15 (1853): p. 131.
9. M. G. Nichols, "To the Women Who Read the Water Cure Journal," *Water Cure Journal* 14 (1852): p. 68.
10. M. G. Nichols, "Old School Medical Journals," *Water Cure Journal* 9 (1850): p. 181.
11. M. G. Nichols, "Woman, the Physician," *Water Cure Journal* 12 (1851): pp. 73–74.
12. M. G. Nichols and T. L. Nichols, *Marriage: Its History, Character and Results* (New York: T. L. Nichols, 1854).
13. As she promised, the secrets of the women who wrote to Pinkham were never divulged by her or her company.

14. R. L. Numbers, "Do-it-yourself the Sectarian Way," in G. B. Risse, R. L. Numbers, and J. W. Leavitt, eds., *Medicine Without Doctors: Home Health Care in American History* (New York: Science History Publications, 1977).
15. A Berman, *The Impact of the Nineteenth-Century Botanico Medical Movement on American Pharmacy and Medicine* (Ph.D. dissertation, Univ. of Wisconsin, 1954).
16. From the *Thomsonian Recorder* of Ohio, Preface to Vol. 2 (1833): p. v.
17. O. W. Holmes, some more recent views on homeopathy, quoted in H. L. Coulter, *Divided Legacy* (Washington, D.C.: McGrath, 1973).
18. R. L. Numbers, *Do-it-yourself the Sectarian Way.*

Chapter 15: The Warriors

1. The Women's Medical Association of New York City, eds., *Mary Putnam Jacobi, M.D.: A Pathfinder in Medicine* (New York: G. P. Putnam, 1925), p. 397.
2. H. S. Hunt, *Glances and Glimpses,* 1856 (Boston: reprinted 1970).
3. Ibid., p. 270.
4. Ibid., p. 272.
5. Ibid., p. 217. Quote from *Boston Medical & Surgical Journal.*
6. E. T. James, *Notable American Women* (Cambridge: The Belknap Press of Harvard University Press, 1971), p. 165.
7. Woman's Medical College of Pennsylvania (Transactions of the Alumnae Association, 1906), p. 61.
8. From the *Philadelphia Evening Bulletin,* quoted by G. F. Alsop in *History of the Woman's Medical College,* Philadelphia, Pennsylvania, 1850–1950 (Philadelphia: J. B. Lippincott, 1950), pp. 54–55.
9. R. Morantz, "The Connecting Link: the Case for the Woman Doctor in Nineteenth Century America," in J. W. Leavitt & R. L. Numbers, eds., *Sickness and Health in America* (Madison: University of Wisconsin Press, 1977), p. 118.
10. Ibid.
11. E. H. Clarke, *Sex in Education: or, A Fair Chance for the Girls* (Boston, 1873), p. 41.
12. Morantz, *Sickness and Health in America,* p. 119.
13. H. Storer and R. J. Abram, "Will There Be a Monument?" in R. J. Abram, ed., *Send Us a Lady Physician* (New York: W. W. Norton, 1985).
14. R. Morantz, "Female Student Has Arrived," in Abram, ed., *Send Us a Lady Physician.*
15. E. Blackwell, *Address on the Medical Education of Women* (New York, 1856), pp. 8–9.
16. J. P. Chesney, "Woman as a Physician," *Richmond and Louisville Medical Journal* 11 (1871): p. 4.
17. M. P. Jacobi, *The Question of Rest for Women During Menstruation* (New York: G. P. Putnam, 1877).

18. E. Pope, E. L. Call, and C. A. Pope, *The Practice of Medicine by Women in the United States* (Boston, 1881).
19. Walsh, *Doctors Wanted, No Women Need Apply*, p. 85.
20. M. P. Jacobi, "An Address Delivered at the Commencement of the Women's Medical College of the New York Infirmary," 1883.
21. Women's Medical Association of New York City, eds., *Mary Putnam Jacobi*, pp. 494.
22. This discussion is summarized from information in Walsh, *Doctors Wanted, No Women Need Apply*.
23. Editorial, *Journal of the American Medical Association*, 31 (1898): pp. 932–933.
24. Editorial, *Journal of the American Medical Association*, 44 (1905): p. 1933.
25. Walsh, *Doctors Wanted, No Women Need Apply*.
26. F. Nightingale, "Notes on Nursing: What It Is, and What It Is Not," (New York: Appleton, 1860), p. 3. See also the chapter by B. Melosh, "Every Woman is a Nurse: Work and Gender in the Emergence of Nursing," in Abram, ed., *Send us a Lady Physician*.
27. R. F. Hume, *Great Women of Medicine* (New York: Random House, 1964), p. 71.
28. F. Nightingale, *Florence Nightingale to Her Nurses: A Selection from Miss Nightingale's Addresses to Probationers and Nurses of the Nightingale School at St. Thomas's Hospital* (1915), p. 303.
29. R. H. Shryock, "Nursing Emerges as a Profession," *Clio Medica* 3 (1968): pp. 131, 147.
30. B. Melosh, *Every Woman is a Nurse*, p. 121.
31. G. E. Wolstenholme, "Florence Nightingale: New Lamps for Old," *Proceedings of Royal Society of Medicine*, 63 (1970): p. 1283.
32. *Boston Medical and Surgical Journal*, 76 (1897): p. 214.
33. Quoted in Walsh, *Doctors Wanted, No Women Need Apply*, p. 142, from F. A. Washburn, *The Massachusetts General Hospital: Its Development 1900–1935* (Boston), pp. 443–444.
34. M. R. O'Connell, "The Roman Catholic Tradition Since 1545," in *Caring and Curing*, R. L. Numbers and D. W. Amundsen, eds. (New York: Macmillan, 1986), p. 136.
35. Ibid.
36. Ibid., p. 137.
37. G. Wacker, "The Pentecostal Tradition," in R. L. Numbers et al., eds., *Caring and Curing*, p. 519.
38. Quoted by Wacker, ibid.
39. W. James, *Varieties of Religious Experience* (London and New York: Collier Books, 1961), p. 110.
40. Ibid., pp. 90–91.
41. R. B. Schoepflin, "The Christian Science Tradition," in R. L. Numbers, et al., eds. *Caring and Curing*.

42. L. Dossey, *Space, Time and Medicine* (Boston: Shambhala, 1982).
43. A. Vietor, *A Woman's Quest: The Life of Marie E. Zakrzewska, M.D.* (New York and London: D. Appleton, 1924), pp. 84–85.

Chapter 16: Woman as Health-Care Provider

1. J. H. Knowles, ed., *Doing Better, and Feeling Worse: Health in the United States* (New York: W. W. Norton, 1977), and D. S. Sobel, ed., *Ways of Health* (New York: Harcourt Brace Jovanovich, 1979).
2. G. Null, *Healing Yourself Naturally* (New York: McGraw-Hill, 1988).
3. G. S. King, "The Flexner Report of 1910," *Journal of the American Medical Association*, 251, no. 8 (February 24, 1984).
4. Shryock, "Nursing Emerges as a Profession," pp. 131–147.
5. V. M. Driscoll, "Movement to Secure Legal Recognition of Nursing as an Independent Profession," *Journal, New York State Nurses Association*, 19, no. 1 (March, 1988).
6. C. Crossen, "Nurses, tired of answering to doctors, begin to treat patients on their own," *Wall Street Journal* (January 7, 1986), p. 31.
7. B. Bullough, "Barriers to the nurse practitioner movement: Problems of women in a woman's field," *International Journal of Health Services*, 5, no. 2 (1976): pp. 229–230.
8. Reported in Nursing News, *Nursing 88* (August, 1988), p. 10.
9. Quoted in B. Rider and R. M. Brashear, "Men in Occupational Therapy," *The American Journal of Occupational Therapy*, 42(4) (April 1988), p. 232.
10. *Allied Health Education Directory* (Chicago: American Medical Association, 1988).
11. Quoted in C. B. Inlander, L. S. Levin, and E. Weiner, eds., *Medicine on Trial* (New York: Prentice Hall, 1988).
12. F. E. Korbin, "The American Midwife Controversy: A Crisis of Professionalization," *Bulletin of the History of Medicine*, 40 (1966): pp. 350–363.
13. E. Declercq and R. Lacroix, "The Immigrant Midwives of Lawrence: The Conflict between Law and Culture in Early Twentieth-Century Massachusetts," *Bulletin of the History of Medicine*, 59 (1985): pp. 232–246.
14. J. Baker, "The Function of the Midwife," *Woman's Medical Journal*, 23 (1913): p. 197.
15. R. Goodell and J. Gurin, "Where Should Babies Be Born?" *American Health* (January–February 1984).
16. Declercq and Lacroix, "The Immigrant Midwives," p. 233.
17. I. H. Butter and B. J. Kay, "State Laws and the Practice of Lay Midwifery," *American Journal of Public Health*, 78 (September 1988), p. 9.
18. Complete tables on state laws are available from Butter and Kay at Department of Public Health Policy and Administration, University of Michigan School of Public Health, Ann Arbor, Mich. 48109–2029.
19. D. A. Sullivan and R. Weitz, "Obstacles to the Practice of Licensed Lay Midwifery," *Journal of Social Science and Medicine*, 19, no. 11 (1984): pp. 1189–1196.

20. Figures from *Physician Characteristics and Distribution in the U.S.*, 1987 Edition, prepared by Department of Data, American Medical Association.
21. M. L. Gonzalez and D. W. Emmons, eds., *Socioeconomic Characteristics of Medical Practice* (Center for Health Policy Research, 1986), from the AMA Socioeconomic System.
22. Audrey Fried, Employment Coordinator, National Association for Social Workers, from July 1986–June 1987 salary survey; personel communication with author.
23. A. Muller, J. J. Vitali, and D. Brannon, "Wage Differences and the Concentration of Women in Hospital Occupations," *Health Care Management Review,* 12(1) (1987): pp. 61–70.
24. Ibid., p. 64.

Chapter 17: Life in the Balance

1. Sr. Miriam Theresa McGillis, director of Genesis Farm, is most articulate on these points, which are derived from an audio tape of her talk, "Fate of the Earth," presented at the Wellness Conference, University of Wisconsin, Steven's Point, July, 1988. Her work is based on the writing of Thomas Berry (*Dream for the Earth,* San Francisco: Sierra Club, 1988). Equally important to this thesis is the work of Matthew Fox.
2. In addition to the classic sources for the masculine and feminine traits mentioned in the text, many of the words were suggested by people who have attended the "Woman as Healer" seminars, and especially by Dr. Rachel Naomi Remen and Marion Woodman.
3. This suggests the notion of "partnership" as described in Riane Eisler's text, *The Chalice and the Blade* (San Francisco: Harper & Row, 1987).
4. C. Gilligan, *In a Different Voice* (Cambridge: Harvard University Press, 1982).
5. The burgeoning professional and lay literature on the role of the mind in health suggests this point, and as been reviewed by J. Achterberg, *Imagery in Healing,* 1985; E. Rossi, *The Psychobiology of Mind-Body Healing* (New York: W. W. Norton, 1986); B. Justice, *Who Gets Sick?* (Los Angeles: Jeremy P. Tarcher, Inc., 1988); and many others.
6. J. Achterberg, "The Wounded Healer: Transformational Journeys in Modern Medicine," in G. Doore, ed., *Shaman's Path: Healing, Personal Growth, and Empowerment* (Boston: Shambhala, 1988).
7. T. McClellan, "Whether Art Is Useful," unpublished manuscript (Dallas, Tex.), p. 4.
8. T. Roszak, *Person/Plant* (New York: Doubleday, 1978).

Bibliography

Abram, R. J., ed. *Send Us a Lady Physician*. New York: W. W. Norton & Co., 1985.

Achterberg, J. *Imagery in Healing: Shamanism and Modern Medicine*. Boston: Shambhala, 1985.

———."The Wounded Healer: Transformational Journeys in Modern Medicine." In *Shaman's Path: Healing, Personal Growth, and Empowerment*, edited by G. Doore. Boston: Shambhala, 1988.

Agrippa, H. C. *Three Books of Occult Philosophy or Magic*. Chicago: Hahn & Whitehead, 1898.

Alexander, W. *The History of Women: From the Earliest Antiquity to the Present Time Giving Some Account of Almost Every Interesting Particular Concerning That Sex, Among All Nations, Ancient and Modern*. London: printed for W. Strahan & T. Cadell in the Strand, 1779.

Allied Health Education Directory. Chicago: American Medical Association, 1988.

Alsop, G. F. *History of the Woman's Medical College, Philadelphia, Pennsylvania, 1850–1950*. Philadelphia: J. B. Lippincott Company, 1950.

Anderson, B. S., and J. P. Zinsser. *A History of Their Own: Women in Europe*. New York: Harper & Row, 1988.

Aquinas, St. Thomas. *Contra gentiles* and *Quodibet*. Translated by E. Frettle and P. Mare. *Opera omnia*. Paris, 1871–1880.

———.*Opus tertium*. Edited by A. G. Little. Aberdeen, 1912.

———.*Summa theologica*. 22 vols. London 1916–1938.

Arnald of Villanova. *Antidotarium, Brevarium, De epilepsia*. From edition of his complete works, published in Lyons, France, 1532.

Aveling, J. H. *English Midwives: Their History and Their Prospects*. London: Churchill, 1872.

Baas, J. H. *History of Medicine*. 2 vols. Translated by H. E. Anderson. Huntington, N.Y.: R. F. Krieger Co., 1971.

Bacon, R. *Opus tertium*. Edited by A. G. Little, Aberdeen, 1912.

Baker, J. "The Function of the Midwife." *Woman's Medical Journal* 23 (1913): 197.

Berman, A. *The Impact of the Nineteenth-Century Botanico Medical Movement on American Pharmacy and Medicine*. Ph.D. dissertation, University of Wisconsin, 1954.

Berry, T. *Dream for the Earth*. San Francisco: Sierra Club, 1988.

Bishop, M. *The Middle Ages*. New York: American Heritage, 1985.

Blackwell, E. *Address on the Medical Education of Women*. New York, 1856.

Boorstin, D. J. *The Discoverers*. New York: Random House, 1983.

Boulding, E. *The Underside of History*. Boulder: Westview Press, 1976.

Braudel, F. *The Structures of Everyday Life: The Limits of the Possible*. Translation. New York: Harper & Row, 1981.

Brothwell, D. *The Bogman and the Archaeology of People*. London: British Museum Publications, 1986.

Bulfinch, T. *Myths of Greece and Rome*. New York: Penguin, 1979.

Bullough, B. "Barriers to the Nurse Practitioner Movement: Problems of Women in a Woman's Field," *International Journal of Health Services*, 5, no. 2 (1975): 229–230.

Bullough, V. *The Subordinate Sex*. Chicago: University of Chicago Press, 1973.

Butter, I. H., and B. J. Kay. "State Laws and the Practice of Lay Midwifery." *American Journal of Public Health* 78 (September 1988).

Bücher, K. *Die Frauenfrage im Mittelalter*. Tübingen, 1910.

Campbell, J. *Occidental Mythology: The Masks of God*. New York: Penguin, 1964.

———. *Primitive Mythology: The Masks of God*. New York: Penguin, 1987.

Carroll, B. A., ed. *Liberating Women's History: Theoretical and Critical Essays*. Urbana, Chicago and London: University of Illinois Press, 1976.

Celsus. *De medicina*. Translated by W. G. Spencer. Cambridge: Harvard University Press, 1938.

Chesney, J. P. "Woman as a Physician." *Richmond and Louisville Medical Journal* 11 (1871): 4.

Christ, C. P., and J. Plaskow, eds. *Womanspirit Rising*. San Francisco: Harper & Row, 1979.

Clark, E., and H. Richardson. *Women and Religion*. New York: Harper & Row, 1977.

Clarke, E. H. *Sex in Education: or, A Fair Chance for the Girls*. Boston, 1873.

Cohn, N. *Europe's Inner Demons*. London: Paladin, 1975.

Corbin, A. *The Foul and the Fragrant*. Cambridge: Harvard University Press, 1986.

Cott, N. "Passionlessness: An Interpretation of Victorian Sexual Ideology, 1790–1850." *Signs: A Journal of Women in Culture and Society*, vol. 4, 21 (1978): 219–236.

Cott, N. *The Bonds of Womanhood*. New Haven: Yale University Press, 1977.

Coulter, H. L. *Divided Legacy*. Washington, D.C.: McGrath Publishing Company, 1973.

Crossen, C. "Nurses, Tired of Answering to Doctors, Begin to Treat Patients on Their Own." *Wall Street Journal* (January 7, 1986).

Cutter, J. S. and H. R. Viets. *A Short History of Midwifery*. Philadelphia: W. B. Sanders, 1964.

Daly, M. *Gynecology: The Metaethics of Radical Feminism*. Boston: Beacon Press, 1970.

————. *The Church and the Second Sex.* Boston: Beacon Press, 1985.

Davidson, H. R. E. *Gods and Myths of Northern Europe.* New York: Penguin Books, 1964.

de Beauvoir, S. *The Second Sex.* Translated by H. M. Parshley. New York: Alfred A. Knopf, 1953.

de Renzi, S., ed. *Collectio salernitana.* 5 vols. Naples, 1852–59.

Declercq, E., and R. Lacroix. "The Immigrant Midwives of Lawrence: The Conflict between Law and Culture in Early Twentieth-Century Massachusetts." *Bulletin of the History of Medicine* 59 (1985): 232–246.

Donegan, J. B. *Women and Men Midwives: Medicine, Morality, and Misogyny in Early America.* Westport, Conn.: Greenwood Press, 1978.

Donnison, J. *Midwives and Medical Men.* New York: Schocken Books, 1977.

Doore, G., ed. *Shaman's Path: Healing, Personal Growth, and Empowerment.* Boston: Shambhala, 1988.

Dossey, L. *Space, Time and Medicine.* Boston: Shambhala, 1982.

Driscoll, V. M. "Movement to Secure Legal Recognition of Nursing as an Independent Profession." *Journal, New York State Nurses Association,* 19, no. 1 (March, 1988).

Dubos, R. *The Mirage of Health: Utopias, Progress, and Biological change.* New York: Harper & Row, 1959.

Duerr, H. P. *Dreamtime.* New York: Basil Blackwell Ltd., 1986.

Duncan, J. M. *Mortality of Childbed.* London, 1870.

Ehrenreich, B., and D. English. *Witches, Midwives, and Nurses: A History of Women Healers.* Old Westbury, N.Y.: The Feminist Press, 1973.

Eisler, Riane. *The Chalice and the Blade.* San Francisco: Harper & Row, 1987.

Eliade, M. *Shamanism.* New York: Pantheon, 1964.

Ewell, T. *Letters to Ladies, Detailing Important Information Concerning Themselves and Infants.* Philadelphia: W. Brown, 1817.

Ewen, C. L. *Witchcraft and Demonism.* London: Heath Cranton, Ltd., 1933.

Farrington, B. *The Philosophy of Francis Bacon.* Chicago: Phoenix, 1964.

Fiorenza, E. S. "Women in the Early Christian Movement." In *Womanspirit Rising,* edited by C. P. Christ and J. Plaskow. San Francisco: Harper & Row, 1979.

Flanagan, S. *Hildegard of Bingen, 1098–1179.* London and New York: Routledge, 1989.

Fox, M. *Illuminations of Hildegard of Bingen.* Santa Fe: Bear & Co., 1985.

————. *The Coming of the Cosmic Christ.* San Francisco: Harper & Row, 1988.

Frazier, J. G. *The Golden Bough,* 1890. New York: Avenel Books, 1981.

Gage, M. *Women, Church and State.* 1893. Watertown, Mass.: Persephone Press, 1980.

Gies, F., and J. Gies. *Life in a Medieval City.* New York: Harper & Row, 1969.

————. *Women in the Middle Ages.* New York: Barnes & Noble, 1978.

Gifford, G. *A Dialogue concerning Witches and Witchcraft,* 1593, 1603, 1842. Edited by Beatrice White, Oxford: Oxford University Press, 1931.

Gilligan, C. *In a Different Voice*. Cambridge: Harvard University Press, 1982.

Gimbutas, M. *The Goddesses and Gods of Old Europe*. Berkeley: University of California Press, 1982.

Glob, P. V. *Denmark*. Ithaca, N.Y., and London: Cornell University Press, 1967.

———. *The Bog People*. London: Faber and Faber, 1969.

———. *The Mound People*. London: Paladin Books, 1983.

Gonzalez, M. L., and D. W. Emmons, eds. *Socioeconomic Characteristics of Medical Practice*. Center for Health Policy Research, 1986.

Goodell, R., and J. Gurin. "Where Should Babies Be Born?" *American Health* (January–February 1984).

Graham, H. *Eternal Eve*. London: W. Heinemann, 1950.

Griffin, S. *Woman and Nature*. New York: Harper & Row, 1978.

Hancar, F. "Zum Problem der Venusstatuetten im eurasiatischen Jungpaläolithikim." *Praehistorische Zeitschrift*. XXX-XXXI Band, 1/2 Heft, 1939–1940.

Harner, M. *Hallucinogens and Shamanism*. New York: Oxford University Press, 1973.

———. *The Way of the Shaman*. San Francisco: Harper & Row, 1980.

Harris, M. *Cows, Pigs, Wars and Witches: The Riddles of Culture*. New York: Vintage Books, 1978.

Harrison, J. E. *Myths of Greece and Rome*. London: Earnest Benn Ltd., 1927.

———. *Themis*. 2nd rev. ed. Cambridge: The University Press, 1927.

Hartman, F. *Paracelsus: Life and Prophecies*. Blauvelt, N.Y.: Rudolf Steiner, 1973.

Harvey, W. *Anatomical Exercitations, Concerning the Generation of Living Creatures*. London, 1653.

Heer, F. *The Medieval World*. New York: New American Library, 1961.

Hooker, M., ed. *Descartes*. Baltimore: Johns Hopkins University Press, 1978.

Hopkins, D. *Princes and Peasants: Smallpox in History*. Chicago: University of Chicago Press, 1983.

Horowitz, M., and C. Palmer. *Shaman Woman, Mainline Lady*. New York: Quill, 1982.

Huizinga, J. *The Waning of the Middle Ages*. Harmondsworth, England: Penguin Books, 1985.

Hume, R. F. *Great Women of Medicine*. New York: Random House, 1964.

Hunt, H. S. *Glances and Glimpses*. Boston: John P. Jewett & Co., 1856.

Hurd-Mead, K. C. *A History of Women in Medicine*. Haddam, Conn.: Haddam Press, 1938.

Inlander, C. B., L. S. Levin, and E. Weinder, eds. *Medicine on Trial*. New York: Prentice Hall, 1988.

Jacobi, M. P. *The Question of Rest for Women During Menstruation*. New York: G. P. Putnam's Sons, 1877.

James, E. T. *Notable American Women*. Cambridge: The Belknap Press of Harvard University Press, 1971.

James, W. *Varieties of Religious Experience*. London and New York: Collier Books, 1961.

Johnson, A., ed. *Dictionary of American Biography*. Vol. 2. New York, 1951.

Johnson, B. *Lady of the Beasts: Ancient Images of the Goddess and Her Sacred Animals*. San Francisco: Harper & Row, 1981.

Justice, B. *Who Gets Sick?* Los Angeles: Jeremy P. Tarcher, 1988.

Keller, E. F. *Reflections on Gender and Science*. New Haven: Yale University Press, 1985.

King, G. S. "The Flexner Report of 1910." *Journal of the American Medical Association* 251, no. 8 (February 24, 1984).

Knowles, J. H., ed. *Doing Better and Feeling Worse: Health in the United States*. New York: W. W. Norton & Company, 1977.

Korbin, F. E. "The American Midwife Controversy: A Crisis of Professionalization." *Bulletin of the History of Medicine* 40 (1966): 350–363.

Kramer, S. N. "Poets and Religious and Anthropological Aspects of the Legacy of Sumer." In *The Legacy of Sumer: Invited Lectures on the Middle East,* edited by D. Schmandt-Besserat. Presented at the University of Texas at Austin, 1976.

Kursh, H. *Cobras in the Garden*. Wisconsin: Harvey Press, 1965.

Landsberger, B., and M. Reiner, eds. "Old Babylonian Proto-Lu List." *Materials for the Sumerian Lexicon*. Vol. 12. Rome, 1969.

Larner, C. *Enemies of God*. Baltimore: Johns Hopkins University Press, 1981.

Leavitt, J. W., and R. L. Numbers, eds. *Sickness and Health in America*. Madison: The University of Wisconsin Press, 1977.

Lerner, G. *The Creation of Patriarchy*. New York: Oxford University Press, 1987.

Leventhal, H. *In the Shadow of the Enlightenment*. New York: New York University Press, 1976.

Lipinska, M. "Histoire des femmes médicine." Thesis: Ecole Paris, 1900.

Lyons, A. S., and R. J. Petrucelli. *Medicine: An Illustrated History*. New York: Harry N. Abrams, Inc., 1978.

Magnus, Albertus. *Sleep and Waking*. Translated by Petrus de Prussia, 1621.

Maple, E. *Magic, Medicine and Quackery*. New York: A. S. Barnes & Co., 1968.

Maubry, J. *The Female Physician*. London: James Holland, 1724.

Majno, G. *The Healing Hand: Man and Wound in the Ancient World*. Cambridge: Harvard University Press, 1975.

McGrew, E., and M. P. McGrew. *Encyclopedia of Medical History*. New York: McGraw-Hill, 1985.

Meigs, C. *Females and Their Diseases*. Philadelphia: Lea & Blanchard, 1848.

———. Lecture on some of the distinctive characteristics of the female, delivered before the class of the Jefferson Medical College, January 5, 1847. Philadelphia: Collins, 1847.

Melosh, B. "Every Woman is a Nurse: Work and Gender in the Emergence of Nursing." In *Send us a Lady Physician,* edited by R. J. Abram. New York: W. W. Norton, 1985.

Merchant, C. *The Death of Nature*. New York: Harper & Row, 1980.

Michelet, J. *Satanism and Witchcraft*. Translated by W. R. Allinson, 1860. Secaucas, N.J.: Citadel, 1939.

Miller, G. "Putting Lady Mary in Her Place: A Discussion of Historical Causation." *Bulletin of the History of Medicine* 55 (1981): 2–16.

Miriam Theresa, Sr. "Fate of the Earth." Audiotape of lecture presented at the Wellness Conference, University of Wisconsin, Steven's Point, July, 1988.

Moore, K. *Victorian Wives*. London and New York: Allison & Busby, 1974.

Morantz, R. "Female Student Has Arrived." In *Send Us a Lady Physician,* edited by R. J. Abram. New York: W. W. Norton & Co., 1985.

———. "Making Women Modern: Middle Class Women and Health Reform in 19th Century America." *Journal of Social History* 10 (Summer 1977): 490–507.

———. "The Connecting Link: The Case for the Woman Doctor in Nineteenth-Century America." In *Sickness and Health in America,* edited by J. W. Leavitt and R. L. Numbers. Madison: The University of Wisconsin Press, 1977.

Morantz, R. M., C. S. Pomerleau and C. H. Fenichel. *In Her Own Words*. New Haven: Yale University Press, 1982.

Muller, A., J. J. Vitali, & D. Brannon. "Wage Differences and the Concentration of Women in Hospital Occupations." *Health Care Management Review* 12(1) (1987): 61–70.

Murray, M. *The God of the Witches,* 1931. Oxford: Oxford University Press, 1970.

Nichols, M. G. "Old School Medical Journals." *Water Cure Journal* 9 (1850): 181.

———. "To the Women Who Read the Water Cure Journal." *Water Cure Journal* 14 (1852): 68.

———. "Woman, the Physician." *Water Cure Journal* 12 (1851): 73–74.

Nichols, M. G., and T. L. Nichols. *Marriage: Its History, Character and Results*. New York: T. L. Nichols, 1854.

Nightingale, F. "Florence Nightingale to Her Nurses: A Selection from Miss Nightingale's Addresses to Probationers and Nurses of the Nightingale School at St. Thomas's Hospital." 1915.

———. "Notes on Nursing: What It Is, and What It Is Not." New York: Appleton, 1860.

Null, G. *Healing Yourself Naturally*. New York: McGraw-Hill, 1988.

Numbers, R. L. "Do-it-yourself the Sectarian Way," In *Medicine Without Doctors: Home Health Care in American History*. Edited by G. B. Risse, R. L. Numbers & J. W. Leavitt. New York: Science History Publications, 1977.

Numbers, R. L., and D. W. Amundsen, eds. *Caring and Curing*. New York: Macmillan, 1986.

Nursing News. *Nursing 88*. August, 1988.

Nutting, M. A., and L. L. Dock. *History of Nursing*. Vol. 1. New York: Putnam, 1907.

O'Connell, M. R. "The Roman Catholic Tradition Since 1545." In *Caring and Curing,* edited by R. L. Numbers and D. W. Amundsen. New York: Macmillan, 1986.

O'Keefe, D. *Stolen Lightning*. New York: Vintage, 1983.

Ochshorn, J. "Ishtar and Her Cult." In *The Book of the Goddess,* edited by C. Olson. New York: Crossroad, 1983.

Odman, S. "An Attempt to Explain the Berserk-Raging of Ancient Nordic Warriors through National History." *Nya Handlingar,* Vol. 5 (Kungliga Vetenskaps Akademien: Stockholm, 1784): 240–247.

Olson, C., ed. *The Book of the Goddess*. New York: Crossroad, 1983.

Pagels, E. "What Became of God the Mother?" In *Womanspirit Rising,* edited by C. P. Christ and J. Plaskow. San Francisco: Harper & Row, 1979.

Penman, W. R. *The Public Practice of Midwifery in Philadelphia*. Transactions of the College of Physicians of Philadelphia 37 (October 1869).

Perkins, William. *A Discourse on the Damned Art of Witchcraft*. Cambridge, 1608, 1610.

Physician Characteristics and Distribution in the U.S. Department of Data. American Medical Association, 1987.

Pope, F., E. L. Call, and C. A. Pope. *The Practice of Medicine by Women in the United States*. Boston, 1881.

Power, E. "Some Women Practitioners of Medicine in the Middle Ages." *Proceedings of the Royal Society of Medicine*. History of Medical Section 6 (1922): 21.

Pressel, W. *Hexen und Hexenmeister*. Stuttgart, 1860. Reprinted in R. H. Robbins, *Encyclopedia of Witchcraft*.

Pugh, B. A. *Treatise on Midwifery, Chiefly with Regard to the Operation, with Several Improvements in That Art*. London: J. Buckland, 1754.

Quackenbush, J. van Pelt. An address delivered before the students of the Albany Medical College, Introductory to the Course on Obstetrics, November 5, 1855. Albany: B. Taylor, 1855.

Rider, B., and R. M. Brashear. "Men in Occupational Therapy." *The American Journal of Occupational Therapy* 42(4) (April, 1988).

Risse, G. B., R. L. Numbers, and J. W. Leavitt, eds. *Medicine Without Doctors: Home Health Care in American History*. New York: Science History Publications, 1977.

Robbins, R. H. *Encyclopedia of Witchcraft and Demonology*. 1959. New York: Bonanza Books, 1981.

Robertson, J. H. "Valerius Terminus on the Interpretation of Nature." In *The Philosophical Works of Francis Bacon*. London: Routledge & Sons, 1905.

Roesdahl, E. *Viking Age Denmark*. London: British Museum Publications, 1982.

Rogers, F. B. *A Syllabus of Medical History*. Boston: Little, Brown, 1962.

Rossi, E. *The Psychobiology of Mind-Body Healing*. New York: W. W. Norton, 1986.

Rowland, B. *Medieval Woman's Guide to Health: The First English Gynecological Handbook*. Kent, Ohio: Kent State University Press, 1981.

Röesslin, E. *The Byrthe of Mankynd, Otherwyse Named the Woman's Boke*. Translated from Latin by Thomas Raynalde. London, 1545.

Russell, J. B. *History of Witchcraft*. London: Thames & Hudson, 1980.

Salzman, M. R. "Magna Mater: Great Mother of the Roman Empire." In *The Book of the Goddess*, edited by C. Olson, 60–67.

Schmidt, W. *Der Ursprung der Gottesidee*. 12 vols. Munster in Westfalia: Aschendorff, 1912–1955.

———. "The Position of Women with Regard to Property in Primitive Society." *American Anthropologist* 37 (1935): 244–56.

Schoepflin, R. B. "The Christian Science Tradition." In *Caring and Curing*, edited by R. L. Numbers and D. W. Amundsen. New York: Macmillan, 1986.

Scot, Michael, *Liber introductorius*, Bodlein 266 manuscript. 15th century.

———. *Physionomia (De secretis natural* [alternate title]). Amsterdam, 1740.

Scot, R. *The Discovery of Witchcraft*, 1584.

Seaman, V. *The Midwives Monitor and Mother's Mirror*. New York: Isaac Collins, 1800.

Selby, S. E. "A Bloomer to Her Sisters." *Water Cure Journal* 15 (1853): 131.

Sharp, J. *The Midwives Book or the Whole Art of Midwifery*. London, 1671.

Shryock, R. H. "Nursing Emerges as a Profession." *Clio Medica* 3 (1968): 131, 147.

Singer, C. "The Scientific Views and Visions of Saint Hildegard (1098–1180)." In *Studies in the History and Method of Science*, edited by C. Singer. Oxford: Clarendon, 1917.

Smellie, W. *A Treatise on the Theory and Practice of Midwifery*. 3rd ed. London: D. Wilson & T. Durham, 1756.

Smith, H. "Gynecology and Ideology in Seventeenth Century England." In *Liberating Women's History: Theoretical and Critical Essays*. Edited by B. A. Carroll. Urbana, Chicago and London: University of Illinois Press, 1976.

Sobel, D. S., ed. *Ways of Health*. New York: Harcourt Brace Jovanovich, 1979.

Sophia, a Person of Quality [Lady Mary Wortley Montague]. 1739. *Woman Not Inferior to Man*. Facsimile reprint. London: Bentham Press, 1975.

Soranus. *Gynecology*. Translated with Introduction by O. Temkin. Baltimore: Johns Hopkins University Press, 1956.

Spretnak, C. *Lost Goddesses of Early Greece*. Boston: Beacon, 1981.

Springer, J., and H. Kramer. *Malleus maleficarum*. Translated by Montague Summers. London: Pushkin, 1948.

Stearns, R. P. "Remarks upon the Introduction of Inoculation for Smallpox in England." *Bulletin of the History of Medicine*. 24: 103–22. 1950.

Stephens, M. *Domestic Midwife, or the Best Means of Preventing Danger in Childbirth Considered*. London, 1795.

Stone, M. *When God Was a Woman*. New York: Harcourt Brace Jovanovich, 1976.

Storer, H., and R. J. Abram. "Will There Be a Monument?" In *Send Us a Lady Physician*, edited by R. J. Abram. New York: W. W. Norton, 1985.

Sturluson, S. *Prose Edda*. Translated by L. M. Hollander. Austin: University of Texas Press, 1962.

Sullivan, D. A., and R. Weitz. "Obstacles to the Practice of Licensed Lay Midwifery." *Journal of Social Science and Medicine* 19, no. 11 (1984): 1189–1196.

Tacitus. *Germania*. Translated by H. Mattingly, reviewed by S. A. Handford. Harmondsworth and Boston: Penguin Classics, 1948.

Thicknesse, P. *Man-Midwifery Analysed and the Tendency of that Practice Detected and Exposed*. London: R. Davis, 1764.

Thompson, R. C. "Assyrian Medical Texts." *Proceedings of the Royal Society of Medicine* 17 (1924): 1–34.

Thorndike, L. *Magic and Experimental Science During the First 13 Centuries of Our Era*. 2 vols. New York, 1923.

Uhlein, G. *Meditation with Hildegard of Bingen*. Santa Fe, NM: Bear & Co., 1982.

Vietor, A. *A Woman's Quest: The Life of Marie E. Zakrzewska, M.D.* New York and London: D. Appleton, 1924.

Wacker, G. "The Pentecostal Tradition." In *Caring and Curing*, edited by R. L. Numbers and D. W. Amundsen. New York: Macmillan, 1986.

Walker, B. *The Crone*. New York: Harper & Row, 1985.

———. *The Women's Encyclopedia of Myths and Secrets*. San Francisco: Harper & Row, 1983.

Walsh, M. R. *Doctors Wanted, No Women Need Apply*. New Haven: Yale University Press, 1977.

Wasson, R. G. *Soma: Divine Mushroom of Immortality*. New York: Harcourt Brace Jovanovich, 1968.

White, C. *Treatise on the Management of Pregnant and Lying-in Women*. London, 1773.

Wilder, C. "Pulmonary Consumption, Its Causes, Symptoms and Treatment." *Medical Communications of the Massachusetts Medical Society* 7, 2nd series. Vol. III. Boston, 1848.

Willughby, P. *Observations in Midwifery. As Also the Countrey Midwifes Opusculum or Vade Mecum*. Edited by H. Blenkinsop. Warwick, England, 1863.

Wolkstein, D., and S. Kramer. *Inanna: Queen of Heaven and Earth*. New York: Harper & Row, 1983.

Wolstenholme, G. E. "Florence Nightingale: New Lamps for Old." *Proceedings of Royal Society of Medicine* 63 (1970): 1283.

Woman's Medical College of Pennsylvania. *Transactions of the Alumnae Association*, 1906.

Women's Medical Association of New York City, The, eds. *Mary Putnam Jacobi, M.D.: A Pathfinder in Medicine*. New York: Putnam, 1925.

Wood, H. C. "The Heroic Treatment of Idiopathic Peritonitis." *Boston Medical and Surgical Journal* 98 (1878): 555–560.

Wortley, Montagu, M. *Letters of the Right Honourable Lady Mary Wortley Montagu: Written During Her Travels in Europe, Asia and Africa to Persons of Distinction, Men of Letters, etc., in Different Parts of Europe*. 3 vols. London: printed for T. Beckett, 1717.

Yates, F. *The Rosicrucian Enlightenment*. Boston: Shambhala, 1978.

Zilboorg, G. *The Medical Man and the Witch During the Renaissance* (1935). New York: Cooper Square, 1969.

Zimmern, H. "Babylonische Hymnen und Gebete in Auswahl." *Der Alte Orient.* 7 Jahrgang, Heft 3. Leipzig, 1905.

Index

Abelard, 54, 58–59
  Héloïse and, 54, 59
Abortion, 37, 42, 121, 199
Agnodice (Gk. physician), 32
Agrippa von Nettesheim, 92, 105
Albertus Magnus, 71, 74, 110
Alexander, William, 27–28
Allopathic medicine, 136–137, 171,
  180, 193
Altered states of consciousness, 30,
  92, 94
Amanita muscaria, 22, 208 n. 5 (chap.
  3)
American Medical Association
  (AMA), 173, 174
  Council on Medical Education,
  174
American medicine, 171–186
  masculinization of, 171, 178–
  179, 181
American Nurses' Association (ANA),
  162, 175–176, 178
Amulets, 44
Anesthesia, 109–110
"Angel in the House," 128, 134–136
Antidotarium (Arnald of Villanova),
  72
Antiochis (Roman healer), 36
Aristotle, 31, 32, 48
  Pythias and, 31
Arnald of Villanova, 70–73, 110
Artemsia (Gk. Queen/healer), 32
Asclepius, 30, 31, 34

caduceus and, 30
Hippocratic Oath and, 30
Aspasia (Roman healer), 36–37
Athena, 30
Augustine, Saint, 67

Bacon, Francis, 92, 93, 102–103
Bacon, Roger, 70, 74, 111
Bible (King James version), 90–91
Birth control, 37, 136, 138, 199
Black Death, 77–78
Blackwell, Elizabeth, 146, 147–148,
  151, 153
Blackwell, Emily, 146, 147–148
Blanche of France, Queen, 45
Boston Female Medical College, 131
Botanic(s), 21–22, 43, 72–74, 89–
  90, 93–95, 139, 142
  alkaloids, 21–22, 42, 90, 94, 109
  Hildegard and, 56–57
  lore, women's, 92–95
  medical schools, 141
  pain-relieving, 121
Brevarium (Arnald of Villanova), 72
Browning, Elizabeth Barrett, 138
Bullough, Bonnie (nursing leader),
  177
Burning of women, 83–86, 90
Byrthe of Mankynd, 119

Campbell, Joseph, 11
Canterbury Tales, 53
Caring/curing, 4, 173, 192–193

Cartesian theory, 100–101
Catholic Church, 54, 69
　decadence and, 54
　heretics and, 68–70
Cato, 34
Celsus, 35
Childbirth, 199
　medieval, 42, 47
　See also Midwifery
Christian cosmology, 39, 65–75
　early, 38–40
　medieval, 41–59, 101, 115
　persecution of women and, 65–75
Christian Science, 142
　healers, 167
Church and state, 98
　psychopathology of, 97–98
　witch-hunts and, 98
Cleopatra (Gk. healer), 32–33
Clinical psychologists, 179
"Clockwork universe," 101
Compassion, 50, 200
Conscious responsibility, 5, 185–186, 188, 197, 204
　and changes in health care, 204–205
Cosmology
　definition of, 2–3
　of Denmark, 22–23
　of Greece, 29–33
　healing ingredients and, 44
　crises and, 63
　new, 188–199
　scientific, 63, 101, 104, 115
　of Rome, 34–37
　of Sumer, 14–19
　of Western civilization, 63, 164, 188, 189–190
　women healers and, 2–3, 19, 25, 188
　See also Christian cosmology
Country Justice (Dalton), 91
Courtly love myths, 53, 135

Creation myths, 11, 66
　Original Sin and, 66
　types of, 11
Crises, 63, 76–78
　cosmology and, 25, 28, 63
The Crusades, 50–51
Curing, 4, 173, 193
Cybele (Magna Mater), 34–35
　and Attis, 35

Dame Julian, 64
Dark Ages, 41–44
　devaluation of women in, 42
　diseases of, 41–42
De Beauvoir, Simone, 53
Deities, female, 23, 24, 28, 38–39, 53
Deities, male, 25–26, 28, 38, 39
Delphi, 31
Demons, 74, 93
Denmark, ancient, 12, 90, 20–28
　Gundestrup cauldron/Holy Grail, 25
　women's healing lore, 20–22
Descartes, Rene, 100–101, 174
Devaluation of women, 65–75
　Christianity and, 97
　devil worship and, 66, 68–70
　economic/political regimes, 66–75
　male gods and, 65–66
　Original Sin and, 66–68
Devil (Satan), 66, 68, 110, 115
　use of herbs and, 87, 89–90, 92
　witchcraft and, 66, 68, 70, 74, 81, 83, 85–90, 92, 96
　worship of, 66, 68–69
Digitalis, 108
Disease(s), 4, 22, 41, 46–47, 76–78
　caring/curing of, 4, 173, 192–193
　cause of, 193, 196
　Christian Science idea of, 167
　germ theory of, 110–111
　mind and, 106
　patterns, 105

Diseases of Women (Paracelsus), 106
"Doctoresses," 115, 146
Domesticity, cult of, 133–134
Dreams, 73
Dualism, 66, 68–70
    vs. monotheism, 68–70
Duncan, Gilly (wise woman), 90

Ea (sun god), 16, 19
Earth Mother/Goddess, 11, 23, 25–
    26, 27, 31, 52, 65, 96, 189
    religions of, 53
    war gods and, 25
Ecosystem, 188
Edda (Scandinavian epics), 53
Eddy, Mary Baker, 142, 145, 166–
    167
    Christian Science and, 166
Eleanor of Aquitaine, 45, 51
Empiricism, 43–44
Enki (god of wisdom), 16
Epic of Gilgamesh, 16–17
    Ishtar and, 17
Epione (Gk. healer), 30
Eugerasia (Roman healer), 36
Evil eye, 74

Fabiola, 39, 42
Faith healing, 164–165
    mind-cure movement and, 165–
    168
Fathers of medicine, 29, 31, 32, 36,
    105–106
    women healers and, 32–33
Fear, 98, 101
    of power, 95, 96, 101
    of women, 135, 149, 164
Felicie, Jacoba, 79–80
Felicity of Carthage, Saint, 7
Feminine healing consciousness, 1–5,
    173, 197–198
Feminine healing energy, 30
Feminine healing mythology, 3–5,
    34–35, 64, 106, 193, 195
Fertility, 11
    cult(s), 96

Flexner Report, 173–175
"Flying Oyle," 92–95
Forceps, 126, 154
Freyja (goddess), 26
Fumigation, 121, 217 n. 9

Gaia (earth goddess), 31
Galen, 32, 36, 48, 101–102
    women healers and, 36–37
Gender
    and health professions, 115–117
    gods', 10–13, 14–19, 164, 165,
    188
Geography (Strabo), 27
Germania (Tacitus), 23
Germ theory, 110–111
God(s), 38
    and devil, 96, 164, 165, 188
    as dyadic being, 38
    the Father, 39
    gender of, 10–19, 164, 165, 188
    the Mother, 19, 23, 38–39
    punitive, 26
    as trinity, 38
    of war, 25–26
Goddess(es), 13, 28, 65, 68
    of Denmark, 22–28
    of Greece, 29–33, 209–210 n. 3
    of Rome, 34–37
    of Sumer, 14–19
Gospel of Philip, 39
Gospels, gnostic, 38–39
Graham, Sylvester, 140
Great Goddess, 65, 68
Great Mother, 13, 28, 188
Greece, 29–33
    healing goddesses of, 29–33,
    209–210 n. 3
Gregory, Samuel, 131
Gudrun (German epic), 53
Guilds, 79, 126, 173
    gender and, 98–99, 173
    women healers and, 98
    women's, 202

Gula (goddess of death/resurrection), 16

Hampton, Isabel (nursing leader), 162
Harrison, J. E. (on mythic traditions), 11
Harvey, William, 106
Healer(s), 188, 196–198
    divine image and, 10–13, 14–19, 164
    hierarchy of, 18, 24–25
    wounded, 197–198, 205
    See also Women healers
Healing, 1–2, 42, 47–48, 101, 193–194
    codification of, 122–123
    dehumanization of, 101
    feminine, mythology, 1–2, 3–5, 34–35, 64, 106, 193
    goddesses (Gk.), 29–30
    magic and, 18
    metaphysical, 165–168
    ministry, 115
    mythology, 34–35
    practices and health, 104–105
    redefinition of, 193–194
    religion and, 163–165
    rituals, 4, 9, 22, 24, 49, 93, 211 n. 11
    tools, medieval, 52–55
Healing arts
    balancing, 198–203
    changes in, 205
    Descartes and, 100–101
    Jews and, 80
    medieval, 47–59
    professionalization of, 115
    Roman, 35–37
    science and, 75
    theology and, 75
    witchcraft and, 83
Healing consciousness (new), 187–205
    the feminine and, 187–199

The Healing Hand . . . (Majno), 19
Healing ingredients, 35–37, 43, 50, 73–75, 92–95
    complexity of, 43
    cosmology and, 44
Healing system, new, 194–196
Health, 2, 104, 138
    balancing art/science of, 204–205
    definition of, 194
    healing practices and, 104–106
    holistic, 180
    mind and, 106
    religion and, 163
Health professions, 78–81, 115–117, 173
    allied, 179–180
    gender and, 1, 115–117
    professionalization of, 175
    proliferation of, 179
    wage inequity and, 186
Health professions, women's, 144–168, 173, 178–185
    gilded age, 144–156
    legislation on, 78–81, 178, 187, 203
    money and, 155–156
    witchcraft and, 81
Health reform, 137–139
    Flexner Report and, 173–175
    women and, 137–139
    women's clothing and, 139
Heer, F. (historian), 59, 211 n. 1
Helen of Troy, 29, 36
Héloïse, 54, 58
Herbs, 50, 56–57, 74, 110
    devil and, 56, 74, 87, 89, 90, 92
    women and, 42, 53, 110
    See also Botanic(s)
Heretics, 68–70, 71
    Cathars, 69–70
    Templars, 69
Heroic medicine, 136, 137, 141–143, 167, 177
High Middle Ages, 44–59

elevation of women in, 45
  healing arts of, 47–48
Hildegard of Bingen, 54–58, 100, 106–107
Hippocrates, 31, 32, 48
Hippocratic Oath, 30
The History of Women (Alexander), 27–28
Holistic health movement, 172, 180
Holistic Nurses' Association, 178
Holmes, Oliver Wendell, 137, 142, 146, 173
Homeopathy, 140, 142
Honoring life, 198–199
Horace, 37
Hospital(s)
  industry, 171, 174, 176
  medieval, 51–52
Hunt, Harriot, 146–147, 150, 153
Hurd-Mead, Kate Campbell, 19, 209–210 n. 3
Hydrotherapy. *See* Water cure
Hygeia (goddess of healing), 30–31, 44, 147
  Asclepius and, 30

Inanna (goddess), 15–16, 22, 23
Industrialization, 134, 164
Infanticide, 42, 199
Innocent VIII, Pope, 86
The Inquisition, 68–71, 85, 86, 98
Integrating masculine and feminine, 190–193
  healers, 196–198
  healing system, 194–195
Ishtar (goddess), 15, 16, 22, 23

Jacobi, Mary Putnam, 145, 151–152, 154–155
Jerome, Saint, 39–40
Jesus of Nazareth, 38, 67
John of Burgundy (physician), 77
Johns Hopkins University Medical School, 156, 162, 175, 202

Judeo-Christian myth, 66
  serpents and, 66–67
Julius Caesar, 27

Keller, Elizabeth (physician), 148
Kempe, Margory (wise woman), 64
Kramer, Samuel Noah, 19

Larner, Christine, 95–96
Liber introductorius (Scot), 73
Lucy, Saint, 52

Magiae naturalis (Porta), 93
Magic, 18, 31, 57–58, 71, 73, 77
  and countermagic, 57
  healing and, 18
  heresy and, 71
  natural (*magia licita*), 92–93
  science and, 71–75, 99–112, 212 n. 7
Magical arts, 28
Magna Mater (Cybele), 34–35
Malaria cure, 108
Male gods, 11, 14–15, 19
Male midwives, 123–130
  mortality rate and, 126–127
Malleus maleficarum (Hammer of Witches), 86–88, 90, 97
  Rev. Montague Summers and, 87–88
Margareta (Roman healer), 36
Mary idolatry, 53, 135
Mary Magdalene, 38
"The Masculine Birth of Time" (F. Bacon), 103
Masculine/feminine, myths of, 191
Mater Matuta (goddess), 34
Matilda of England (Empress), 45
Medical texts, 48
Medicine
  allopathic, 136–137, 171, 180, 193
  American, 171–186

heroic, 136, 137, 141–142, 167, 172
  magic and, 74
  preventive, 150–151
  science and, 99
  women in, 144–168
Medicine, modern/scientific, 63–64
  birth of, 63–64
  women and, 63–64, 144–158, 185–187
Medicine: An Illustrated History (Lyons and Petrucelli), 19
Medieval cosmology (Christian), 41–59
  Dark Ages, 41–44
  Middle Ages, 44–59, 76, 88
Meigs, Charles, 128
Men's lodges, 10
  Hebrew tribes and, 10
  Ona tribe (Tierra del Fuego), 10
  Norse, 26
Menstrual blood, 32, 210 n. 6 (chap. 4)
Menstruation, 150, 151–152
Mesopotamia. *See* Sumer
Metaphysical healing, 165–168
Metrodora (Gk. healer), 33
Middle Ages (High), 44–59, 202
  The Crusades, 51–52
  healing arts in, 47–48
  public health, 45–47
  women in, 45, 54–55
Middle Ages (late), 76, 88
Midwifery, 18, 47, 71, 79, 87, 88, 111, 115, 116, 120, 181–185
  in America, 130–132
  definition of, 118–120
  legislation on, 122–123, 132, 182–185
  men and, 123–130
  modesty/fashion and, 127–130
  witchcraft and, 121
  witch-hunts and, 118
Midwifery Analysed (Thicknesse), 129

Midwives, 181–185
  certified nurses (CNMs), 182–183
  lay, 182–184
  male, 123–130
The Midwives' Book (Sharp), 122
The Midwives Monitor & Mother's Mirror (Seaman), 130
Mind/body
  connection, 4, 167
  separation, 100–101, 103, 174
Mind-cure movement, 165
Mind medicine, 21–22
Misogeny, 39–40, 55, 98
Monotheism, 11, 12, 68
Montagu, Lady Mary Wortley, 107–108, 115
  smallpox vaccination, 107
Mother goddess, 11, 19
  Namu, 19
Mutilative surgery, 136

National League for Nursing, 175
Natura (goddess), 58
Nature, 12, 58, 63
  Cartesian theory and, 101
  healing and, 4
  women and/as, 99–100, 102–103
Nerthus (Danish goddess), 22–23, 25–26
  rituals of, 23–24
New England Hospital for Women and Children, 154
New York Infirmary for Women and Children, 153
Nichols, Mary Gove, 139–140, 141
Night flight, 92
Nightingale, Florence, 138, 145, 158, 159–161, 202
Njord (god), 26
Nurse(s), 149, 150
  definition of, 176, 177

practitioners, 177
  as women, 161–162
Nurse Healers Cooperative, 178
Nurse Practice Act, 176–177
Nursing, 18, 51–52, 115
  orders, 158, 163
  professionalization of, 176–178
  secular, 163
  sisters, 158, 163, 164

Observations on Midwifery (Willughby),
  119
Octavia (Roman healer), 36
Odin, 26
Odyssey (Homer), 29
"Old wives," 72, 74
Oldenburg, Henry, 102
On Sleep and Waking (Albertus Magnus), 73
Origenia, 36
Original Sin, 54, 66–68

Paracelsus, 105–106, 110
Patriarchal religions, 10, 53
  Mary and, 53–54
Patriarchy, 38
Peirsoun of Byrehill, Alison, 90
Penis, as object of worship, 10
Persecution of women, 10–11, 63,
  65–75, 96
  Albertus Magnus and, 70, 73
  Arnald of Villanova and, 70, 71,
    72, 73
  Roger Bacon and, 70, 74, 110
  Guy de Chauliac and, 78–79
  Church/state, 65–75, 98–99
  dualism and, 68–70
  economic/political, 66
  Pope Innocent VIII and, 86
  Original Sin and, 65, 66–68, 70
  William Perkins and, 89
  philosophical basis of, 65–75
  science and, 70–75
  Michael Scot and, 70, 71, 73

St. Thomas Aquinas and, 70, 71,
    74–75, 88
  See also Witch-hunts
Pharmacy, 9, 92
  See also Botanic(s)
Physicians, women, 144–158, 185–
  187
Physionomia (Scot), 73
Pinkham, Lydia, 140
Pisan, Christine (early feminist), 64
Plagues/Pox, 76–78
Pliny the Elder, 34
Popular health movement, 115, 131,
  133–143, 144, 172
Pornography industry, 136
Preston, Ann (physician), 146, 148
Preventive medicine, 150–151
Priestesses of Delphi, 31
Prose Edda (Sturluson), 26
Psychopathology, 97–98
Public health, medieval, 45–47
Pythias (at Delphi), 31, 32

Reflections on Gender & Science (Keller), 102
Relics, healing, 44, 52–53
Religion(s),
  health and, 163–165
  pagan, 96–97
  science and, 64, 99, 102
Renaissance, 99–104, 124
Ritual, 4, 9, 24, 49, 93, 211 n. 11
Rome, 34–37
  decline of, 36–37
  women healers of, 34–37
Roszak, Theodore, 198
Royal College of Midwives, 130
Royal Society, 102, 104, 106
Runestones, 53

Sacred sites, 11, 188
  orientation of, 11, 188–189
Salerno Medical University, 48, 50,
  72, 80, 83

Satan. *See* Devil
Science,
    birth of experimental, 63–64,
        70–77, 101–102
    magic and, 71–75, 99, 212 n. 7
    religion/theology and, 63–64,
        70–75, 99, 102
Science and Health . . . (Eddy), 166
Scientific Revolution, 99–104, 111–
    112
    witch-hunts and, 103, 111–112
Scribes, 48, 200
    structuring of reality by, 19, 48,
        200
Seaman, Valentine (on midwifery),
    130
Semmelweiss, Ignaz, 110–111
Seventh-Day Adventists, 141
*Sex Education; or, A Fair Chance for the
    Girls* (Clarke), 149, 151
Shadow, confronting the, 203–204
Shaman, female, 20, 24–28, 209 n. 18
    as wounded healer, 198
Shamanic practices, 24–25, 91–92,
    94, 209 n. 18
    accusation of, 91–92
    Christian Era/Denmark, 26–27
Sisterhood, 201–203, 204, 205
Sloane 2463 (manuscript on mid-
    wifery), 120, 121
Smallpox vaccination, 107–109
    Lady Mary Montagu and, 107–
        108
Snake(s), 10, 30
    caduceus and, 30
    feminine healing energy and, 30
Social work, 179, 202
Soranus, 35, 120
Springs/wells, healing, 21, 26, 28, 52–
    53
Stones, sacred, 26, 35
    See also Runestones
Strabo (historian), 27
Sumer (Mesopotamia), 14–19

healing legacy of, 17–18
    women's divinity and, 14–17
    women healers of, 17–19
Summers, Rev. Montague, 87

Tacitus, 23, 27
Tetrabiblion (Aëtius), 37
Thomas Aquinas, Saint, 68, 70, 71,
    74–75, 88
Thomson, Samuel, 140, 141–142
Thomsonians, 141
Thor, 26
Thorbioga (Danish shaman), 27–28
Torture of women, 83–84, 90
Tristan and Isolde (legend), 53
Trotula of Salerno, 48–51, 72

Vagina, as object of worship, 10
Vanir (goddess/shaman), 26, 209 n. 18
Venus of Willendorf, 10
Virgin Mary, 67
    See also Mary idolatry

Wage inequity, 186, 203
War(s), 25–26, 76–78
    male gods of, 25–26
Water cure, 140, 141
Water Cure Journal, 139
Wellness, 116, 190, 194
Western civilization, 63
Western medicine, 31, 33
Weyer, Johannes, 92–93, 95
White, Ellen, 141, 145, 166
Willughby, Percivall, 119, 124, 125
Wise women (*femina saga*), 76–99
Witch(es), 81–82, 90–91, 93
    devil and, 81, 83, 85–90, 92,
        115
    "flying Oyle" of, 92–95
    "good," 88–91
    identifying, 83–86, 88, 91–92
    night flight of, 92
    trials of, 82–88, 209 n. 18

Witchcraft, 68, 70, 74, 81, 83, 88, 89, 90, 97
   healing and, 83, 88–89
   healing professions and, 81
   midwifery and, 123
   psychiatry and, 97
   sociopolitical aspects of, 88, 95–96
Witch craze, 95–99
   explanation of, 95–98
   nobles/clergy and, 96
Witch-hunts, 68, 81–88, 116–117
   as business, 84
   end of, 98–99
   and the Scientific Revolution, 103, 111–112
   as women-hunts, 81–82, 115
Woman Not Inferior to Man (Montagu), 108
Woman's Medical College of Pennsylvania, 148
Women, 9
   devaluation of, 65–75, 97
   elevation of, 45
   fear of, 86–87, 95, 96, 149, 164
   herbs/oils and, 9, 42, 53, 88–95, 110
   as nature, 102–103
   physicians, 144–158, 185–187
   as prophets, 163–168
   in religious life, 54–55
   as scribes, 17
   written works of, 120–122, 200-201
Women healers, 5, 58, 66, 112, 117, 135, 143, 146, 158, 168, 187–188, 205
   cosmology and, 12, 19, 25
   courtly love myths and, 53
   definition of, 39
   disappearance of, 18–19
   flowering of, 38, 50–51
   gods' gender and, 10–13, 14–19, 164
   vs. health-care providers, 173
   as heretics, 65–75
   integrating masculine/feminine, 191, 196–199
   legislation and, 78–81, 98
   Mary worship and, 53–54
   money and, 155–156, 202
   sisterhood and, 201–203
   social decline and, 17–18
Women healers, Danish, 20–28
Women healers, Greek, 29–33
Women healers, Roman, 34–37
Women healers, Sumerian, 17–19
Women health-care providers, 171–186
Women's healing practices (U.S.), 116–117
Women's "place," 27–28, 35, 44–45
Woodworth-Etter, Maria B., 164
Wounded healer(s), 197–198, 205
Wurzburg, Prince-Bishop of, 86

Zakrzewska, Marie, 131, 146, 152, 153–154, 168
Zilboorg, Gregory, 97